AT THE MOUNTAINS' ALTAR

In high-Andean Peru, Rapaz village maintains a temple to mountain beings who command water and weather. By examining the ritual practices and belief systems of an Andean community, this book provides students with rich understandings of unfamiliar religious experiences and delivers theories of religion from the realm of abstraction. From core field encounters, each chapter guides readers outward in a different theoretical direction, successively exploring the main paths in the anthropology of religion.

As well as addressing classical approaches in the anthropology of religion to rural modernity, Salomon engages with newer currents such as cognitive-evolution models, power-oriented critiques, the ontological reworking of relativism, and the "new materialism" in the context of a deep-rooted Andean ethos. He reflects on central questions such as: Why does sacred ritualism seem almost universal? Is it seated in social power, human psychology, symbolic meanings, or cultural logics? Are varied theories compatible? Is "religion" still a tenable category in the post-colonial world?

At the Mountains' Altar is a valuable resource for students taking courses on the anthropology of religion, Andean cultures, Latin American ethnography, religious studies, and indigenous peoples of the Americas.

Frank Salomon is the John V. Murra Professor Emeritus of Anthropology at the University of Wisconsin–Madison, USA, and Adjunct Professor of Anthropology at the University of Iowa, USA.

AT THE MOUNTAINS' ALTAR

Anthropology of Religion in an Andean Community

Frank Salomon

Routledge
Taylor & Francis Group

LONDON AND NEW YORK

First published 2018
by Routledge
2 Park Square, Milton Park, Abingdon, Oxon OX14 4RN

and by Routledge
711 Third Avenue, New York, NY 10017

Routledge is an imprint of the Taylor & Francis Group, an informa business

British Library Cataloguing-in-Publication Data
A catalogue record for this book is available from the British Library

Library of Congress Cataloging-in-Publication Data
A catalog record for this book has been requested

ISBN: 978-1-138-03746-5 (hbk)
ISBN: 978-1-138-03750-2 (pbk)
ISBN: 978-1-315-17788-5 (ebk)

Typeset in Bembo
by Swales & Willis Ltd, Exeter, Devon, UK

Some names and identifying details have been changed to protect the
privacy of individuals.

To Alexander Kai Niño, his family and his generation

Great things are done when Men & Mountains meet
This is not done by Jostling in the Street
(William Blake, *Notebook*, p. 43; 1807–1809?)

CONTENTS

PREFACE

I have spent a lot of time bumping along in buses under the glittering snowline of Andean peaks. Looking out the window, I often remembered a soaring phrase from Isaiah (58:14): "I will cause thee to ride upon the high places of the earth."[1] What a vocation it was, I thought, to be an Andean scholar, and travel where an ancient prophetic feeling for landscape connects with American sacred geography.

But that thought was a naïve one. It implied that a "natural symbol" invented over and over by different cultures—the sacred mountain—implied underlying uniformities of meaning. The mountain as a metaphor for exaltation or sacredness is indeed common to many cultures, and it is among the notions anthropologists have most often nominated for the ever-elusive title of "natural symbol" (Winzeler 2012, 78–79). Edwin Bernbaum's survey of sacred peaks worldwide (2006) describes mountain cults in India, Tibet, Israel, Kirghizia, Japan, New Zealand, Arizona, and Peru, with Aztec Mexico and Greco-Roman Europe also relevant. Richly dressed Inka human sacrifices on the icy tops of Mounts Ampato (Peru) and Llullaillaco (Argentina), as well as a massive modern Christian-Andean pilgrimage to the glacier Qoyllur Rit'i, have made the Andes perhaps the most famous single example of reverence for altitude (Besom 2013; Ceruti 2003; Reinhard 2010).

That feeling also belongs to secular modernity. Some ostensibly non-religious subcultures, such as mountain climbers and nation builders, revere their favored snowcaps in ways that resemble religiosity. One exemplary devotee was Simón Bolívar, whose prose poem *My Delirium on [Mount] Chimborazo* attaches the Ecuadorian cordillera to romantic nationalist ideology:

> No human foot had ever blemished the diamond crown placed by Eternity's hands on the sublime temples of this lofty Andean peak. . . . Caught up in a spiritual tremor . . . which seemed to me a kind of divine frenzy I . . . began to leave my own marks on the eternal crystals girding Chimborazo.
>
> *Bolívar 2003 [1822], 135*

My mistake lay in thinking that because mountains are strong candidates for "natural symbols" they have "naturally" shared broad meanings. I could have been right to hear Isaiah as voicing a repeated tendency of human imagination and yet wrong in supposing this tendency pointed to a pan-human sense of nature. To their sacred summits various cultures attach varied meanings: purity, centrality, primordial genesis, beauty, divinity, danger, and much more. It is only supreme salience that mountains have in common. Like religiosity itself, mountain veneration is a human response whose underpinnings are not obvious.

Churches and states sometimes attach summits to supposedly universal metaphysical postulates. Bolívar located the seats of Time and Destiny atop Chimborazo. But popular mountain cults usually derive from local rather than cosmic attachments. In many places, including the Andes, they tend to signify origin of particular peoples and their relations with a territory. For instance, the ancient Peruvian people of Huarochirí province dedicated their mummified dead to immemorial ancestors at their totemic mountain, the double-peaked snowcap Pariacaca, and they claimed Pariacaca as the patron of their conquests. In such roles Andean mountains usually have superhuman personalities. They "own" the weather and control the local biosphere.[2] Yet they never were, and are not now, transcendental gods above and beyond this world. Mountain cult has always condensed local interests including territoriality, resource needs, environmental knowledge, and ethnic feeling. Like ritual in general, mountain veneration may not have much to do with God or gods.

In the Biblical tradition, Hebrew *har*, "mountain," can carry the positive epithet "holy," as well as geographical meanings. Biblical mountains are often the scenes of encounters with God: the binding of Isaac on Mount Moriah (Genesis 22:2); the burning bush on "Horeb, the mountain of God" (Exodus 3:1); the giving of the commandments on Mount Sinai (Exodus 19:20); and other episodes.[3]

But when I looked into the many instances of "high places" (*bamoth*), I found they had as context calls to stamp out a class of local hill shrines and elevated altars that seemed disloyal and idolatrous in the eyes of priests affiliated with Jahweh's Second Temple sacrificial cult. As priests and scribes codified past revelations and demanded centralized sacrifice at Jerusalem's Temple Mount,[4] they forbade Hebrew sacrifice at public and private "high places." Some texts went as far as to advocate wrecking the "high places" of other groups: "Destroy all the places where the nations whom you shall dispossess served their gods, upon the high mountains and upon the hills and under every green tree" (Deuteronomy 12:2).

At a later age, however, Talmudic rabbis looking back on Biblical history judged that *bamoth* where Hebrews had sacrificed had been legitimate up to the moment when the central temple replaced them (Zevin 1969, 342–356). King Solomon himself supposedly acquired his miraculous wisdom after sacrificing at the *bamah* of Gibeon (1 Kings 3:4). Both Orthodox Christianity and Judaism went on to retain the metaphor of a high place by relocating it in the topography of sanctuaries. In a synagogue the name of the elevated platform for reading Torah scrolls, *bimah*, derives from the singular of the old word whose plural once meant the proscribed high places.

Andean mountains, like the hill shrines of ancient Near Eastern communities, often embody the migrations and politics of their local or regional devotees, and thus have among their valences a streak of resistance to centralized ecclesiastical power.

James C. Scott, in his 2009 book *The Art of Not Being Governed*, observes that priesthoods and states that claim power over mountainous regions almost everywhere work hard to curb resistance from entrenched, localistic highlanders, even after the latter have given formal allegiance. It seems that almost anywhere one looks—from Appalachia to Ethiopia, Scotland to Viet Nam—mountainous regions tend to produce frictions with the state and tenacious local religions differentiated from state cult. Such montane religions are often associated with combative loyalties to descent groups and their terrains. "Idolatry" is often a name for worldviews in which a fractionated realm of the superhuman reflects montane societies themselves organized in fractions (lineages, clans, etc.) settled in different valleys or ranges. These segments have their own engines of solidarity. Their systems of cult and sacredness—in short, of religion—emerge from experiences separable even now from the centralizing process of state and literate priesthood. Scott's cases concern highland Southeast Asia, but he takes note of New World parallels.

I too perceive some resemblance between Old World religious dynamics and the Andean case insofar as mountain cults at certain times came into conflict with centralized priesthood. With few exceptions, the Catholic clergy who implanted Christianity in the Americas arrived already believing that "the demon, expelled by the presence of Christ—and with him the idolater—took refuge in the Indies" (Duviols 1977 [1971]). Nine years before the conquest of Peru the crown ordered royal officers to destroy "pagan altars and places of worship" (Duviols 1977 [1971], 18, 54). Yet it was not the shock of first contact with "the people called Indians"[5] that aroused a faction of the clergy to attack rural Peruvian ritual life. It was rather the persisting vitality of local highland shrines a century later despite the Archbishopric of Lima's ever-growing claim to central religious control.

In 1608, a curate influenced by Jesuits launched a series of campaigns to "extirpate idolatry" by attacking shrines which often were built on the high slopes of mountains, lodged inside caves and shelters in high cliffs, and often expressly named or dedicated for particular peaks. To Andean devotees these were ancestor shrines, but also political shrines in the sense that they marked spots where a power of the nonhuman world installed original ancestors of lineages—that is, the first node of each segment's family tree. They marked the point where ancestry linked with superhuman progenitors like lightning or a great mountain. The cults of mountain-emplaced ancestors endured in some places up to the 18th century. Peter Gose has argued that mountains as such in post-extirpation times "wholly absorbed ancestral functions previously lodged in mummies and statues" (2008, 231). The holiness of mountains changed from a matter of ancestry to a matter of sacred territories and their animated natural setting, sometimes absorbing apparitions of Christian divinity too. And it persisted to become the group of sacred practices this book describes.

Losing interest in idol-breaking, the Catholic Church eventually adopted solutions parallel to what the Inkas had practiced some four centuries earlier. The Inka empire affiliated politically powerful local shrines with central power by inviting the former to send delegated symbols and persons to the highest temple in the imperial city. Catholicism too has adopted "the high places" by endorsing syncretistic apparitions of Jesus or Mary at mountains, caverns, and monoliths, outfitting them with pilgrimage chapels, and allowing their veneration even from afar.

In this book I hope to bring readers close to life as lived (part of the time) in mountain veneration. I want to refresh our acquaintance with habits of mind and practice that have been vital to agrarian societies in many ages, but are now unfamiliar to most of us except through retrospective stereotypes, including the fatally inflammatory word "idolatry." What is it we were thinking *against* all this time?

To be literate and "Western" is to grow up bathed in literary evocations and theological denunciations of destroyed agrarian worlds: worlds with attributes such as personalized land features and sacrifice to them. Few processes have been more central to the evolution of Abrahamic religions than the intellectual struggle against pluralistic ideas of superhumanity. Few arguments in the emergence of science were more fundamental than the gradual rebuttal of ideas about social relations between humans and the nonhuman. Now, we see the kind of society Ernest Gellner (1988) called "Agraria" primarily through archaeology, philology, and art history. Up to a point, its characteristic ideas nonetheless still live in parts of some cultures. As an ethnographer, I want first of all to simply pay close, real-time attention once more: to listen to a part of the discourse our great-grandteachers learned to think by thinking against.

In doing so we step into an intellectual stream called anthropology of religion. Anthropology of religion shares with religious studies and similar fields the goal of showing broadly what range of human sacred practices exist. But anthropology asks a further question: why does the cultural domain of the sacred exist at all? The anthropological discussion of religiosity consists of several deep-rooted conversations about why most or all societies create areas of sacredness, and why humans are inclined to people them with special, powerful beings. As an instructor in anthropology of religion, I have often taught such conversations. As a private person whose life is peopled by believers as well as academic secularists, I never stop thinking about them.

This book is not a full-scale ethnographic treatise. On the contrary, it paints the merest miniature of a world known through research. Nor is it a full-scale theoretical book, in the sense of a book deliberating on all major theories or offering a new theory. Instead we will briefly tag along with one ethnographic project, frequently pausing to think about theories that claim to explain things seen along the way. The text connects with theoretical literature by offering "handles": critical openings and short theoretical sketches that relate each chapter to some canonical and some innovative theories. "Handles" are just invitations to apply various theories to the ethnographic matter.

Anthropology of religion courses are splendid fora for major theoretical ideas, but they also are fora where we question the cross-cultural worth of "religion" as a category. Rapacinos who run the weather temple Kaha Wayi don't speak of the temple's work as a "religious" matter. They reject any suggestion that it competes with Catholicism, or calls into question their standing as Christians. We visitors feel an impulse to call Kaha Wayi religious because the little temple evokes a powerful sense of the sacred in its local constituency: it is walled off from other domains and demands specialized, stereotyped, respectful behaviors. Yet if we ask people who serve Kaha Wayi the usual first question about religion, "what do you believe?", people take the question as relevant to the village church or to Protestant denominations, not to Kaha Wayi.

This mismatch reminds us that the common-sense usage of the word "religion" as referring to "faith" organizations with doctrines about gods, is nowhere near adequate to cover the range of groupings that carry on the world's ritual work. Many ritual communities explain their agenda under non-theological rubrics like compliance to law or practical engagement with land and climate. Instead of making that wispy and provincial idea "belief" the object of study, we concentrate on the observable deeds that all communities of the sacred have in common, namely ritual. That is why actual practices at the mountain altar form the touchstones of each chapter here.

The anthropology of religion, then, puts before us one first and last big question: why is there any religion as opposed to no religion? Starting from the ethnographic experience of one mountain cult, this book approaches various theories that try to tell us why. We will think about these theories selectively, with a taste for variety and tolerance for contradiction. Seeing social theory as a conversation that questions our own time vis-à-vis other kinds of life, rather than as a cumulative science, I'm content to be an indecisive writer. Instead of swearing by one overarching explanation or another we will try on many theories and try to carry them all lightly. Ethnography seems to me the durable wealth of anthropology. For this reason I point in references to some further Andean research. How theories shape ethnographic encounters, and how they condition what we get out of them, is for readers to assess.

The long encounter from which this book emerges was first and last the gift of Comunidad Campesina San Cristóbal de Rapaz, a place I hope always to revisit in gratitude. Everything is owed to so many kind Rapacinos that I can only thank a few in print: Fidencio Alejo; Mario Alejo; Tomás Alejo Falcón; Antonio Cajachagua and his wife Sonia; Néstor Cóndor, his wife Catalina Alejo, and his mother Basilia; Cecilio Encarnación; Juan de Dios Evangelista and his wife Presilia; Elisa Falcón, Martín Falcón, Melanio Falcón and his daughter Ruth; Teodora Falcón Altamirana and her sister "Shanta"; Teodosio Falcón and his wife Teodora; Margarita Flores Romero; Alicia Gallardo, Anita Gallardo, Toribio Gallardo and Víctor Gallardo with his wife Noemí; Melecio Montes; Epifania Montes Flores; Rosa Santosa Pomazón; Felipe Nery Racacha; and Wilfredo Ugarte.

I am especially grateful to Dr. Arturo Ruiz Estrada of Lima's San Marcos University, the pioneer archaeologist of the upper Huaura basin and the first scientific visitor to Kaha Wayi. His good will toward this latecomer has been heartening.

To my main co-researchers, some of whom became co-authors in various works, I owe a decade of research pleasures and a wealth of expertise: the linguist

Luis Andrade Ciudad; the mathematician-textile specialist Carrie Brezine; textile conservationists Rosa and Rosalía Choque Gonzales; conservation architect Gino de las Casas; archaeologist Víctor Falcón Huayta; and archaeological museologist Renata Peters. Many technical specialists and consultants also lent their talents: Edgar Centeno, architectural conservation technician; archaeologist Reymundo "Tony" Chapa; camp cook Valeria Evangelista; museum designer Nelly Faustino; zoologist Patricia Maita Agurto; draftsman Humberto Maraví; publicist Erica Tuesta; and the incomparable curator of ancient Peruvian mummies, Sonia Guillén.

Many institutional sponsors are cordially thanked: the National Science Foundation Archaeology Program under grant 0453965; the Fulbright Commission of Peru; Fundación Telefónica del Perú; Instituto Nacional de Cultura; Centro Mallqui; the Wenner-Gren Foundation for Anthropological Research; University College of London Graduate School, and the same University's Institute of Archaeology. The University of Wisconsin-Madison generously granted all the leave and insurance support a long-term researcher could wish for.

The Obermann Center at the University of Iowa gave me what I finally needed most: a 2014 resident fellowship to write this work, and meanwhile to continue enjoying the company of scholars after I retired from the University of Wisconsin. What a blessing. Warmest thanks to Director Teresa Mangum and her staff.

The Scurrah-Mayer family of Miraflores, hearth of many a great research conversation, afforded a warm place to stop, discuss, and laugh. At their house my son Abraham and daughter Malka were kindly treated by Liduvina Vásquez Umboni. My wife, Mercedes Niño-Murcia forgave a lot of fieldwork absenteeism. Now that she too knows Rapaz, I feel she is a part of this book; I hope it pleases her. I salute everyone who kept me going *spe et bona mente*, as my Latin-loving grandfather Richard Georg used to say: "with hope and a good attitude."

Notes

1 Biblical citations in this Preface are to the King James Version.
2 A famous archaeologist of Inka-era human sacrificial sites on the highest snowcaps, Johan Reinhard, reminds us in *Inca Rituals and Sacred Mountains* (2010, 1, 81) that mountains really "do control meteorological phenomena" of their landscapes.
3 The Solomonic temple mount (1 Kings 6:1), Elijah versus Ba'al on Mount Carmel (1 Kings 18:20).
4 The noun Romanized as *bama* primarily denotes high places, such as mountains tops or ridges (Micah 3:12; Ezekiel 36:2). The Biblical expression "riding/treading the high places" can signify controlling the land (Deuteronomy 32:13; Amos 4:13; Isaiah 58:14). But more usually *bama* meant a local high place of worship. The centralizing of cult apparently begun under King Hezekiah of Judea (c.715–687 BCE) and after 622 BCE became a main tenet of the new Deuteronomic code proclaimed during King Josiah's reign. The destruction of "high places" is a frequent mytho-historic motif in 1 and 2 Kings (1 Kings 3:2, 14:23, 15:14, 22:43; 2 Kings 12:3, 14:4, 15:4, 15:35, 16:4, 17:32, 23:5, 22:8) and 2 Chronicles (11:15, 14:3, 14:5, 15:17, 17:6, 20:33, 28:4, 33:17, 33:19).
5 *Runa yn[di]o ñisca*, "the people called Indians," is how the author of the Huarochirí Quechua manuscript of 1608 alluded pluralistically to the many societies lumped as "Indians" in Spanish (Salomon and Urioste 1991, 41).

References

Bernbaum, Edwin. 2006. "Sacred Mountains: Themes and Teachings." *Mountain Research and Development* 26(4): 304–309.

Besom, Thomas. 2013. *Inka Human Sacrifice and Mountain Worship: Strategies for Empire Unification.* Albuquerque, NM: University of New Mexico Press.

Bolívar, Simón. 2003 [1822]. "My Delirium on Chimborazo." In *El Libertador: Writings of Simón Bolívar*, edited by Frederick H. Fornoff and David Bushnell. New York: Oxford University Press. 134–136.

Ceruti, María Constanza. 2003. *Llullaillaco: sacrificios y ofrendas en un santuario inca de alta montaña.* Salta, Argentina: Ediciones Universidad Católica de Salta.

Duviols, Pierre. 1977 [1971]. *La destrucción de las religiones andinas (durante la conquista y la colonia)*, translated by Albor Maruenda. México DF: Universidad Nacional Autónoma de México.

Gellner, Ernest. 1988. *Plough, Sword and Book: The Structure of Human History.* Chicago: University of Chicago Press.

Gose, Peter. 2008. *Invaders as Ancestors: On the Intercultural Making and Unmaking of Spanish Colonialism in the Andes.* Toronto: University of Toronto Press.

Reinhard, Johan. 2010. *Inca Rituals and Sacred Mountains: A Study of the World's Highest Archaeological Sites.* Los Angeles: Cotsen Institute of Archaeology Press.

Scott, James C. 2009. *The Art of Not Being Governed: An Anarchist History of Upland Southeast Asia.* New Haven, CT: Yale University Press.

Winzeler, Robert L. 2012. *Anthropology and Religion: What We Know, Think, and Question*, 2nd ed. Plymouth, UK: Altamira Press.

Zevin, Shlomo Josef. 1969. *Encyclopedia Talmudica, Vol. 4.* Translated and edited by Isidore Epstein and Harry Freedman. Jerusalem: Talmudic Encyclopedia Institute.

INTRODUCTION

In the high-Andean village of Rapaz stands a tiny stone house in a walled and locked precinct. Its windowless interior is lined by stone benches around an altar piled high with coca leaf. The woolen ponchos of generations sitting around it have polished the stones of the wall to a blackish sheen. This is Kaha Wayi, a temple to the snowcaps, lakes, and springs of the Cordillera Negra in central western Peru. It is the place where men (and some women) of traditional authority retreat to deliberate about nature and society.

For at least a millennium Andean people in high villages from Peru to Chile and Argentina have venerated mountains as the "owners of water" (Castro and Aldunate 2003, 73). The unusual thing about Rapacinos is that they still do organize mountain cult in the form of a temple. As far as I know, this is the only such temple still functioning. It is said to be the engine of fertility: "Everything within it is destined to grow." This book hopes to bring readers inside Kaha Wayi's ethos and to suggest its relevance to some (not all) theoretical approaches to religiosity.

It was an enormous surprise to find, in 2004, a working temple of Andean mountain veneration because Rapaz is in the very area where Christendom strove hardest to stamp out pre-Christian sacred culture. And there are additional surprises. A collection of *khipus*, the knotted-cord records that formed the information base of Andean societies in prehispanic times, exists here as nowhere else in its original house.

This book tells about an eight-year encounter with the people who conduct rites in Kaha Wayi, about a partnership with the community that treasures it, and about the continuing enigma of its origin. It chooses Rapaz as a place from which to wonder why the domain of the sacred exists at all. It takes into view the question of how well the category "religion" applies to this stubbornly surviving legacy of ancient lifeways, and in doing so examines basic anthropological theories about religiosity.

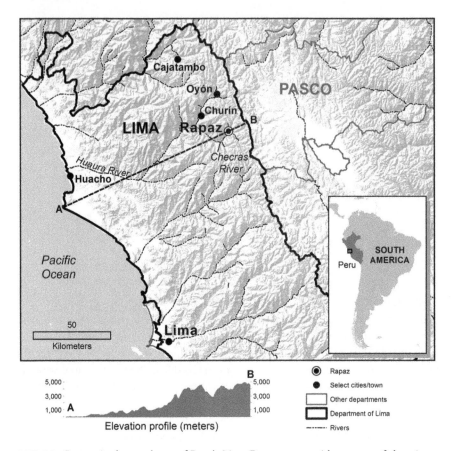

MAP 0.1 Rapaz, in the northeast of Peru's Lima Department, with transect of elevations.

Introducing a village

The west face of the cordilleras of northern Lima Department (see Map 0.1), where this story takes place, is better known to mining engineers than to tourists. Multi-metal mines built up in the 20th century by North American, European, and now Chinese companies, have gashed the slopes and generated bleak cities above the treeline. Rapaz village belongs to the coal and metal-mining District of Oyón in the province of the same name. Oyón had 12,812 inhabitants in the 2007 census. Although Rapaz is the most spacious of Oyón's districts, it houses only 5.5% of its people.

Rapaz is a free peasant village, one that has fought successfully to keep up a demanding regime of commons together while also providing some business latitude. It is home to 711 people,[1] many of whom are usually absent. Within their memory, its agropastoral system has been transformed by successive conflicts. One was an interminable lawsuit, running from the 18th century up to 1962. The lawsuit in its later stages became a fight with a famous latifundio or herding estate belonging to the Fernandini family and called Algolán. Algolán was part of a central highlands complex built around the then USA-owned Cerro de Pasco Corporation mines. Spreading from the intermontane basin up and over the western cordillera like latter-day Llacuaces, Algolán's aggressively technical managers in the middle of the 20th century took over about a third of Rapaz's historic lands by dubious purchase and rental. Older Rapacinos remember working as Algolán peons. In the early 1960s, Rapacinos joined with many other villages in coordinated resistance to latifundism, invading and occupying such estate lands. In a fight they remember as heroic, Rapacinos won back the vast tract called Lot 29, secured its recognition by President Fernando Belaúnde Terry in 1963, and reserved it to make room for a greatly increased communal herd. It tripled the area of Rapaz.

A number of Rapacinos initiated a cooperative called Los Andes in 1965 to capitalize this asset. In that era, the USA's Kennedy and Johnson presidencies hoped to forestall the spread of Cuban revolutionism by favoring non-Communist land reforms. One Rapacino, Neri Racacha, secured a Farm Union fellowship in 1966 to study cooperative administration at the University of Wisconsin and other places. (I was astonished in 2004 to meet Neri: an Andean horseman in full cowboy gear who greeted me in rusty English and reminisced about Madison professors of my acquaintance.) The cooperative enjoyed substantial success and yielded advances some remember with nostalgia, such as a community store offering basic goods at low prices.

But independent cooperatives became unpopular with the state in the era of Peru's radical, top-down, bureaucratic experiment in agrarian reform (1968–1973). In such an environment the cooperative had an Achilles' heel: it did not benefit comuneros equally. Only those with enough initial assets to invest in it at the beginning gained full benefits. Partly as a result of changes in Ministry of Agriculture and Livestock policy, opponents of the Cooperative prevailed. In 1977 it was dissolved by ministerial order. Five-thousand-plus sheep and 200-plus cattle passed into a Community Enterprise owned by the jural Peasant Community. That corporation has had its own ups and downs. It came under pressure from Shining Path terrorists during the 1982–1992 insurgency, and at one point the Maoists forced the Enterprise at gunpoint to sell off their cattle and divide the proceeds. The memory of the terrifying days when guerrillas sealed the village off for indoctrination and "justice" is still alive. But veterans feel they got the better of Shining Path and are proud of the armed self-defense patrol that (together with the army) kept it at bay in the later stages of the war.

Rapaz continues to enforce its collective regime by restricting land use rights to comuneros, or stakeholders in the corporation of the commons. Only children of the village are eligible. In 2007, there were 82 full comuneros, plus over 80 who had finished their duties and passed to the status of semiretired comunero (*pasivo*). Traditionally, in each household the senior male is the titular comunero, but women become comuneras in their own right if they are single mothers, widowed, or caring for elders. There can be only one titular comunero per household. The number of female comuneras has been rising steadily with the "feminization of agriculture" everywhere in the Andes, reaching about half the total among Rapacinos by 2011.

To join the Peasant Community is a huge commitment, dwarfing military service and equal in gravity to marriage. Every *socio* ("partner," i.e., stakeholding member) has to serve thirty years and carry out at least fifteen *cargos* or offices before becoming eligible for semi-retired status. Cargo responsibilities include expensive ritual duties such as festival sponsorship, which is indispensable for building up political credibility.

For a long time, Rapaz took a stand-offish position in the face of neoliberal pressures of the post-Shining-Path era. When the Department of Lima built up its rural electrical network, Rapaz insisted on remaining off the grid—not because it failed to appreciate electricity, but because it had already built its own local hydroelectric system by installing a second-hand generator from Canada. At the time when most of the ethnography in this book was compiled, Rapaz had abstained from contracting with any mining enterprise. But that has changed in recent years.

From 2012 onward, Rapaz's state-recognized Community engaged in a barter-like relationship with the predominantly Swiss-owned mining corporation Los Quenuales. As of 2016, in return for allowing the mine to extract nonferrous metals from some of its highest lands (4,500–5,000 meters over sea level), the Community received funding for seven new civic projects directed to quality-of-life issues.[2] Unlike many highland communities, Rapaz has so far generated no public controversies over metallic water pollution. Quenuales transports the ore to a concentration plant in another town. But neither has Rapaz earned community capital in monetary form from mining (Falcón Huayta 2014). Meanwhile, above the village a blackish tailings pond holds back potentially toxic sludge, which some find worrisome.

As Peru moved into the ranks of middle-income countries in the 2010s, villages like Rapaz sat insecurely, as did small towns in the USA, Russia, Spain, and a host of other countries. Export-oriented agroindustry in a globalized marketplace makes it hard for villages anywhere to find competitive advantage. Rapaz's government-recognized Community bets partly on mine benefits, which have markedly improved public facilities but provide little steady employment. Daily, helmeted Rapaz workers troop down to their foaming river ravine, where Quenuales is also supporting construction of a major hydroelectric plant. Future income from selling power is the Community's other main development bet.

Even when villages do find new economic niches, agropastoral communalism is becoming hard to maintain. In much of the countryside the lifeways and knowledge that anthropologists have enshrined as Andean, Nahuatl, or Mayan "traditional" or "indigenous" culture are being neglected out of existence. This happens unintentionally when urban-oriented education and technology make rival demands. Protestant preachers' campaigns to stamp out rural traditions as pagan also have some influence. At rural schools, traditions are folklorized to insignificance by presenting them as quaint rather than powerful.

Rapaz has been trying to find another outcome, and as it happens, its comuneros recruited this anthropologist to be a part of it. Rapaz is no exception to erosive tendencies, but still, its tenacity in "custom" stands out.

The presence of a living temple to beings like the mountains Yara Wayna, Saqsar Wayna, Qumpir Wayna, and Lake Punrún raises so many questions that as a veteran anthropologist I feel trepidation about even reporting it. Sophisticated historians will immediately suspect that the temple called Kaha Wayi and its companion-structure Pasa Qulqa are recent "reinventions": attempts by a modern people to install in their culture a re-imagined past, as other Andean towns have "discovered" themselves to be bearers of an Inka solar religion. Skeptical archae-ologists will warn that too many years and changes have gone by for Kaha Wayi to be relevant for interpreting prehispanic temple ruins. Well-read ethnographers will suspect that the temple might only look non-Christian if you artificially leave other practices out of focus.

Nobody says Kaha Wayi is a miraculously enduring outcrop of prehispanic religion. As a lifetime practitioner of ethnohistory, I'd be the first to say that we can never walk around the back of 480 years' Euro-Andean history to encounter, as it were, a world without us. But experience does persuade me that in Rapaz indigenous sacred institutions different from Christianity were somehow car-ried forward, adapted, and protected, and are still practiced amid 21st-century civilization. Jesuits of the 17th century proposed to tear such cults out by the roots. Shining Path Communism had similar leanings, and some Evangelical and Pentecostal Protestants of our time are still hoping to do so. But there is the Andean temple—in a little stone-walled precinct under the glaciers, across from a modern schoolhouse and catty-corner to a huge colonial church. How did this happen? How does it gives meaning to the "vertical" way of life? What may come of it as Rapacinos enter the global diaspora?

A word with the sophisticates

So let's have a word with those who necessarily wonder whether it makes sense to study the past by studying the present: historians, archaeologists, and ethnographers.

During the later 20th century it became hard for historians to credit even the possibility of deep continuity. In 1983 Eric Hobsbawm put us on alert about "invented tradition" by collecting "traditions," such as the clan plaids of Scotland, which turned out to have been recent innovations packaged as immemorial folkways for ideological and commercial purposes (Trevor-Roper 1983). When historiography set out to understand nonwestern peoples as active populations, it undercut western notions of living archaism. The Africanist Edwin Wilmsen asserted that South Africa's !Kung San Khoisan people, anthropologically famous as enduring exponents of the Paleolithic "old way," were actually refugees recently buffeted to the desert margin by Bantu expansion (Wilmsen 1989). The potlatch of the Pacific Northwest, which Marcel Mauss had taught us to see as primordial gift economy, turned out in Philip Drucker's research to have been stimulated by mercantile inflation a scarce few years prior to Mauss' own *Essay on the Gift* (Drucker 1967). Multiplied by a hundred examples, such critiques made skepticism about continuities a default. We demoted the durability of social arrangements from a self-evident premise to a stage effect in ideological dramas, or even to illusion.

The problem of how to plausibly recognize the old was not a theoretical problem. All the high theorists of my formative era, including Bourdieu, Wolf, and Sahlins, did in their disparate ways make room for diachronic concepts of culture. Even the Foucauldian model, which seems to make the weave of dominant discourse in any given era as impermeable as Superman's leotard, does provide a powerful theory of both discontinuity and continuity.

Rather than being a theoretical matter, our leeriness about attributing long continuity was mostly an ethical scruple. To the degree that the waning of colonialism made it urgent to recognize all peoples as actors in history, scholars repudiated arguments imputing to some people a slow-track historicity. Insistence on deep continuity might smack of the bias that Fabian called "denial of coevalness" (2002). By this he meant removing our ethnographic subjects from frameworks of shared modernity by treating them as living fossils of bygone lifeways.

I went with the pack—and was repeatedly astonished to find in central Peruvian society elements of deep continuity. The kinds of "social structure" that my 1970s PhD cohort had learned to dismiss as "ideology," such as unilineal clan organization and moiety dualism, could not be dismissed as fictitious ideals once I saw them in operation. As the Andeanist Paul Gelles put it, distinctively Andean models were still in some places society's "gameboard," doing important work such as organizing people to maintain livelihood. Apparently there was something wrong with grad-school suppositions about the way people inhabit time and change. The endurance of the Rapaz temple is an example. The point is not that Andean ways are archaic after all, but that organizational resources older than any of the successive empires and states have demonstrated generative usefulness through the imperial centuries.

To sophisticated ethnographers, the historians' diagnoses of amnesia and invention were not the only ones that made the claims about endurance of ancient nonwestern culture seem fishy. There was also the matter of indigenism and "othering." In many parts of the ex-colonial world, writers who pulled together strands of local practice—especially expressive culture, such as dance, costume, ritual, and music—and packaged it as integrally "native" or "indigenous" culture, became suspect of "orientalism." That is, so the argument went, by editing out of the picture the internet café, the leftist peasant union, the Adidas, and the state inoculation campaign, ethnography created illusory images of a deeply separate, innocent, and exotic version of humanity. That kind of ethnography, we were told, was part and parcel of global structures of inequality. Ethnographers were accused of taking conflict off the agenda, the better to reinstate old social distances under new labels. Orin Starn, an emulator of Edward Said, influentially put studies of Andean cultural continuity under sentence of "andeanism" by analogy to orientalism (1991). Sackcloth and ashes were suddenly the height of anthropological fashion.

But the unforeseen victories of "neo-Indianist" political movements from 1990 (in Ecuador) through the Peruvian and Bolivian elections of the new millennium, made it clear that many Andean citizens had themselves dismissed the dismissals.

By 2000, as Alcida Ramos has observed, many young people born into South American indigenous families appropriated cultural anthropology's language as their own (Ramos 2008, 470–472). Everybody talked about "culture" in the North American multiculturalist sense. In Peru, the self-ethnographic attitude seems to have taken root among people whose relation with the Andean legacy is no longer governed by the old rural habitus. Their experience of being Andean became self-reflective as they experienced travel in diaspora, made careers that included higher education, and interacted with people who no longer accepted the equation between Quechua and backwardness. Such experiences relocated the whole Andean matter into critical consciousness. For the generation that logged its experience under the formerly anthropological but now omnipresent heading of "*cultura*," it became possible to treat Andean continuities as an inheritance one might optionally interiorize—or change, or abandon.

The cultural voltage of researching sacred things

To sit in somebody else's holy place, to set off photo flashes in the dim chamber where barely a candle had been allowed to burn for untold years—these are weighty steps. Is anthropological curiosity a good enough reason for inquiry that someone else might think desecration? Anthropological curiosity was a passion for me. But in the eyes of the men who formed the community's inner cabinet that motive was not sufficient—not even reasonable. They would never let an outsider, however plausible his credentials, barge in and handle things that they themselves considered too holy to touch. Yet they didn't say no, either. Instead, they pushed this investigation in a direction I had never foreseen. It evolved into a pact that put research under the mandate of a tradition and its ritualist.

In 1994, I was doing field research in Tupicocha (Huarochirí Province), a high-altitude village four river basins south of Rapaz. This province casts a spell over anthropologists because it is the home of the 1608 Quechua Manuscript of Huarochirí. It is the only known early book that explains pre-Christian Andean religion in an Andean language. When Tupicochans showed me their communal khipus, I was riveted. Khipus as parts of the ongoing governance of a modern village were an unusual find. Their study consumed me for ten years (Salomon 2004).

In the course of the study, I read an old published report (1981) by the Peruvian archaeologist Arturo Ruiz Estrada. In his archaeological surveys among the crags of Peru's central region, Ruiz Estrada had found numerous prehispanic villages and some Inka sites. Together with three students, he went to investigate a hearsay report about khipus in Rapaz in 1978. There, for the first time ever, villagers hauled the huge tangle of wool that they called their khipu out of its sacred dwelling and allowed an outsider to take a scientific look at it. Ruiz Estrada took the first picture (1981, 23).

The cords' emergence from their house was an unprecedented moment because of what Ruiz called "the secrecy in which they kept [the khipu] and still do keep it." He wrote that:

> still in these times [the community] continues carrying out native magico-religious practices, for which reason nobody is allowed to go inside the precinct, except the officiant of the rites and his helpers, and some of the local authorities when they took inventory of the number of quipus in order to care for them . . . Several Rapacinos told us that when they were children their parents forbade them to enter Cajahuay and Colca, and so they looked on these buildings with unease, fear, and respect. A sort of taboo applied to them.
> *Ruiz Estrada 1981, 25–26*

As my Tupicochan work wound down in 2003, I felt the need to find out if Rapaz's patrimony still existed. I looked for a way to contact the owners of Kaha Wayi. In Tupicocha, an ex-mayor's wife turned out to be from the area, and she mentioned a Rapacino who lived in Lima; I tracked the man down and asked him if Rapaz had a telephone. It did, and with his counsel I began to contact the village's elected authorities. Might I hope for a visit? On the strength of one call, in August 2003, I packed myself in with twenty Rapacinos and their bundles and set out in a beat-up rural mini-bus.

That trip led to a negotiation about access to the khipu collection in exchange for conservation work. The pact and its execution is explained in Chapter 5. I delighted in it, yet remain puzzled about how this intervention might stand in the long-term judgments of my discipline. I also wonder how future Rapacinos may some day feel about it.

Like many anthropologists who study religion, I take seriously the question of whether research constitutes a "defacement" of a cultural resource whose value depends on its hiddenness. In such cases, we may ask ourselves what rule governs—the cosmopolitan ethic of research and humanism, or the local ethic of respecting hierarchies and "cultural privacy" (Brown 2009, 27–59)? One example from early South American ethnology is Martin Gusinde's narrative about the last performance of a Fuegian group's coming-of-age ritual in 1923, a ritual in which the secret was that the aggressive spirits who threatened women actually were their own men (Gusinde 1961 [1937]; Chapman 1982). Gusinde felt scruples about publicizing a purported secret, but decided that since he witnessed what was expressly to be the last enactment in a devastated society, it was justified. Other anthropologists (Bellman 1984) have described West African secret societies from the insider perspective of membership and discussed ethics of disclosure.

Is Kaha Wayi this kind of a case? I don't think so. There is no secret, in the sense that no "insider" knowledge reveals the sacred context to be other than what outsiders think it is. Deception plays no part. Kaha Wayi is a reserved place that one enters gradually, by a series of public duties that inculcate specialized knowledge. Nor are the things done inside Kaha Wayi so unfamiliar to people outside it. Many times I was told that its officiants perform rites that householders themselves practice in smaller, private versions. The "taboo" climate that Ruiz Estrada mentions seems to me to derive from the confidential climate of intimacy with the mountains and the political intimacy of peer-leaders, rather than from any mystery that may not be revealed. It is as with a court: everyone is to fear the solemnity of the law and respect its confidential dialogues, but all know its basic principles, practices, and materials.

In what follows I refrain from expounding particulars within confidentiality, such the words exchanged in sacrificial encounters or political conversations inside Kaha Wayi. It is true, however, that conservation work lays cultural things bare. I wince when I think about my camera flash, or about revered objects laid out like surgical patients on a white lab table. Their home is the smoky, murky chamber of Kaha Wayi, and seeing them outside it made people nervous. But I hope that in the last consideration, ethnographic detail amounts to an homage whose effect will be the opposite of disenchanting.

About this book: ethnography and Western theories of religiosity

Although this book presents fresh research, it is not a full-dress specialist monograph. Rather it is meant to put before students' eyes one case, an Andean temple, and treat it as an example for pondering the possibly pan-human matter of sacred ritual. How shall we explain the sacred-ritual conjunction? Why is there any religion as opposed to no religion? In other words, how shall we study Anthropology of Religion?

As much as we feel that we know religion when we see it, defining religion has turned out to be a labyrinth. When speaking of religion, social scientists usually mean a collection of human behaviors and ideas that tend to occur together in many societies and are often perceived by inhabitants as forming a coherent complex with special rules and importance. Western definitions of religion typically include such features as:

- Disembodied or physically anomalous agents and discourse about their character;
- Objects that correspond to these beings such as icons, relics, vestments, etc.;
- Ritual practices addressed to them, usually including special language;
- Moral notions about right and wrong attributed to them;
- Sacredness, i.e., rules that mark them as privileged and separate;
- Ways of inducing contact and communication with them;
- Models for interaction that often include sacrifice;
- A sense of "we" thus generated by group practice.

Obviously the edges of the religious constellation are cloudy. It is easy to think of borderline cases. We see groupings where most of these attributes coincide yet people don't call the result a religion (this book being about one such). We also see groupings where participants claim the word religion while disclaiming some or most of these traits. We should leave our own definition loose if we want to bring into our discussion the many theorists who want to explain religiosity using not only different theories but different baseline definitions.

We also need to think a bit about the conceptual basis for supposing "religion" is a natural class. Benson Saler's odyssey through proposed definitions ends with a reminder that religion is not a thing, not a trait, but an abstraction on the observer's part: religion is "a pool of elements that more or less tend to occur together" in worshipful complexes. And since "the observer" in anthropology, comparative religion, and so forth becomes an observer by virtue of a critique occurring inside the orbit of Abrahamic thinking, the choice of things we want to study inevitably partakes of theological priorities if only by defying them. We extend the term religion to non-Abrahamic traditions by finding "elements that we deem analogous to . . . our reference religions, the Western monotheisms" (Saler 1993, 225). Every anthropology of religion book, including this one, uses terms that rest on such analogies: sacrifice, belief, sacredness, priesthood, etc. An ethnographic-minded reader should be ever-ready to question them.

For a time, the notoriously difficult job of defining religion was set aside with a gentle shrug. But in recent times the point that Saler concedes, namely that the observer abstraction called religion is relative to Western monotheism, has come under suspicion of being a fatal pitfall. When less-Western scholars made their claims in anthropology, all eyes were called to the fact that secular-minded study of religion became institutional within Western Christendom.

This observation has, in recent years, triggered a controversy questioning the very validity of anthropology of religion as a subdiscipline (Chapter 7). If the secular forum is itself a locus within and derived from Christianity's intellectual life, what claim can secularists have to defining a domain of religion worldwide? Should they give up the claim to have built a platform outside of and independent from what they call "religion"? What right have they to segregate under the rubric of "religion" a range of practices which their respective owners recognize as authoritative without deferring to Western premises about the bounded separateness of religion?

Taken a little further, this challenge requires us to wonder what sort of description—what ethnography—would convey qualities of a foreign sensibility without asking the usual out-of-place questions like "what do they believe?" In the pages that follow, we will study a complex of Andean rituals and ideas that appear religious by the usual criteria, yet are not classified as religion by their owners. I confess to not being able to avoid terms such as "sacredness," "ritual," and "sacrifice" in unfolding what I beheld in Rapaz. Perhaps there would have been some other "translation domain"—law, science or ethics?—sufficient to convey the "not-exactly-religious" character of culture in and around Rapaz's sacred precinct. But with that proviso, I would suggest that the varied theoretical postures sketched in the chapters provide enough alternatives within the western ethnographic posture to let the reader envision Andean practice as something more distinctive than just another flavor within the familiar range of "religions." To the prior question of defining religion—and whether it should be defined at all—we will return below and in the Conclusion.

The characteristic question anthropologists bring to the religious studies arena is, why do so many peoples and ages incline to be religious in the first place? Why are reverential poses, ritual and the sacred, sacrifice, and magical bonds so endemic to humanity? Here is one sociologist's inventory of the basic explanations for religiosity that Western scholarship has devised since the 16th century:

> "Religion as a *gift of reason*" (Herbert of Cherbury; Kant);
>
> "Religion as an experience of *revelation*" (Schleiermacher; Otto; van der Leeuw; Eliade);
>
> "Religion as *projection*" (Marx);
>
> "Religion as *proto-science*" (Tylor; Frazer; Boyer);
>
> "Religion as *affect and as a way of controlling affects*" (Marett);
>
> "Religion as *brain function*" (Newberg; Ramachandran);
>
> "Religion as *sacralised society*" (Durkheim; Luckmann, Luhmann);
>
> "Religion as an *interest in salvation*" (Weber; Bourdieu);
>
> "Religion as *commodity*" (Stark).
>
> *Stausberg 2009, 267, summarizing a 2007*
> *work of the sociologist Martin Riesebrodt*

To cover anthropological interests, one would have to add a few more:

> Religion as *adaptation to environments* (Vajda; Rappaport);
>
> Religion as *matrix of meanings* (Geertz; Douglas);
>
> Religion as *symbolic engine of social reproduction* (Bloch; V. Turner);
>
> Religion as *foreign ontology* (Viveiros de Castro; Pedersen).

Could there be greater dissensus about anything? Yet just about all these ideas are upheld by one anthropologist or another.

Ethnographers, like philosophers, sociologists, psychologists, and evolutionary biologists, hold spectacularly divergent ideas about why people are religious. They disagree about even the most basic question: is "religion" a universal phenomenon, an objectively present attribute of the human world? Or is "religion" just a theoretical construct, that is, a classifying category set up by observers to group phenomena by criteria that interest them?

Maybe half a millennium of unrelieved non-consilience suggests just how far humanity still is from having its own number. But the question of religiosity remains both urgent and engrossing. It is urgent because religions' fantastic destructiveness in conflictive settings, together with their humanitarian potential, make them a central theme of 21st-century debate. This is not a particularly political book, but after reading it, a secular-minded reader may feel less perplexed about the tendency to sacralize political life. Religiosity is also especially engrossing today because, as rarely in history, major parts of humanity have choices about whether to "be religious." Now that we ourselves must *decide* how far from or near to religiosity we will dwell, we have the option of beholding religiosity as compared to being held by it.

An alternative definition of the object: ritual studies and Bell's fusion engine

Taking "religion" as the object of study gives anthropology fantastic color and resonance—actually, too fantastic to be trustworthy. Discussions of religion-as-such usually end up dragging in imponderable terms such as "belief," "spirituality," and "the ultimate." Good theories don't leave such jokers in the deck. Seeking a more orderly conceptual life, certain modern scholars advise us to choose as our object of study something easier to recognize on the ground: "ritual."

Ritual is a type of action: action with an underlying script. Wikipedia's sturdy old definition of ritual will do for a start: "a sequence of activities involving gestures, words, and objects, performed in a sequestered place, and performed according to set sequences . . . prescribed by a community" and characterized by "formalism, traditionalism, invariance, rule-governance, sacred symbolism, and performance" (as of 2017). Compared with the improvisations of everyday life, ritual looks like culture in a state of hyper-structure.

Anthropologists and sociologists usually discard "sequestered place" as diagnostic of ritual. Rituals can be ordinary and tiny, as with minimal social protocols that set the frames for our everyday improvisations (a handshake or leave-taking). Ritual is the dramaturgic aspect of culture everywhere, not just in sanctuaries. Social-psychological theory sees the stagecraft of daily ritual as the very way we build up (or undercut) each other's selfhood. Greetings, courtship, sports, legal process, shows, exams, and politics, for example, are ritual frames. Gambling seethes with ritual. Nothing is too profane or too minor for ritual.

But nothing is as ritual as religion. A great ethnohistorian of Iroquoian peoples, Anthony F.C. Wallace,[3] defined religion as "a set of rituals, rationalized by myth, which mobilizes supernatural powers for the purpose of achieving or preventing transformations of state in man and nature" (1966, 107). While the concept of the supernatural has fallen out of favor (because it only makes sense for cultures that posit a delimited notion of nature), many ethnographers still think Wallace's definition is unusually effective.

Let's start by saying that for this book religion is the area of intersection between ritual practice and the domain of the sacred.

When authors say that religion is a human universal, what they really mean is that ritualism is one of the strongest candidates for being a pan-human behavior, and sacredness tends to go with ritual (Brown 1991, 139). Making sense of what people "believe in" (Needham 1972) may be inherently hard, but one thing anthropologists do agree on is that every known society alternates between ordinary states and ritual states. The conjuncture between ritual and sacredness may or may not be truly universal, but it is so widespread that one may reasonably suspect it to reflect something fundamental. One reason to think so is that sacred ritual has some amazingly far-flung regularities across cultures, and these regularities correspond to rather specific conjunctures in the affairs of people, such as birth, sickness, the onset of adulthood, installation of authority, and death. Another reason is that purportedly non-sacred rituals like sports events, legal process, political rallies, and commercial fairs seem to almost automatically attract sacred attitudes and gestures whether they are invited or not.

When sociocultural anthropologists read that something is pan-human they sit up and take notice—the more so if that "something" is an observable, conscious part of life (rather than a gene, etc.). Maybe instead of chasing that ghostly thing "belief" we should be concentrating on a part of religiosity that is both more concrete and more universal: ritual behavior. As Don Handelman's manifesto put it, we should get to work on *Ritual in its Own Right* (2004).[4]

That mission implies many things we should *not* do. We should stop assuming that rituals are secondary expressions of something else, something purportedly more fundamental. For example, we should leave aside the notion that "mere ritual" is a secondary acting-out mechanism of deeper, primary things in the mind (myth, emotions, binary structures, biases, archetypes, etc.). Likewise, we also should set aside the two dominant 20th-century notions about ritual: on one hand, that it is a functional mechanism that helps society reproduce its order (Chapter 3), and on the other hand, that it is a distraction that helps people delude themselves about the crushing cost of society (Chapter 5). Although many call ritual a type of communication, it must be a most peculiar one, for (by some accounts) the less information it conveys the better it works. In rote unison, all it "says" is that a certain form of group life is happening. Bell thinks ritual's "thoughtlessness" is its strength.

And Frits Staal, a specialist in Hindu ritual, went as far as saying that in the end rituals don't mean anything at all. That is, a ritual act doesn't stand for something exterior to itself, such as group allegiance, etc. To ritually perform Vedic sacred fire is to forget all other purposes and concentrate only on perfecting a "self-contained and self-absorbed" rule-bound activity. Like playing chess, performing a ritual is a consummate activity with no end but itself. It does not matter if celebrants of the Vedic fire cannot understand the language they chant. Ritual steps out of the referential and utilitarian realms altogether. "Activity itself is all that counts . . . [and] ritual is one up on most games, because you cannot even lose" (1979, 3, 10).

Staal does make room for ritual's attachment to many extra-ritual functions, but he argues that rituals' roles in enforcing ethics, explaining the mysterious, and so forth are secondary. Religion seems to him an accretion on a primary ritual faculty that evolved primordially and autonomously. It began with humans' self-recognition as creatures with shared agency: rejoicing in agency by perfecting it. Staal's speculative argument about primordial origin and his Hindu-centrism are obvious faults. But he makes one powerful and valuable point. Anyone who uses the phrase "merely ritual" is hard put to explain why humans (apparently, all humans) enjoy and desire ritual for its own sake, as we do games and music.

After demanding these renunciations of ordinary social-scientific wisdom, the ritual studies approach asks us to start on something different: to home in on *what actually happens* in rituals. Apart from their purported role as handmaidens to other institutions, what do these "impractical" yet universal activities achieve *in and of themselves*?

Catherine Bell was a religious studies scholar who specialized in Chinese religions. Perhaps it is no accident that she produced her anthropologically influential book *Ritual Theory, Ritual Practice* (1992) during her immersion in a culture whose philosophical and ritual orientations are sometimes said to fit poorly under the rubric of religion.

In *Ritual Theory*, Bell stood very far back from both ethnography and theory, the better to offer a "meta" perspective in relation to the anthropology of her moment. She builds up her answer about what actually happens in ritual in an unusual way: instead of comparing ethnographic cases, she compares the dominant theoretical explanations of ritualism in general. And she discovers a surprising thing about them: they are all underlyingly alike. Even when they dispute each other on many dimensions they share a common tacit basis, all being "structured by the differentiation and subsequent reintegration of two particular categories of human experience: thought and action."

To unfold just a little: human activity consists in part of "mental content or conceptual blueprints: 'beliefs, creeds, symbols and myths' that direct, inspire, or promote activity, but themselves are not activities." Simultaneously, every activity also consists in part of actions to effect things (that is, of agency in more recent terminology). Ritual transcends the though/action distinction by being sacred, which at root means set apart from both normal intellectual questioning and normal utilitarian action. In a sacred setting, the two are melded. Ritual is a special "type of functional or structural mechanism to reintegrate the thought-action dichotomy." Kaha Wayi's array of altar objects expresses an environmental schema, and it is at the same time the scene of actions to affect environment (Chapter 2). It is a scheme activated as a deed. Rituals always consist of ideas and agency in process of fusion.

But the really unusual thing about Bell is how she likens worshipers to researchers and cults to studies. For Bell the "the naturalness of the thought-action dichotomy" does not stop at ritual. Discussing Milton Singer's ethnography of Hindu ritualism, Bell discovers that that a separate, parallel thought-action fusion engine has also been at work *inside the ethnographer*:

> [B]ecause . . . the rite is already implicitly construed as effecting an integration for participants between a supposed conceptual totality (Hinduism) and the

practical needs of a particular time and place (the dispositions within the ritual context), the researcher easily sees in the exhibition of these rites for theoretical interpretation an equally effective convergence of theory and practice on another level—our conceptual abstractions integrated with their theoretical practices. . . . The dichotomy between a thinking theorist and an acting actor is simultaneously affirmed and resolved. It is this homologization that makes ritual appear to provide such a privileged vantage point on culture.

1992, 31

In short, ritual "appears to prove . . . a privileged vantage point on culture" because ethnography, far from being the alien expropriation of culture that post-imperial polemics allege, actually contains within it a program shared with ritual (1992, 31). The man burning llama fat and the man taking ethnographic notes seem to Bell to be doing, at a very high level of abstraction, the same thing. It is because the host, the ethnographer, and the whole human race share a universal agenda of fusing orderly thought and contingent action that ritual is *inevitable*.

Is Bell's central thought/action antithesis really the heart of the matter? Is it too widely applicable to be useful? (For after all, non-ritual life is also thought plus action.) Is her argument about ritual as culture's fusion engine too providential to be believable? Are we willing to make the great renunciations? And is ritual a broad enough concept to account for the myriad works of sacred culture? We will be in a better position to decide after trying out other theories. But we will not forget her first point. Ritual will remain the ethnographic center of gravity.

About this book in context of courses: programs and chapters

Undergraduate and lower graduate courses titled Anthropology of Religion are usually either theoretically partitioned surveys of the more respectable among the above theories, or else ethnologically partitioned overviews of sacred practices (shamanism, priestly religion, etc.). This book is an ethnographic case study fashioned to meet such course strategies halfway. Each chapter concerns one facet of a single close-up ethnography and combines it with one or more "handles" or minimal theoretical discussions connecting the topic to a currently active vein of theorizing. Each chapter is relatively free-standing so as to allow reading in whatever order a course's logic may suggest. The book is not a brief for any one theory, nor does it innovate in theory. It only offers ways to go.

"Handles" connect with some but not all of the major anthropological veins of theorizing about religiosity. To make up for its selectivity, this book might be complemented by any of the several overviews that systematically survey "families" of theories about religion: materialist, intellectualist, emotionalist, sociological, structuralist, phenomenological, cognitive-evolutionary, and ontological. Among such books are James. S. Bielo's compact yet inclusive *Anthropology of Religion: The Basics* (2015), Daniel Pals' historically rich *Nine Theories of Religion* (2014), and

Fiona Bowie's British-based *Anthropology of Religion: An Introduction* (2006). The same purpose might be served by Robert L. Winzeler's *Anthropology and Religion: What We Know, Think, and Question* (2012), or Jack Eller's *Introducing Anthropology of Religion: Culture to the Ultimate* (2nd ed., Routledge, 2014). These last two are textbooks structured by typologies of religious practice, but each is marbled through with commentaries on major theoretical contributors.

Better suited to higher-level courses is Michael Lambek's compendious 2008 *Reader in the Anthropology of Religion*, which gathers excerpts with both ethnographic and theoretical impact, and sorts them according to an idiosyncratic "Aristotelian" map of the subdiscipline. Lambek and Janice Boddy have also orchestrated a second sophisticated guide to current theoretical discussions. It is composed of 28 mostly recent research-plus-theory excerpts, under the title *A Companion to the Anthropology of Religion* (2013).

Chapter 1, "A single nest," concerns how the peoples of the Andean Pacific slope have understood their environment: as a livelihood and simultaneously as a joint human-animal-plant-mountain society. They did so through a peculiar representation of humanity and nature known as the Huari-Llacuaz model. Its essence is the notion of society as not a unitary organization but an antagonistic interdependence between two poles of human and superhuman power. Rapaz has a predominantly Llacuaz legacy, implicating altitude, wildness, and herding. Llacuaz settlements like Rapaz saw themselves as descendants of the highest peaks, owing their pasture and water rights to glacial lords. But why should natural features be seen as lords at all? The question exemplifies a universal question about worship. Faced with the apparently pan-human inclination to see nonhuman phenomena as persons, recent anthropology asks if the social view of nature might not reflect some *brain function*. One cognitive-evolutionary stream of argument holds that humans almost everywhere perceive the world as full of "strange" beings like jealous mountains not because cultures freely invent such imaginings, but rather because all cultural activity is constrained by an underlying, evolved psychological disposition to see such beings. For some, this disposition is a mere "byproduct" of cognitive evolution; religiosity is then a curious side effect of other cognitive-evolutionary processes. But others think it an adaptive trait selected for its own value. The latter tendency proposes that natural selection has favored worshipful societies simply because religiosity imparts *survivable, "prosocial" habits*. In this chapter "handles" point to cognitive-minded anthropology by Guthrie, Boyer, Pyysiäinen, Atran and others.

Chapter 2, "A little palace of analogies," is about the ritual work done within Kaha Wayi. It addresses attachments and fights among people and mountains, with emphasis on how to manipulate weather by ritual. Kaha Wayi's formal, politicized cult of mountain lords exemplifies a wide Andean tradition, but stands out insofar as it exists today as a temple priesthood. Conceptually, the chapter sketches how the Kaha Wayi priesthood might look within Philippe Descola's recent innovative reworking of inquiries about the *a priori* structures of culture as shared mental life. This addresses another fundamental debate about religiosity: do all mythologies and rituals manifest deep uniformities of cultural logic? Or do cultures differ in *fundamental premises for organizing experience into categorical structures*? Developing a new variant of structuralism, Descola argues for a reclassification of humanity's basic alternatives for ordered thought. In rituals of governance, sacrifice, and gender-structured political economy, Rapaz often expresses what Descola calls "analogism," a way of knowledge characteristic of agrarian state-level societies.

Chapter 3, "Children of the mummy Libiac Cancharco," ethnohistorically sketches Rapaz's domain of the sacred as it was in post-Inka times: ancestor-focused mummy veneration, with sacrifices, oracles, and kinship celebrations. The mid-colonial Church campaigned to "extirpate" ancestral mummy cult in the Rapaz area, and these campaigns seem to have produced a boomerang effect by empowering Rapaz's socially potent magical leaders and weather-mastering *bendelhombres*. It also shifted their ritual arena from mummies to mountains. Anthropological theories about ancestor cult exemplify a classic but still productive vein of theorizing to the effect that religion is the way society makes itself visible to itself: it is *society sacralized*, as taught by Durkheim and Hertz. "Handles" here attach to the ongoing discussion of what death means to society and why the dead must be made to live on.

Chapter 4, "Songs for herds and crops," samples the verbal part of Rapaz's modern ritual life. It begins with a resumé of Rapaz's little-documented variety of the Quechua language and considers its status in a Spanish-dominated yet persistently diverse land. The ethnographic emphasis here is on the fieldwork of listening: ritual considered as a work in the media of sound and words. Focusing in on herdsmen's ritual all nighter at a remote cattle station, we consider the emotional power of songs in praise of famous cow and bull archetypes (*ila*). Such ritual intensity forms another of the durable central themes in the anthropology of religion: why do many—but not all—religions foster "altered" mental experience, rich in emotion and straining at the limits of "normal" thought? Song and rite generate "affect and . . . a way of controlling affect" through extraordinary mental states, a theme central to several theories of religiosity including those of William James and Tanya Luhrmann.

Chapter 5, "Mending their sacred things," focalizes the materiality of religious life. It is partly a chronicle of hands-on involvement with Rapaz's sacred objects: khipus, altar objects, dried birds, sacred vital stones, and offered animals. Unwilling to let sacred patrimony decay, but also unwilling to disrupt ritual work, authorities assigned to the authors *in situ* technical conservation of the sacred things. Cleaning and shoring up the material infrastructure of mountain cult brought to the fore a hidden cargo of symbolism. These were symbolic things par excellence. But why are symbols revered as the very source of human well-being? This venerable question brings us to a triple theoretical choice. From Clifford Geertz we inherit the idea that people "make sense out of experience [and] give it form and order" through the play of *symbolism* in a "text" of emblems, gestures, etc. Thus is meaning assigned to action. But this idea has rivals equally central to anthropology: the notion of religiosity as a "primitive science" as developed by E. E. Evans-Pritchard and Robin Horton, and the rival idea of religion as *a manifestation of power.* Two variants of the "power" thesis are those of Maurice Bloch and by Talal Asad.

Chapter 6, "A temple by night," returns to the larger question of how we, as "foreign" onlookers, are to make sense of Rapaz's mountain veneration complex— or of any body of beliefs not contained within our familiar notions of science and religion "proper." During the years of Rapaz research, this continued to be the anthropologist's central disquiet. But the concern took a new direction as cultural anthropology generated a radical variant of cultural relativism known as the "ontological turn." As one way to consider whether "ontology" helps capture the Rapaz ethos, we consider whether Rapacinos, with their major religious differences among themselves, display ontological diversity. Worries about profanation accentuated friction among three mentalities: the "old allegiance" to Kaha Wayi; social-cum-technical modernism with its cosmopolitan view; and Protestant conversion, which challenges both. Do these divergences express differences in the deep foundations of culture? Are sacred things iceberg tips of alternative tacit philosophies? We engage thoughts about the transience of "ontological" objects, drawing on recent work by Marisol de la Cadena, Guillermo Salas Carreño, G.E.R. Lloyd, and Morten Pedersen.

Chapter 7, "The ground trembles," returns to the Introduction's query about making the notion of religion anthropologically useful. We consider Talal Asad's assertion that secularism is an implicit, but not impartial, background to the ethnography of religion, and we take note of current challenges to religion as a viable field of study. How might the not-exactly-religious ritual life of Rapaz look minus its formerly steady subdisciplinary frame? We consider recent proposals to distance the study of sacred culture from its traditional basis, such as "posthumanist" or "new materialist" approaches. One is that of Bruno Latour, who proposes annulling social sciences' nature-versus-culture premises. We close with a coda on whether anthropologists' own religious participation, or lack of it, has a bearing on the anthropological vocation.

A note about research and norms

The research was done by a team of specialists, with myself as the principle investigator of the ethnographic part and Víctor Falcón Huayta of the archaeological part. Different chapters have different subdisciplinary agendas. The exposition brings forward these and other participants' respective contributions, but the text as a whole, together with any errors that it might contain, are mine.

In representing the Quechua language, I have distinguished between two practices: on the one hand linguistic transcription using Peru's "official" orthography (devised by a semi-governmental commission in the 1970s and later updated), and on the other, the homemade transcriptions that literate Rapacinos invent for purposes like making rehearsal books or drawing sketch maps. The former is used when transcribing from scratch, but when quoting local writers who use the latter I do not "correct" it. Translations not otherwise attributed are by the author.

In research, people were asked if they would prefer to be mentioned by their real names or pseudonyms. Almost everybody preferred real names, so I use real names except when mentioning something confidential or potentially harmful to someone's interests. The entire project was carried out under daily supervision by Rapaz's *Comunidad Campesina* or legally recognized corporation of the commons, which owns the Kaha Wayi-Pasa Qulqa complex and its contents. The architectural conservation and archaeological parts of the project were licensed by Peru's Instituto Nacional de Cultura, the ministerial agency responsible for material national patrimony.

Notes

1 According to the 2007 census.
2 New community meeting hall, new municipal offices, improvements in the Health Center including lodging for medical staff, stadium bleachers, upgraded hydroelectric generator, new public bathrooms, and new artisanal weaving workshop.
3 Anthony F.C. Wallace, an ethnohistorian of the Iroquoian peoples in New York and Ontario, viewed ritual as the bootstrap by which the Seneca saved their polity from extinction. Out of this research he originated a theory that ritual revival is itself the source of new religions (1966).
4 The ritual studies platform was first proclaimed in 1977 and has offered a journal of its own for thirty years (Grimes 1987, 1). Some of its exponents are anthropologists, but most teach in cultural studies, religious studies, drama or liturgy departments, or else in groups where area and language expertise are paramount (for example, Asian studies or Classics).

References

Bell, Catherine. 1992. *Ritual Theory, Ritual Practice*. New York and Oxford: Oxford University Press.

Bellman, Beryl. 1984. *The Language of Secrecy: Symbols and Metaphors in Poro Ritual*. New Brunswick, NJ: Rutgers University Press.

Bielo, James S. 2015. *Anthropology of Religion: The Basics*. London: Routledge.

Boddy, Janice, and Michael Lambek, eds. 2013. *A Companion to the Anthropology of Religion*. Chichester, UK: John Wiley.

Bowie, Fiona. 2006. *Anthropology of Religion: An Introduction*, 2nd ed. Oxford: Blackwell.

Brown, Donald. 1991. *Human Universals*. Philadelphia, PA: Temple University Press.

Brown, Michael F. 2009. *Who Owns Native Culture?* Cambridge, MA: Harvard University Press.

Castro, Victoria, and Carlos Aldunate. 2003. "Sacred Mountains in the Highlands of the South-Central Andes." *Mountain Research and Development* 23(1): 73–79.

Chapman, Anne. 1982. *Drama and Power in a Hunting Society: The Selk'nam of Tierra del Fuego*. Cambridge: Cambridge University Press.

Drucker, Philip. 1967. *To Make My Name Good: A Reexamination of the Southern Kwakiutl Potlatch*. Berkeley, CA: University of California Press.

Eller, Jack. 2014. *Introducing Anthropology of Religion: Culture to the Ultimate*, 2nd ed. London: Routledge.

Fabian, Johannes. 2002. *Time and the Other: How Anthropology Makes Its Object*. New York: Columbia University Press.

Falcón Huayta, Víctor. 2014. "San Cristóbal de Rapaz: Hacia un enfoque comunitario del patrimonio y su gestión." Unpublished academic paper. Maestría en Gestión del Patrimonio Cultural, Universidad Nacional Mayor de San Marcós.

Gusinde, Martin. 1961 [1937]. *The Yamana: The Life and Thought of the Water Nomads of Cape Horn. Vol. V*, translated by Frieda Schütze. New Haven, CT: Human Relations Area Files.

Handelman, Don. 2004. "Why Ritual in Its Own Right? How So?" *Social Analysis: The International Journal of Social and Cultural Practice* 48(2): 1–32.

Lambek, Michael. 2008. *A Reader in the Anthropology of Religion*, 2nd ed. Oxford: Blackwell.

Needham, Rodney. 1972. *Belief, Language, and Experience*. Oxford: Basil Blackwell.

Pals, Daniel. 2014. *Nine Theories of Religion*, 3rd ed. New York: Oxford University Press.

Ramos, Alcida Rita. 2008. "Disengaging Anthropology." In *A Companion to Latin American Anthropology*, edited by Deborah Poole. Oxford: Blackwell. 465–484.

Ruiz Estrada, Arturo. 1981. *Los quipus de Rapaz*. Huacho: Centro de Investigación de Ciencia y Tecnología de Huacho.

Saler, Benson. 1993. *Conceptualizing Religion: Immanent Anthropologists, Transcendent Natives, and Unbounded Categories*. Leiden, Netherlands: E.J. Brill.

Salomon, Frank. 2004. *The Cord Keepers: Khipus and Culture in a Peruvian Village*. Durham, NC: Duke University Press.

Staal, Frits. 1979. "The Meaninglessness of Ritual." *Numen* 26(1): 2–22.

Starn, Orin. 1991. "Missing the Revolution: Anthropologists and the War in Peru." *Cultural Anthropology* 6(1): 63–91.

Stausberg, Michael. 2009. *Contemporary Theories of Religion: A Critical Companion*. London: Routledge.

Trevor-Roper, Hugh. 1983. "The Highland Traditions of Scotland." In *The Invention of Tradition*, edited by Eric Hobsbawm. Cambridge: Cambridge University Press. 15–41.

Wallace, Anthony F.C. 1966. *Religion: An Anthropological View*. New York: Random House.

Wilmsen, Edwin. 1989. *Land Filled with Flies: A Political Economy of the Kalahari*. Chicago, IL: University of Chicago Press.

Winzeler, Robert L. 2012. *Anthropology and Religion: What We Know, Think, and Question*, 2nd ed. Plymouth, UK: Altamira Press.

1

A SINGLE NEST

(and some theories about cognitive-evolutionary foundations of religiosity)

"Rapaz—it's where the condor put on his scarf." Thus neighboring villagers jest about the high, cold, rugged village, which stands on a triangular ledge at 4,040 meters (13,255 feet)[1] over sea level (see Figure 1.1). Indeed, daily at lunch time a condor glided over our lab, close enough to flash its "scarf" of snowy neck feathers. As it sailed out over the abyss of the Checras River canyon, the condor made me remember Wallace Stevens' lines:

> The pensive man . . . He sees that eagle float
> For which the intricate Alps are a single nest.
>
> *Stevens 1954 [1942], 216*

Seen from Rapaz, subsidiary ranges of the Andean cordillera unfold westward as intricate as crumpled paper. Foaming melt-off from the snowcaps rolls down the Checras River, a silver thread at the bottom of a chasm. Two miles vertically down—perhaps fifty miles on the road's zigzagging descent—the water is still glacier cold. It flows past bright green asparagus fields, crosses a ruin-strewn coastal desert, and dives down into the Pacific depths.

This chapter concerns how one population made of the soaring, plunging Andean landscape a "single nest," and whom they feel themselves to be as its inhabitants. Making a home involves both physical adaptive work and cultural work to guide and motivate labor.

We emphasize the cultural more than the physical infrastructure. We seek to highlight an Andean view of geographic features as person-like presences, with whom humans reckon through ritual and negotiation. In perceiving the world as full of person-like superhuman agents, Andean people resemble much of humanity. But why should this be so?

FIGURE 1.1 Rapaz village seen from Cerro Calvario. Photo by Víctor Falcón Huayta.

In a first round of theorizing, this chapter will take note of recently proliferating theories that answer, "evolution." In one branch of evolutionary theorizing about religiosity, the disposition to perceive mysterious agents is explained as an almost random side effect of cognitive faculties that evolved by serving other functions. A rival group of theorists agrees that religiosity has preconditions in brain evolution but denies its randomness. Rather, they see in it adaptive value: "prosocial" neural dispositions that enhance ability to live in groups. A third tendency suggests that evolutionary selection does indeed underlie religiosity but the selection involved is not brain evolution. Instead, they suggest, what has been selected is groups themselves. Which groups? Groups that that have invented (consciously or otherwise) a uniquely durable device for establishing loyalty, namely, sacred symbols.

Llacuaces, the "Children of Lightning"

Historically, Rapaz typifies the high part of an apparently unique Andean adaptive system, famously called "verticality."[2] This term refers to a politically coordinated society built of stacked "islands" on the land, so that political societies of varied scale "sampled" the resources of high and low landscape. The articulation of high with low involved military pressure and conquest. Societies from irrigable coastal valleys fought upward to control water sources, and societies native to the inland heights fought downward to acquire cultivable land. Early legend sometimes figures the relationship as multiethnic interdependence, exemplified as the marriage of high with low and of water with earth.

Like most mountain dwellers, Rapacinos (who numbered 711 in the 2007 census) move around the landscape. They live part of the time in their high-lying village, partly because that is where the government provides compulsory school for their children. The nuclear village remains the place for reunions and festivities. But, apart from holidays, on any given day under half of the Rapacinos are in town. Many roam up on the high slopes (*puna*) with animals: llamas, alpacas, cows, sheep, and a few horses and donkeys. As one follows them to the highest pastures, grass gives way to cliff-growing lichens that look like gaudy petroglyphs, then to bare rock and snow. Puna life is life at the very end of the biosphere. At night, shivering under millions of stars, one feels the chill of interstellar space disturbingly close.

FIGURE 1.2   On the puna. Corral and herders' house at Pampas, over Rapaz. Photo by Víctor Falcón Huayta.

FIGURE 1.3   Puna and cordillera over Rapaz in wet season, with herders' corrals and houses in the distance. Photo by the author.

Yet Rapacinos don't experience the heights as inhospitable. When I asked which they like better, their herding life up on the high pastures (*puna*) or their life as village-based farmers, almost everyone said "I'd rather be on the puna, that's a beautiful life." Tawny grass waving in the wind, brawny bulls and graceful alpacas, meals of sizzling meat, brilliant sunlight and starlit nights, cozy sleep in thatched stone igloos—these are images of well-being, and not at all the freezing privation that lowlanders imagine (see Figures 1.2, 1.3). Using solar electric panels, people on the remote slopes even enjoy media appliances. Animals bred on rough puna grasses are loved and bragged about. From adolescence, people prove their valor by fighting anything that hurts the herds: condors, foxes, and pumas, and also rustlers. They devote offerings and invocations to their mighty neighbors, the living mountains who "own" rain and thereby give or withhold this kind of well-being.

This condor's-eye view of society historically takes a form often called the Huari-Llacuaz model. It is most clearly expressed in 17th-century testimonies. One reason for anthropologists to be interested in it is that, unlike so many occidental models, this Andean notion does not posit an antithesis between nature and culture. It divides the world otherwise. Another is that it does not see society as unification (as in "United States"). Rather it imagines society as a field of interaction between antagonistically interdependent poles. In "dual society" (a concept invented to characterize Amazonian and Andean America), difference itself is the source of society.

"The West" met the Huari-Llacuaz formation over 400 years ago. It became prominent in literate discussion not during the Spanish conquest era, 1532–1569, but at a later time when Catholic churchmen realized that a half century of indoctrination had failed to inculcate Catholic orthodoxy. Rather, a hybrid and innovative Andean ritualism had taken shape. From about 1608 through the 1670s, and again in the 1720s, Spanish clergy invented a kind of missionary ethnography for researching the non-Christian beliefs of Andean "Indians," the better to uproot what clerics (especially, but not only, Jesuits) saw as Satan's fraud on gullible neophytes. Rapaz forms part of the region where these extirpators of idolatry hit hardest and most repeatedly.[3] Trial records of "idolaters," together with the unique Quechua book of Huarochirí,[4] vividly show how the ancestors of Rapacinos (and many other highlanders) thought about heights and valleys, herding and farming, mountains and lowlands.

Pierre Duviols, a pathbreaking researcher on colonial Peruvian religion, noticed that in many communities along the western range of the Central-Peruvian Andes, the extirpators heard people talk about the nature of society in a manner different from European suppositions (1971).

The Andean model perceived no boundary between nature and culture (or environment and society). Rather, in Andean eyes, nature and culture together were formed upon the opposing poles of montane or celestial altitude and riverine or oceanic depth. Human society, seen as one aspect of the "vertical" world, lives suspended between the poles, that is, between the ice and rock of the cordillera crest and the green oases near sea level. Life was, and in some respects still is, a conversation, a fight, a wedding, between contrasting kinds of people: people of the heights called *Llacuaz* (*llaqwash* in a modern Quechua transcription) and valley people called *Huari* (*wari*).

In his 1973 article "Huari y Llacuaz," Duviols limelights a 1621 passage from the extirpator Arriaga:

> in a town in the sierra, the Indian should be asked if he is a *llacuaz* or a *huari*, for they call a huari or *llactayoc*[5] anyone native to the town of his ancestors and who have no recollection of having come from outside. All those whose fathers and ancestors were born elsewhere they call llacuazes, even if they themselves were born in the town. . . .
>
> The llacuazes, like persons newly arrived from somewhere else, have fewer *huacas* [shrines, superhuman beings]. Instead, they often fervently worship and venerate their *malquis*, which . . . are the mummies of their ancestors. They also worship huaris, that is, the founders of the earth or the persons to whom it first belonged and who were its first populators. These [huaris] have many huacas and they tell fables about them . . . there are generally divisions and enmities between the clans and factions and they inform on each other.
>
> *Arriaga 1968 [1621], 116*

This is a pregnant paragraph. It asks us to imagine a society (of several thousand people) that sees itself as a banding together of multiple corporate lineages called *ayllus*, something like clans. Each ayllu thought its founders emerged separately out of the earth at a unique "dawning place" or *pacarina*. Huari ayllus were felt to descend from ancient dwellers in the western valleys. Huari descent was associated with antiquity, with agriculture, with stability, with plant fertility, and with wealth. Huaris had many shrines that were themselves parts of the earth: monoliths, cliffs, springs, caves, etc. They were sometimes called *llactayoc*, "possessors of the village," with implication of possessing its very divinities. Huari groups were often considered to belong ethnically to the now-extinct coastal or Yunka peoples, and as of 1657 one such group was still said to conduct worship in the ancestral coastal tongue (Duviols 1973, 182). In "biethnic" villages where Huari and Llacuaz lineages coexisted, Huari sacred beings were often female, embodying the depth and fecundity of the earth.

Llacuaz ayllus, by contrast, thought themselves descended from the llama-alpaca herders of the high punas. Llacuaces were said to have entered society as invaders, or guests, or sometimes vagrants. The word Llacuaz connoted alien origin and rude customs as well as pastoralism. Lacking local origin shrines, Llacuaces remembered and worshiped their mummified progenitors in faraway places of origin. The protectors of the ancient Llacuaces were the powers of sky and altitude: the storm and the snowcapped peaks called *jirka* in Central Peruvian Quechua or *apu* in the Inka heartlands (Híjar Soto 1984). Llacuaz ayllus revered "destructive hail, frightening thunder, and gloomy clouds, but also the rain that makes the wild pasture sprout and turn green" (Duviols 1973, 171). They called themselves "the children of lightning." Llacuaz people identified with llamas, guanacos, and deer of the high puna. They propitiated the high lakes out of which these fleet, cold-loving animals mythically emerged—especially the giant highland lake Chinchaycocha or Lake Junín. When the Llacuaz wak'as coexisted with Huaris of seaward-facing valleys, there was a tendency to give Llacuaz male gender valence.

Does the Huari-Llacuaz worldview reflect a historic sequence? The archaeologist Augusto Cardich thinks the people called llacuaces had in fact arrived as invaders (1985). Their ancestors seem to have originated on the inland high plains of Junín and Pasco Departments, at 12,000-plus feet over sea level, just as their myths affirmed. Duviols thinks it was about 1350 CE that Llacuaz forces surged over the mountain crests and spread downward, conquering warmer, more fertile lands, and a newer archaeological inquiry suggests even later dates (Chase 2015). Their original homeland, the "plain of Junín," was (and still is) a rich land for camelids but a miserable one for agriculture. For that reason they became aggressive and migratory.[6]

Like armed pastoralists in many parts of the world (inner Eurasia and East Africa especially), Peru's alpaca and llama drivers proved efficient aggressors. They apparently pushed their way westward and downward into old, settled agricultural areas at lower and warmer altitudes. Recent scholars see fortified remains of the Late Intermediate Period (i.e., immediately pre-Inka times) as reflecting an age of widespread local warfare in which even small settlements had to defend themselves and their crops against other small polities—circumstances typical of a period without imperial peace.

On the western slope from about 11,000 feet (3,500 meters) downward, people during most of the colonial era saw their world as the result of confrontations between these two ancient lifeways. The outcomes varied. In mixed villages, Llacuaz lineages—we can almost say clans—saw themselves as victors but also as parvenus in need of deeper legitimation. Members attended the mummy cults of Huari ancestors, not unlike *nouveaux riches* of our times who try to work their families into the high society descended from "founding fathers." A situation like this was expressed, in the idiom of myth, by the Quechua narrators whose legacy is the great Manuscript of Huarochirí (Salomon and Urioste 1991).

In other places, stable arrangements of economic exchange established a pattern of Llacuaz dominance in animal economy (wool, meat, yarn, clothing) balanced with Huari dominance in agriculture (corn, squash, greens, and the luscious fruit of the lower valleys). Coca leaf (Erythroxylon coca) was the vital vehicle for ritual maintenance of high-low sociability, so arrangements around coca-producing lands in the "middle yunka," or irrigable subtropical altitudes, tended to become the hinge issue in Llacuaz-Huari politics. In one valley not so far from Rapaz, scuffling about coca lands continued not only throughout Inka times but on into the first three decades of the Spanish colony (Rostworowski and Marcus 1988).

Llacuaz derives from the word *llaqwa*, meaning vicuña (Lama vicugna). An eloquent word! Nothing could be more emblematic of high mountain life than this elfin camelid, so skinny, skittish, and wild, but at the same time so robust and valuable. The prehispanically rooted vicuña surround hunt is the very symbol of Llacuaz prowess. With nets and poles, shears and drums, Rapacinos hike en masse up the freezing ridges to encircle, shear, and then release vicuñas. Vicuña wool is worth more by weight than gold. It occasionally sufficed to pay for major improvements like the community bus. But by 2016, poachers had killed all of Rapaz's vicuñas.

Llaqwas in Quechua and *avicuñado* in Spanish mean a volatile, unreliable person. "*Llaqwas llaqwanunmi*" a Rapacino said to me, meaning, "The unstable man took off like a vicuña." Inhabitants of nearby Junín say *llaqwash* to mean "people without manners, people of the puna"(Cerrón-Palomino 1976, 81). To Huánuco Quechua speakers, *lagwas* means a person who relishes meat, meat-rich diets being the privilege of herdspeople (Weber et al. 1998, 294). In Ancash, *llakwash* means the sap of the giant bromeliad Puya Raimondi, a high-altitude plant so memorably strange it has become an emblem of the puna lifeway (Parker and Chávez 1976, 92). In Huarochirí, the word denotes llama caravaneers who troop down from the highest pastures to trade their animal wealth (wool, leather, tallow, knitted clothes) for crops. Comic dancers called *llacuacos* in the nearby Chancay watershed prance in woolen rags to represent half-wild, Quechua-monolingual herders from the heights (Rivera Andia 2012, 178).

Rapaz seems to have stood out as a Llacuaz outlier derived from higher-dwelling Llacuaz groups around Lake Junín. We can infer this because history has left us an extraordinary source about the ethnic group of which it formed part. In 1614 an unknown parish priest gave the Jesuit extirpator Fabián de Ayala a beautifully composed memo that the priest had written eleven years earlier. Its title is "Errors, Rituals, Superstitions and Ceremonies of the Indians of Chinchaycocha and Others of Peru." Chinchaycocha, or Junín Lake, was the very sanctuary of Llacuaz origins, and it is close to Rapaz—straight up and over the crest of the western cordillera, within a hard day's walking distance from the village nucleus.

This manuscript emphasizes an isolated, double-peaked snowcap named Raco (*raku*, "robust, thick"), near Rapaz's uppermost boundary. From it two brother-deities emerged: Raco, the lord of food according to Chinchaycocha belief, and Yanayacolca, who "went to another province near that one, called Andajes"(Duviols 1974 [Anonymous 1603], 279). Andajes was the colonial name for the province in which Rapaz lies. So the person-mountain avatar Yanayacolca may be the name of the expansive lineage of which Rapaz formed part. Rapaz ceramic, both archaeological and recent, seems to confirm connections in Cerro de Pasco, the basin of Chinchaycocha or Lake Junín (Falcón Huayta 2007, 19, 30–34).

Llacuaz is a relative concept. In recent times, Rapacinos maintained ritualized trading partnerships with herders from still farther up in the Junín basin, and these seemed to them Llacuaz in relation to Rapaz people. Irene Luya said:

They were animal raisers, you see, because they lived way up on the heights. No kind of agriculture can grow up there. Not potatoes, nothing. So they'd come down here in harvest season and take things back. And up there they used to work toward that [trip], they used to make their pots, they'd make wool capes, they'd make ropes, all that. With that they'd come and perform barter here. That's how we lived. [They brought] *chalwa* [fish from high lakes], *kushuru* [edible algae], even clay for washing, because they had clay soil. There was no detergent then, we washed laundry with clay. They'd bring meat, all those products from the heights, from animal raising. They weren't Rapacinos, no, no! They were from other settlements far away! It took them a whole day or two days to arrive here.

Glacial lords: the nature and rules of rainfall-based pasturing

The quest for water is the urgent, worrying concern of agropastoralists in semi-arid western Peru, and it is the central theme of their technology as well as their mythology. Water, considered as a superhuman force, is the unifying part of the world. Water circulating up out of the ocean into the celestial river—that is, the Milky Way—yields life-giving but also destructive rain, which then courses down the mountains and rivers to return to the Pacific. Rain regenerates life by giving grass for herds and irrigation for crops, but it destroys life when it descends in the form of flash floods and earthslides. The Checras Valley is scarred with bare cone-shaped slopes where earthslides have instantly buried whole agropastoral neighborhoods.

The waters of the heights—storms, glaciers, and glacial lakes—are imagined as harsh and wild, generally with a male valence. Llacuaz people of old saw themselves as children and intimates of these powers. The ultimate "owners" of water are the 6,000-meter monster peaks of the Cordillera Waywash and the Cordillera Blanca, including Yerupajá and Huascarán. But most ritual practice addresses smaller, closer mountains whose bodies govern the local flows of water down to individual's pastures and fields. Mountains have personalities and social relationships, feelings and moods. They are often described as if they were a political community. When addressing the mountain range as a whole one speaks to the "*cabildo* (town council) of hills." It has an internal hierarchy, which parallels approximately the hydrographic flow chart.

Rapaz's temple has the mission of propitiating but also making demands of mountains. People and terrain are related through a system of rights and duties more like a constitution than a theology. It is explained in Chapter 2.

When a young Rapacino signs up to become a *comunero*, he gains the right to use a *jirka* or *estancia* (usually his parents') up on the 34,000 hectares of common range.[7] An estancia consists of an oval-shaped, thatched house with a stone-walled corral (see Figure 1.4). It is a base for pasturing on open range. He also acquires a right to pasture a quota of private animals (up to 150 sheep, 20 cattle, 20 alpacas, and five horses, donkeys, or mules).[8] Although the *puna*, or dry grassland, of the

FIGURE 1.4 A herder's house on an *estancia*. Photo by Víctor Falcón Huayta.

high slopes looks endless, wild, and lonely, it is in reality completely measured and socialized; every spot on it has a name as well as use rules, a history of disputes, and specific symbolic associations. The most local capillaries of the mountain-propitiating system are small stone-lined chambers or boxes installed inside high corrals. There herders deposit gifts to a local mountain, including the ear-clippings left from earmarking, to "pay for" the animals' health.

Each comunero also acquires duties to serve at least one turn as a community herdsman, caring for cows, sheep, and camelids that belong to the *Empresa Comunal*. These herds live on a reserved portion of the commons, the slopes of the pyramid-shaped black mountain Chururu. Adult Rapacinos are skilled in birthing animals, shearing, and washing wool. Most resident women, and some men, can spin and hand weave. Wives make beautifully knitted or crocheted clothes for their families and increasingly for sale via the new textile cooperative. A person skilled with animals also knows how to account for the herd. Controlling the increase and commerce of communal herds is one of the main agenda items in village assemblies.

Life with animals, as many ethnographers have shown,[9] is a matter of conviviality—conviviality in a Llacuaz-like tradition. Herding ritual has two climaxes, one in "carnival," that is, the rainy month of February, which is also the camelid mating season, and another in the dry season, usually July. Herdspeople corral their animals for branding (*señalakuy*, *marcación*), medicine, updating of records, and magical fecundation. Ritual transitorily creates a joint human-animal society, far from the disciplines of village and church. We will revisit animal rituals in Chapter 4.

Motherwoman: the nature and rules of irrigation

In the Checras watershed, as in many parts of South America (and some other parts of the world), female sacred beings dwell in spring-fed grottos. Hidden or spontaneously upwelling water tends to have female valence. Some cave springs are Catholic pilgrimage shrines re-founded around a vision of the Virgin. Less Catholicized spring shrines are homes of old aquatic females today called "sirens" or "mermaids": seductive spirit-women.

The town at the mouth of the Checras River, Churín, lives by Lima-based tourist traffic to its hot, mineral-rich springs. Mamahuarmi, "Motherwoman," is the name of the most scenic and beloved spring: a turquoise grotto pool surrounded by greenery and flowerbeds.

Mamahuarmi today looks urbanized and touristic. But an almost forgotten and beautifully written student report brings us close to the older, rural sense of female water. In 1968 Earl Morris, Leslie Brownrigg, Susan Bourque, and Henry Dobyns were working on a doctoral training project in the Checras canyon (about a thousand meters lower than Rapaz, at the hamlet of Mayobamba). There, they saw Motherwoman, "the water principle," guiding irrigation agriculture:

> Before work begins, all pay ritual homage to the water principle. Mama Huarmi, in her home in Poq Mountain. [Its name is an onomatopoeia for burbling water.] Mayobamba's feminine principle of fertility is named "Mother Woman" but she seems more akin to a Teutonic Ondine or a Danish water sprite than to the heavy "earth mother" of early Near Eastern religions.
>
> The Mama Huarmi is invisible, and has no tangible idolic [sic] representation, but she is conceived as being a beautiful, young goddess with long flowing black hair, dressed in the bright colors of mountain finery, yellow, orange, and red, that villagers favor. She lives near the spring Poq where during the rainy season a waterfall miraculously appears spouting out of the earth. She is friendly, playful, bounteous and dependable in her gift of water to the town. Children, who often play in the broad pampa of Nauticocha, the community pasture which lies north of Poq, will sometimes go up to the spring to call to her, and to invent songs for her to hear.
>
> The Mama Huarmi is officially addressed by the community only in the irrigation canal cleaning in the spring. The feline doll and all the workers who clean the ditches present themselves at Poq to explain their task, and to implore that Mama Huarmi will continue to send water rushing down the canals as she has in the past.
>
> Neighboring villagers too have or have had a Mama Huarmi. This deity is specific to the place and brings water and fertility to the land. Canín and

Puñún, neighboring villages where soil exhaustion, poor irrigation systems and over-population tax agricultural resources, explain their crisis by saying that people from Jucul have stolen their Mama Huarmi. The accounts differ on the nature of what was stolen. Those of Canín say their Mama Huarmi was sitting above a landmark rock on the trail to Mayobamba, Puc'ratururumi (red[10] bull rock) dressed in red, her hair long, sunning herself, combing her hair. Two men from Jucul saw her, sneaked up behind and spirited her away. She wept despondently for her Canín, and often tried to escape, but her Jucul guards always overtook her on Mayobamba soil. She is now locked in a strong prison.

Those of Puñún describe their Mama Huarmi as a less-than life size doll which was being given an airing by her keeper when people from Jucul stole her. Told of the Puñún interpretation, a mountain Mayobamba villager voiced assurance that Mayobamba's Mama Huarmi is a spirit, an idea only, and has never been represented. The idea of a Mama Huarmi idol struck her as quaint and backward. A Mama Huarmi is invisible, an idea like that of the Holy Ghost or the auquin [animate mountain being; see Chapter 2].

The Mama Huarmi abstraction reinforces the mythological ethnocentrism of the patron saint complex in each village. A Mama Huarmi is the genius of the town, the personification of its physical resources, its special guardian and benefactor. In like manner, a patron saint is a personification and mystical leader of the people. As each Mama Huarmi has a unique character, so does a patron saint, and this character affects the whole town.

Morris et al. *1968, 249–250*

Rapaz has a spring-fed irrigation system resembling the ones Morris and his fellow students saw. Indeed, Rapacinos consider themselves fortunate to have a relatively ample water supply. As in many Andean places, including Cuzco (Sherbondy 1986), water flow and water governance became the matrix of ritual and a model of social organization. Of late, the installation of PVC pipe (which excludes algae and mud) has rendered most of the traditional works and rites obsolete, so the treatment of water ritual in these pages includes a lot of "memory ethnography."

Ukan Spring and Qiusar Spring bubble forth from opposite sides of a dome-shaped hill overlooking Rapaz. Each has been separately channeled, so as to form two separate hydraulic systems serving the two village halves or moieties (see Figure 1.5). Above the village, an artificial canal and reservoir system connects the two canals, so that flow into the village and down to the fields can be adjusted between them.

Like innumerable Andean societies, Rapaz defines itself as the union of two rival halves or moieties, named Allauca and Lamash, or K'ollana and Huaylapamba.[11] The halves have separate hydraulic systems of approximately equal length, each with its own canal through the village. As it passes through its respective half of the village, each canal had (and Lamash still has) an elaborate tap and basin or *pileta*.

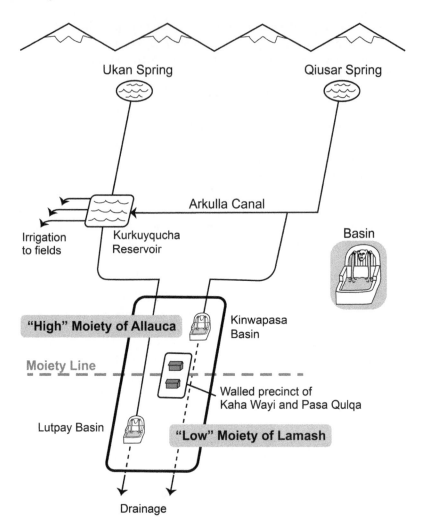

FIGURE 1.5 Main canals of Rapaz according to comunero Juan de Dios Evangelista.

Celebrants welcome their share of water at their respective basins. Like most Andean dual structures, halves are seen as symmetrical in form, complementary in function, and unequal in rank. (Rank refers to ritual precedence, not political superiority.)

Dual organization predating the recent conversion from open canals to pipes was specific to hydraulic matters, not general governance.[12] Ritual rivalry between halves organized the work of canal maintenance. Lamash families and Allauca families formed two teams facing each other in rivalry (*tinkunakuy*, *gananakuy*). Each paraded in pomp up to its spring. Then each cleaned downward, shoveling algae and mud out of the watercourse, racing to finish first. Along the way they danced *wanka* to the sound of a special flute (*shuqush*). When the two teams met, they fought in token of their rivalry. The half whose water first reached its drinking tap was the winner, and it got to lead in the celebrations.

The first water from each side was brought to Kaha Wayi to be magically invoked, and to be saved for a whole year, as a protective essence. Water was collected from each household and added to share in the blessing. This series of acts was called *yaku sariykuy*, "grasping water," and it was believed to help the household's water supply suffice for the year.

As one elder lady remembered:

> At 12:00 exactly, the water was supposed to arrive at the Rapaz water fountain. There we grabbed our water. At midnight it arrived, down the cleaned canals. And the *espensera* (female chief of community), all beautifully dressed in regalia, with her mantle and that big punchbowl, with that bowl she'd receive the first water there. We carried that water and took it to Kaha Wayi and in Kaha Wayi we performed a *mesa* (offering) for it.

The *kamachikuq* (male chief of community) would award the winning moiety a sheep.

As water flows from its path through the village down toward the belt of *chacras* or planted fields, it comes under the routine governance of the Community's Water Judge to make sure irrigation turns are distributed as customary law requires.[13] Rapaz's small-scale irrigated cultivation lies toward the bottom of the village's space and along the Checras riverbank. Some of the water is used to maintain six irrigated paddocks or feedlots on the riverbank.

Chacras: the nature and rules of high-altitude farming

Herding is Rapaz's mainstay, and agriculture supports herding. Only about 10% to 20% of Rapaz is cultivable, and even this consists of tiny fields wedged into steep mountainsides. In Rapaz and neighboring villages, swaths of steep mountainside were terraced in prehispanic antiquity; some of the prehispanic terraces are still in use. Everybody demands an allotment. By the 2010s, villagers practiced less agriculture, leaving some allotments unproductive.

Products include potatoes, of course—this is the very land where potatoes were first domesticated—and potatoes' relatives: the delicious sweet-smoky *oca* (Oxalis tuberosum) and the earthy-crisp *ullucu* (Ullucus tuberosus). The protein-rich grain quinua (Chenopodium quinoa) used to be important, but most families have abandoned homegrown quinua in favor of more prestigious noodles and white rice. For the rest, the green belt just below the village (see Figure 1.6) produces broadbeans, barley, and some onions or carrots. Rapaz produces too little of any one crop to support commercial agriculture. Farming serves rather to hold down food expenses and thereby subsidize herding. Small as it is, farming has a

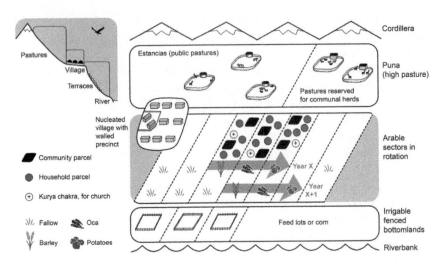

FIGURE 1.6 System of Rapaz communal land use.

most elaborate sacred mystique. It will play a great part in understanding Kaha Wayi's regimen in Chapter 3.

Comuneros have land use rights only at the community's pleasure. The *balternos* (staffholding officers) enforce strict sectorial fallowing, sometimes called *raymi* in Andean literature. This control is necessary because rainfall agriculture (*saki chakra*) at high altitude only works when it respects environmental constraints: thin, easily eroded soil, slow biomass accumulation, and biochemical depletion. Arable land is divided into seven named cultivation sectors (*anqi*), of which only three are in use at any given time. (After agrarian reform the system became eight and three.)

Each sector successively comes into use for a three-year term (*benio* or *ratay*).[14] Each is opened as a potato sector, then continues during the following year as a sector for oca, finishes as a barley sector, and finally is declared closed. At any given time, therefore, Rapaz operates a sector in each of the three crop groups and four (later five) resting zones (*moya*).

Chakras or planted plots (see Figure 1.7) live at the mercy of fluky microclimatic and epidemic effects. To spread risk, villagers receive their land in the form of multiple small parcels within each zone (see Figure 1.8). In a given year each household is working two or three small potato plots and similar numbers of oca and barley plots. Semi-retired members receive one plot less in each sector. As a result, about 300 plots are in use in each of the three active zones. This makes enforcing correct use a big job, and it is the officers of Kaha Wayi who perform it. With herding work taken into account, the amount of hiking involved is huge, yet agronomists have never persuaded people to give up scattered land use. Caring for fields involves frequent ritual work, such as rites to trap evil winds, forestall killing frosts, and chase plant pests, and these favors too depend on the good will of mountains.

FIGURE 1.7 Path from Rapaz village down to terraces presently used as comuneros' parcels in Sector Pueblo.

FIGURE 1.8 Harvesting potatoes in Sector Pueblo.

A traditional inner cabinet rules herding, farming, and ritual

Rapaz has the usual institutions of a state-recognized town, including a small municipality, a justice of the peace, and a *Comunidad Campesina* or legally recognized peasant corporation of the commons. The Comunidad Campesina San Cristóbal de Rapaz is what we translate as the Community. It has its buildings and offices, ledgers, minutes, and computer where elected members do the paperwork of taxes, voting rolls, and collaboration with NGOs, as well as managing finance—all on normal modern lines, in a big new building with three floors.

But what gives the Community gravity and character is an old, more uniquely Andean authority that dwells within this structure. This is the corps of traditional authorities often called *varayos* in Peruvian literature (from *varayuq*, "possessor of a staff of office") or "civil-religious hierarchy." These men and, increasingly, women, form an inner cabinet at the core of ritual and customary agropastoral life. Male members wear the long brown poncho, flowered hat, and decorated coca bag which, as formal regalia, make visible the august force of "custom." (In Andean usage, *costumbre* means unwritten law, not optional traditional practice.) Balternos hold sacred authority as well as delegated managerial power.

Their authority is much older than the jural Community (recognized in 1939). The state-recognized Community has not replaced the varayuq corps but rather created a utilitarian outer shell around it. Translating "custom" into bureaucratic terms, the Community calls its inner cabinet the *Comité Agropastoral* ("Agropastoral Committee").

The Community's vice-president heads the inner cabinet according to a long-standing Andean division of labor. While the President represents the Community in all its exterior relations, the *"vice"* rules its internal life, and he is the one responsible for correct, fruitful relations with the owners of rain. The vice-president inherits the early colonial (or perhaps Inka) title of *kamachikuq* or *kamasichuq*, "the one who creates order."[15] His insignia is a silver-clad wooden staff adorned with carnations (see Figure 1.9). He is elected in odd-numbered years.

The remaining members of the inner cabinet are the six *balternos* ("subalterns"), elected yearly.[16] The balternos perform the public parts of their jobs at assemblies of the community and do their paperwork at the state-recognized community offices.[17] They also gather by night in Kaha Wayi for more private ritual-cum-administrative meetings. This fire-lit, coca-taking meeting is called *rimanakuy*, "the conversation." In it a ritualist leads devotions to the mountains in the form of long invocation chants accompanied by drinks and massive amounts of coca leaf, both as stimulant and as offering (see Chapter 2).

Confidentiality is an important attribute of the rimanakuy. It is remembered that during the long era when authorities were litigating against latifundists, and then again in the early 1960s, they secretly planned the invasion of Hacienda Algolán in Kaha Wayi. As a past ritualist said, "no gossip could leak out of there." The same man recalled that as a child he asked, "Why does my dad visit Kaha Wayi?" and was told "It's the house of the Inkas. People talk there so nobody will hear."

FIGURE 1.9 Procession of balternos, members of an inner traditional government today called the Agropastoral Committee.

Communal endowments and their rites

From panoramic overlooks, older Rapacinos can point out along the sculptured mountainside a few terraces much larger than the rest. Until the 1980s, these were the *kumun chakra*, fields reserved by the Community as its endowment. There were at least two large common fields in each rotation, up to about 120 meters on each side. The work and festivities that took place when comuneros convened to plant, cultivate, and store common harvests underpinned Kaha Wayi and its storehouse Pasa Qulqa.

Common-field tenure had ended before I reached Rapaz.[18] But other ethnographers observed the mountain-oriented festivities of communal fields in nearby villages. Medina Susano saw women at a harvest in the middle Checras

> gather at the center of the field, lay out blankets on the ground to throw the seed [potatoes] down, and begin to drink liquor and chicha. They conduct divinations by coca, they put flowers in their hats, and finally they sing *yaraví* songs to their mountain protectors . . . Men sit around the edges.
>
> *1989, 55*

Earl Morris saw corn planting festivities where women brought and planted garlanded staffs of authority capped with bird images (which are relevant to the Raywan or Food Divinity complex described in Chapters 2 and 3).

The men and women adorn one another with flowers (*huamanripa*, carnations, and chamomile) and the women paint the men's faces white, red, blue, and or green. Some families also paste coca leaves on men's and women's foreheads and cheeks. . . . The staves (varas) function as a kind of digging stick to prepare the actual holes into which the seed is placed after the ground is prepared by the men's garlanded hoes, shovels, and picks.

1968, 119–122

In the upland or pasturing tier the common sector has expanded due to the reconquest of lands formerly claimed by large estates. Land reform reopened a great swath of high puna to Community animals. So it is not surprising that the ritual celebration of animals and their stone image prototypes is an important gathering on the llacuaz-like side of culture. We will encounter the animal powers and their songs in Chapter 4.

Gods in mountains, gods everywhere, gods in the brain: is religiosity an inborn cognitive bias?

At Kaha Wayi, in fields, and on the pastures, the mountain beings are invoked in roster by their names: Saqsar Wayna, Yara Wayna, Qumpir Wayna, Chuqichuqu, Chururu, San Antonio, and San Camilo. Nearby Qisunki, Saqsar Wanka, and Pichilay also receive Rapaz's homage. All these are considered males. Lakes, which likewise receive ritual homage, are sometimes considered female: Cochaquillo, Chaupi Cocha, Churamachay, Chalcó, Anqarayuq, Suerococha Grande and Suerococha Chico, Huytuqucha, Hanka Kuta, Qinwayuq, Wasaqucha, Morococha, Lutacocha, Hawi, Brava Machay, Taho Verde, Uchkumachay, Chiuwriq, and Llaqucha. Nearby Punrún Lake, though belonging to another community, also receives Rapaz's cultic support.

All these beings count as individuals in society and hierarchy. They are referred to with the Quechua third-person pronouns proper to persons— "he/she," not "it."

Mountains and lakes don't seem to resemble people. Yet, in certain contexts, Rapacinos treat them as being persons—persons of a special kind, who have powers that humans lack, and who therefore deserve special propitiation. The traditional structure of authority requires everyone to interact with them in ways that are strictly programmed and different from ordinary communications—in other words, by ritual. Why?

One currently powerful area of theorizing about this is cognitive and/or evolutionary theory of religiosity. Its adherents would see Rapaz as nothing unusual. They would have us note that the mountain cult is an average example of an allegedly pan-human tendency: the tendency to see nonhuman but humanlike personal agents ("gods") behind the impersonal events of life.

Apparently, say some biologists, evolution instilled in humans a disposition to take the evidence of the senses as *incomplete*. Our evolutionary ancestors found advantage in supposing any sound in the grass might indicate animals, or people out of view, or something unfamiliar. They were disposed to receive sense data as signs with multiple possible referents. It is our specialization to live in a world taken as a world of such signs, and to elaborate sign interpretations until we construct in our heads—or better put, among our heads—parallel universes. The shared cognized universe is made of representations that organize inherently ambiguous phenomena.

Cognitive theories of religion, then, have in common the notion that religiosity is a cultural receptacle in which groups hold, share, and elaborate their sense of *something more*. Perception doesn't yield unambiguous results. The sensation that there's *something more* is an unsleeping goad to consciousness. It stimulates curiosity, anxiety, and reasoning. Saqsar Wayna is a mountain, and yet . . . that leaves so much open.

One version of such theory holds that religion elaborates the feeling—perhaps everyone has it intuitively—that when a raincloud rains or a mountain trembles, it does so because somebody or something is *making* it happen.

It's easy to see that the old Andean habit of thought extends society as a web of personal causation outward to include all parts of the world. But it is hard to see why people are so inclined to extend it indiscriminately. Why is impersonal (scientific) causation a hard idea to have, while anthropomorphic causation is an easy one? What is stopping people from simply saying that clouds are rain, instead of introducing an imponderable third party as the author of rain? Why do most societies most of the time systematically steer us into this cognitive detour—and then build up domineering institutions, like Kaha Wayi, that reinforce it?

Could it be that some property of the human cognitive system constrains us to look for humanlike but sensorially elusive agents? Might religious commonalities among far-flung cultures reflect a common inborn predisposition that makes religious ideas easy to generate (Lawson and McCauley 1990)? Psychological explanations of religiosity and evolutionary theories about why they exist became hot foci of research in the last two decades. The arguments summarized below are offered by their authors with a profusion of mostly lab-based experience, but some have gathered ethnographic evidence purporting to show how built-in human cognitive dispositions shape and align the creative power of culture.

Starting in 1980 Stewart Guthrie identified the predisposition as a human tendency to see "faces in the clouds" (1993). Universally, humans interpret ambiguous phenomena anthropomorphically. Caught in a terrifying thunderstorm, we have no intuitive understanding of why atmospheric moisture causes thunder and lightning, or why the storm is endangering us (and not somebody else). But we do have an irresistible intuition: being caught in a storm feels a lot like being the brunt of somebody's rage. And we can easily agree to talk about the storm as that angry "somebody"—Zeus, or Huracán of the Aztecs, or in ancient Peru the lightning-hurling mountain Pariacaca.

Guthrie thinks people easily accept such intuitions as valid simply because anthropomorphism poses a "Pascal's wager": if a person-like power is endangering us, it would be foolish not to get on his right side by gifts and deference. And if not, little is lost; after all, being wrong about storm-persons needn't stop us from building a strong roof. So for Guthrie, religiosity is a pragmatic default.

Starting from this simple (perhaps overly simple) insight, Guthrie became an early anthropological contributor to Cognitive Science of Religion (CSR), a movement connecting psychology's cognitive research to cultural phenomena. He began at a favorable time because experimental neurologists and psychologists were then starting to build a powerful new model of cognition. Instead of seeing the mind-in-brain as a single vast, all-purpose computing engine, they came to see it as a cluster of different, inborn functional systems ("faculties," or "mental organs" in older language), each pre-evolved to neurally represent different domains of experience.

In the 1990s the idea of mental "faculties" was reborn in the form of "modular" theories about brain adaptation (Tooby and Cosmides 1992). Multiple, separately evolved neural "organs" entered broad discussion through an unforgettable simile: "The brain is like a Swiss Army Knife." From handling objects infants develop an "intuitive physics" even if taught none. They register animals as if developing a rough-and-ready zoology. They grasp quantity without prompting. They have a capacity for organizing speech rules even before they begin to master any particular language. They have an untaught "other minds" faculty for estimating dispositions of nearby beings. And these developments emerge in similar ways and similar sequences among all healthy infants, regardless of culture. Because they are working not blindly but with pre-installed principles, young humans can swiftly acquire and organize vast amounts of knowledge.

But are these principles just temporary learning props? For cognitive-minded anthropologists like Pascal Boyer, such "modular" parts of mind do not cease to underlie thought as the adult mind emerges (2001). Rather, they dictate our feeling that experience is full of radically different sorts of "things"—what cognitive science calls "ontological domains" (person, animal, plant, artifact, inanimate object). The sorting of experience into domains that are processed differently makes ideas easy or hard to have, easy or hard to remember, and easy or hard to share. So cultures do not operate on a blank human slate. Rather, they mold human invention onto a bumpy underlying terrain of mental predispositions.

And where does religion fit? In Boyer's view, "religion is based on cognitive processes in which the boundaries between these ontological domains are violated," or to put it more positively, when multiple mental "modules" simultaneously process a phenomenon but in different ways. If a mountain is apprehended by "intuitive physics" as an inanimate object, yet *also* is apprehended by the interpersonal faculty as an interacting being (by getting "angry" and rumbling, by endangering one that gets "angry" and rumbles, one that endangers life while also giving resources), then the impulse to understand it as both object and person simultaneously is the mental process Boyer sees at the root of religiosity. Religious experience is "a violator of ontological domains" (Jensen 2009, 129).

That does not mean every odd mental twitch is a religious idea. Religious notions are usually representations similar to ordinary cognition but with some twist of strangeness that makes them "minimally counterintuitive." An ancestor mummy is a human woman—except that she is immortal. A mountain is a familiar type of earthly matter—except that it (he?) is moody and violent. This category of *partly* abnormal perception is crucial. Routine cognitive moments when things *fully* match their type are forgotten because they bring no new information. At the other end of the spectrum, extreme counterintuitive perceptions are simply discarded as mistakes. But *minimally* counterintuitive cases are memorable and interesting. They form a captivating intermediate zone. To call a mountain a god, a lord (*apu*), etc., is to manifest "a probable but by no means inevitable by-product of the normal operation of human cognition" (Boyer cited in Jensen 2009, 130, 152).

This variety of cognitivism does not posit any inborn organ or module for religiosity. Nor is it party to the chase for a "God gene." Boyer says that religion is, rather, a "by-product" of routine cognition. Yet he recognizes such fluky cognitions as extremely viable products of the mind. Mental representations that span and merge models from two parts of the mind have impactful *specialness*. Like a joke or a catchy tune, they "catch" awareness by making an unexpected yet compelling connection. Since this disposition results from pan-human neural traits, "minimally counterintuitive ideas" (MCIs) are both recurrent and contagious. And if such an idea as the mountain-person is easily shared, it can easily become a vehicle for social practice (Boyer and Bergstrom 2008, 122–124)—eventually, for institutions like Kaha Wayi.

Gods everywhere, for adaptive evolutionary reasons: religiosity as authenticator of "prosocial" commitments

How could such a small fact as minimally counterintuitive perception come to be a core process of social organization? How could a mere subjective anomaly generate such intense loyalty that people will kill and die upholding it?

One starting point is to pick up on Gould and Lewontin's famous "spandrel" analogy in evolutionary theory (1979). In the original architectural sense of the term, a spandrel is simply the triangular space that emerges between two diverging arches. Spandrels began as by-products of structure, not design elements. But in the gothic style, spandrels became functional spaces for adornment, and eventually, decorated spandrels became indispensable parts of the design ensemble. Likewise, many biological traits, having emerged as random consequences of adaptive process, turn out *ex post* to provide selective advantage in some situations. Such a trait is not "adapted," but in the event it turns out "adaptive."

Some evolutionary cognitive theories put religiosity into that category. Whether or not it originated as a random side effect of modular thinking, MCI thinking turned out to have selective advantages because its attention-grabbing character makes it very communicable and eventually "prosocial." (By "prosocial" theorists mean useful in fostering solidarity and cooperation.) Theorists heading in this direction think a disposition toward ritualism and the other traits of religiosity makes humans more able to live in strong groups.

Recently, Léon Turner judged such MCI-based analysis, the dominant idea among evolutionary cognitive researchers on religion (2014, 6). But merely invoking the term "prosocial" can hardly be the end of the argument. Since we always find people in social groups in the first place, it is too easy to simply label anything human as a function of society.

Obviously not every MCI has religious potential. Most are memorable but trivial: we won't forget a truck shaped like a hot dog, but we won't feel reverent toward it either. Common sense suggests that a domain-violating idea has religious potential only if it is powerfully suggestive of something strongly felt or preoccupying. Unlike the Oscar Mayer weiner truck, the human-like mountain resonates with powerful experiences of vital importance. Saqsar Wayna seems a solemn presence because it-or-he embodies our precarious life situation, our love and hate of our place on earth, and our deep, costly local allegiances.

Scott Atran, an anthropologist who does fieldwork among people with extreme belief commitments, goes beyond such common sense. He theorizes in cognitive evolutionary terms routes by which mere MCIs, which after all begin as mere glitches in individuals' "modular" functioning, can become the nuclei of powerfully adaptive, prosocial complexes called religions (Atran and Henrich 2010). Atran's work is a synthesis that unites several explanatory components. It fuses the theory of accidental, non-adaptive MCI perception with attempts to theorize religion as a set of dispositions adaptively selected for their value in promoting social commitment.

Those familiar with biological evolutionary theory will notice that this idea is relatively vague on the important matter of "level of selection": on what does selection operate? On individuals? On populations? While Atran apparently leaves room to consider religiosity as a factor affecting individual reproductive success, his synthesis partakes of the recent trend toward multilevel models of natural selection by admitting the "prosocial" as a cause of group selection.

Minimally counterintuitive entities function well—crucially, Atran thinks—as bits of received culture that betoken common identity. Peculiar and memorable as they are, they function as unlosable I.D. cards. Simply sharing them with others who recognize them opens space for social trust. When a Rapacino speaks of Mount Saqsar Wayna as his irascible neighbor, his interlocutor supposes he belongs on Rapaz's land and understands it, even if one speaker does not know the other. Here is a Rapaz example:

> One foggy morning in December 2005, Cecilio Encarnación said, "Tomorrow I'm going up the mountain to kill those compadres." Compadres means "co-godparents" or close friends.
>
> "What compadres?" I asked.
>
> "The foxes that kill lambs and baby llamas." Cecilio calls the foxes compadres because as wild creatures they are the mountain's ritual kin.
>
> "But how can you aim your gun with the fog covering everything?" I asked.

He smiled. "There's a solution for that. You need to round up some earthworms, about half a kilo. Also lime, or *ichku* as we say, another half kilo. And you need some glowing embers, *shanla*. You set all those things together and put something on top" (meaning, you say an invocation over them). "Everything will be left burned up. After that there'll be beautiful spring weather for a day or two."

"But," I said, "what do the worms have to do with it?"

"The mountain mourns the death of his children the worms. He resents it, so he withdraws his gift, the raincloud. But since they are very tiny children, he only withdraws it for a short time."

When a Rapacino talks in this vein to his neighbors, he implies that both know what sort of person the mountain is: jealous of his "children" (i.e., wild animals). The exchange makes both feel like fellow insiders. They share Llacuaz know-how about how to influence mountains. Such feelings increase the likelihood that the two will trust and help each other. Their mutuality gives a selective advantage to them, and to their group, in winning competition among land users (villages, estates). Conflict rewards groups that are rich in such "prosocial" cultural practices.

But, as anthropologists have long recognized, talk is cheap. Using such low-cost cultural tokens as conversation about MCIs as keys to solidarity is a weak adaptive move because it is open to deceit. When the tokens are cheap, consisting of words or simple gestures, or even an easy ritual like burning worms, they are easy to fake. A man who speaks knowingly of the mountain might not really intend to come through on the help that one Rapaz comunero owes another. We are still far short of explaining the social intensity of religion.

Atran (following the prescient Melanesianist Roy Rappaport, 1999) thinks this is the reason norms involving nonhuman actors like Saqsar Wayna or God demand costly "hard-to-fake" signs of commitment. The person a Rapacino can trust as a more-than-opportunistic user of Saqsar Wayna's land is not the one who merely bandies local words. He is the one who stays up all night fasting and freezing at the ritual altar, the one who donates animals to rituals, the one who has taken the trouble to learn long invocations. For similar reasons, many committed members of churches despise "God talk" but respect consistent ritual practice, however plodding.

Sacred cultures therefore tend to ratchet ritual demands upward. They select or invent paradoxical ideas, not easy ones. They elaborate them challengingly, to inculcate strange, hard-to-credit definitions of reality. As one of its minimum demands, Christianity long ago demanded interaction with a wafer that is at the same time sacred human/divine flesh. Kaha Wayi demands affirmation of sparkling embers that are the speech of a mountain. Innumerable societies require "costly communications" of loyalty such as self-flagellation, cutting off bits of the body, making exhausting pilgrimages, abstaining from sex, embracing poverty, giving expensive donations, and other seemingly irrational mortifications. Kaha Wayi demands of its adepts intervals of celibacy, abstention from salt and tasty food, and austere seclusion in ritual. In some sacred cultures such as Mahayana Buddhism, ascetic Hinduism, or monastic Catholicism, the highest degree of solidarity with the religious community is expressed by wholesale sacrifice of normal social options.

This theory also claims to explain the characteristic intensity of religious communication. Gatherings in which people intensify their allegiances by undergoing severe bodily disciplines together, as the herdsmen of Rapaz do in their cattle-honoring all-nighter (Chapter 4), are another near-universal. Here too it seems selection has encouraged societies to recruit inborn neurological dispositions. Rituals everywhere latch onto a psychobiological, kinetic phenomenon: when people dance together, or sing together, or recite together, or mass their bodies, or do many other synchronized activities, they feel closer. They become excited, fascinated, and desirous of unity. Rhythm creates a compelling sense of shared selfhood and even of ecstatic merging.

But this argument cannot pretend to apply everywhere. Solidarity-generating devices that don't depend on the submerging of self-interest or on renouncing lucid deliberation are also extremely common. Rules for ritual may be very mental, even cerebral, as in the strict unison of litany or in studious text-based prayer, in legal-theologicial disputation, and in preaching. Ritual may be tedious or obscure. "Faith in otherwise inscrutable content is deepened and validated by communion," even when communion amounts to self-denying discipline (Atran and Henrich 2010, 6). In many religious cultures, competence requires time-consuming study of laws, special language, action routines and authoritative texts—another way to raise the price of credible participation. Kaha Wayi too demands quite a lot of unexciting know-how.

Ritual practices, evolutionary-cognitive thinkers hold, function to forge strong feelings of "we." They commit members to an imagined, overarching, permanent virtual entity such as "Rapaz Community," "the Jewish People," "the *Ummah* of Islam," "the Elect of God," or "the Bear Clan." (In Chapter 5, we will encounter a related notion under the term of "the transcendent social.") Commitments to the collective virtual entity are intensely prosocial, in both positive and negative ways. They increase members' willingness to trust and help each other, even if the members are not acquainted or related.

The negative counterpart is that the same religious process that makes people experience themselves as parts of an imagined, transcendent, brotherly whole, also heightens the distinction between "us" and "them." If a ritually reinforced "we" feel "our" vital interests threatened, nothing works better than the combination of ritually induced social intensity with rigid doctrinal framing to generate extreme behavior. It's not accidental that Atran's field studies include many interviews with religiously motivated terrorists.

Reductionism and the retired engineer's parable

Cognitive and evolutionary theorists of religiosity are proud "reductionists." That is, their theories set about to "reduce" religiosity by showing that it amounts to a particular manifestation of more general, basic, and simpler human traits and processes. Most of them reduce religiosity to a specific combination of human neurological predispositions that, under evolutionary pressure of selection favoring the "prosocial," yields the cluster of ideas and behaviors called religion.

In natural science, reduction is the normal strategy for extracting general laws from the infinity of phenomena. Most anthropologists on "the science end" of our nonconsensual discipline favor one or another reductionist way of explaining cultural facts because that strategy puts study of sociocultural facts on the same footing as study of things to which science does not attribute mind or culture—things like genomes or climates. Reductionism is science's path toward what Edward O. Wilson calls consilience, meaning convergence among systems of knowledge. "Social scientists proper" (e.g., methodologically strict sociologists or macroeconomists) also propose characteristic reductions, although the lawfulness they seek concerns properties of society as such and not properties of the mind. Other reductionisms saturate such theoretical traditions as Marxism and structuralism, not all of them discussed in this book.

By contrast, many social and cultural anthropologists, and most specialists in Religious Studies, dislike the evolutionary-cognitive approach to religion. One major objection, now largely outdated but still afloat, has been the charge of "methodological individualism." The simplest possible methodological individualism was Margaret Thatcher's when she said in 1987 that "there is no such thing as society." For her, a society is simply the additive total of individuals and their actions—not an overall entity with properties of its own. She would have us take no account of the society's scale or mode of organization as causal forces in their own right. Guthrie's "faces in clouds" explanation, as initially proposed, similarly tended to jump directly from properties of individual minds to vast collective facts, without taking much account of the variant social setups within which minimally counterintuitive ideas move. Critics object: surely MCI effects must vary depending on differing social circumstances, for example, in a hunter-gatherer band or in a postindustrial state. Otherwise we have little hope of explaining why religions are not all the same!

Another more fundamental objection voiced among cultural anthropologists is that the evolutionary-cognitive tendency drives us away from a core value of ethnography, "the native's point of view." The cognitive framework that people like Atran or Boyer start out with is presented as cosmopolitan scientific knowledge, exterior to religiosity. Its premises include the idea that the local religious insider (or anyone) is governed by biases that a certain kind of outsider (the scientist) can recognize. So insider statements hardly count as knowledge at all. They are interesting as examples of evolved bias and group selection but not as mental-cultural constructions in their own right. Why, then, study details of Rapaz mountain cult—or any religion at all? More traditional ethnographers think that purely evolutionary-cognitive arguments throw the baby out with the bathwater.

Many people sympathetic to Religious Studies (Comparative Religion, History of Religions, etc.) object more broadly to *any* way of reducing religion to non-religious causes, not just the psychological one. In their eyes, social science has been influenced ever since its origins in Renaissance humanism and the Enlightenment by anti-religious doctrines. Most scientific explanations, they allege, are set up against the possibility that religion might be an important phenomenon in its own right. In repudiating revelation as a source of truth, social science's founders illogically closed the door on the possibility that religion might matter in its own right for non-supernatural reasons. The venture of explaining social facts through reduction to underlying nonreligious factors (e.g., cognition, geography, class structure, race, depth psychology) marginalizes religiosity as a curious secondary oddity. Such critics think social science explains religiosity away (as false consciousness, neurosis, or cognitive bias), rather than explaining what it is. For thinkers committed to autonomous religiosity, *any* reductionistic approach tosses the baby out with the bathwater. Mircea Eliade, a South Asianist and still-popular inventor of "*homo religiosus*" (man as bearer of an irreducibly religious inclination), warned that reductionisms eliminate at the start any chance of taking seriously the subject we set out to understand.

The unfortunate thing is that such critiques are usually offered in a rhetoric of resentment. Anti-reductionism oddly unites extremes: on the one hand it pleases those who are most deferential to religion (theologians, Eliade's descendants, Jungians, humanistic historians, and some political or philosophical conservatives). On the other hand, anti-reductionism is also congenial to "cultural construction-ists" generally on the "cultural left." Strong cultural constructionism perceives culture as the activity by which societies become sovereign creators of their own "worlds" (see Chapters 4, 6). Suggestions that this work is constrained by inborn, infra-cultural factors are not welcome. It's a safe bet that some reviewer from one tendency or the other will spank this book for even admitting cognitive evolution-ism to the discussion.

In this observer's judgment, anti-reductionism has popularized a misunder-standing about how anthropology connects to natural science. The suggestion that reductionism is a Bad Thing derives from unawareness that scientific method works in two directions, not just in the "downward" drive called reductionism. Science shows how complexity emerges from simplicity, as well as how simplicity under-lies complexity. In other words, the scientific worldview entertains emergence as complement to reduction. Emergence means the way interaction of smaller, simpler parts produces new levels of complexity or new types of patterning not visible at the underlying level. It is legitimate to reduce atoms' properties to particle physics, but that still leaves the scientist to explain behaviors of bonding atoms that are not like those of subatomic phenomena. That is why particle discoveries do not replace the science of chemistry. New complexities emerge at the chemical level and again at the biochemical level called "life." Why not at the level called culture?

"Emergence," unlike "reduction," is a good-vibe word. But being for emer-gence and against reduction makes exactly as much sense as being for multiplication and against division.

Once a retired audio engineer enrolled in my Anthropology of Religion course. He gave us a parable about reduction and emergence:

"Here are two people who work with music," he said. "One is an audio engineer and the other is a musicologist.

"The engineer says: 'I never take music courses because I already have a sufficient explanation for my purposes: music is a class of sounds. Sounds are a class of waves. We can reduce any wave to simple, general physical properties using a model called wave mechanics. I don't need a special theory of music. I can say quite a bit about music simply as patterned combinations of waves. And someday neurologists will explain how these patterns work in the brain too.'

"The musicologist says, 'Thanks for inventing headphones. But what you're doing doesn't say anything about music *as music*. Surely laws of wave physics do constrain music-making, and surely waves' correlates in the brain must have something to do with the construction of musical rules. But when sounds are organized culturally, the resulting patterns aren't prefigured in a way wave physics or neurology predicts, only in one that they permit. What accounts for a given musical culture's properties as a self-contained musical domain? What I want to do is interpret the qualities of music on the level of music.'"

This parable resembles a classic discussion in the study of language, long since widened to anthropology as well. Do we want to be like "pure" linguists and psycholinguists, who reduce particular tongues and discourses to underlying laws of language as such? Or do we want to be like philologists and literary scholars, who acknowledge the achievements of linguistics yet nonetheless want to unfold the properties of particular tongues and discourses, each on its own plane? Anthropology convinces most when it partakes of the generalizing, explanatory power of reduction and at the same time of the particularizing, enriching power of interpretation. For anthropologists, both options are open, necessary, and hard to combine.

Notes

1 Instituto Geográfico Nacional [del Perú] 2000: mapa 1549 (22-j).
2 So named by the ethnohistorian John V. Murra (1972). Murra's model, based on 16th-century evidence, acquired greater ethnographic nuance in modern field studies such as Mayer (2002 [1985]).
3 The foundational studies of extirpation are those of Pierre Duviols. His monograph on *The Struggle Against Andean Religions* (translated title; 1971) and his transcriptions of idolatry trials (2003) concentrate on the colonial Province of Cajatambo, which includes Rapaz. Meritorious studies of extirpation are many; some English examples include Gose (2008) and Mills (1997), Spanish examples include Gareis (1989), Larco (2008), and Acosta (1987).
4 Salomon and Urioste (1991) offer an English translation. A fuller study apparatus is available in Taylor's Spanish version (1999).
5 *Llactayoc* means "possessor of community." "Community" is a gloss for the Quechua word that means (as Gerald Taylor clarified) three things taken together: land, a human group, and its *wak'as* or shrines.

6 Augusto Cardich has propounded climate change as the reason frustrated cultivators of the Pasco-Junín high plateau became aggressive in westward and downward migration (Cardich 1985).

7 The range is divided into named but unfenced sectors, only for purposes of describing where a herd is, and for organizing sector-by-sector animal censuses that control correct use. The sectors are: Caracancha, Sharín, Jankil, Yaruchinchinchán, Shullpu or Yanatamá, Shushupuín or Antapampa, Shulupampa, Pampa or Cochakillu, and Población.

8 These limits were imposed in recent times; previous to agrarian reform some households ran many hundreds of head. There are still substantial inequalities in herd ownership. Ten percent of families lack livestock; a few of these concentrate on agriculture, and some must work as peons.

9 Flores Ochoa 1977b, Rivera Andia 2005, and many other ethnographers.

10 There may be a confusion between *puka* "red" and *pukyu* "spring." The word *puc'ra* is not attested.

11 Allauca, "right-hand," suggests the side with ritual precedence, while K'ollana seems a version of a Quechua term meaning "preeminent" (Encarnación and Robles 2011, 12). Huaylapamba appears a version of a phrase meaning "green flat."

12 The two "teams" also supplied the barriers for the annual bullfight festival in alternating years.

13 Details of water governance: Most farming is dry farming, but there is community-run irrigation from the two main springs and also from Manantial Cocana and its reservoir. Each comunero requests and pays for the water he needs at s./.50 per day (about USD $.15 c.2005). Irrigation may be used for crops, ryegrass, dáctil, alfalfa, or clover. Water is collected at night and channeled out to one or two users per day. The Community's water judge sets the rotation. He sells water tickets. Each comunero requests the day he prefers. If that day is taken, the water judge will offer a day close to it. Tickets may be sold. This system is very old and has not varied in living memory.

14 *Rata-* "Caer, ponerse (el sol)" (Adelaar 1982, 73) might extend the idea of sunset to the end of a field's fertile time.

15 The Quechua title was the usual one with the lifetime of today's elders, says Agustín Racacha. It is often pronounced in a South-Andean or Quechua II way, "kamachikuq." This, like some other words used in the festival dance Inka Tinkuy, suggests persistence of colonial usages modeled on "Inka" speech.

16 First and second among them are the *campo mayor* ("head rural constable," in charge of the current potato sector), *campo menor* ("lesser rural constable," in charge of the oca sector), and *kasha campo* (in charge of the barley sector), followed by four to six *regidores* ("counsellors") of equal rank whom the kamachikuq can appoint to specific tasks. Two additional offices are held by women: the *llavera* or "keeper of the key," meaning the person who locks up impounded "damager" animals, and the *rematista* or "auctioneer," who sells them off for Community revenue if the owner fails to pay his fine. The "vice" also appoints a *juez de agua* or "water judge" to assign irrigation turns, and a *fiscalejo* or town crier, who stands in the bell tower at dawn rallying citizens to community tasks or calling the owners of captured strays to reclaim them at the pound. (At the time of study, Rapaz had no cell phone coverage.) A variable number of *regadores* water the seven communal feeding paddocks, and one household is assigned to tend the hydroelectric power station. Elder statesmen are sometimes also invited to sit with the inner cabinet because, having finished their careers as officers, they are free to voice politically delicate concerns.

17 For some forty years (c.1970–2010) ethnographers reported steady decline or dissolution of highland "traditional authorities" (Isbell 1971–1972). Based on interviews in 2005–2006, La Serna writes that in war-plagued Ayacucho Department, younger self-defense combatants marginalized the senior men of the vara (2012, 204–205). Yet in the last few years, the youngest active generation seems disposed to rebuild the vara offices with their aura of revindicated local legitimacy. In Rapaz, the vara offices were never interrupted, not even during the Shining Path war.

18 Toward the end of the 20th century, the agricultural commons worked poorly. "Few went to turn the soil, few to sow it, few to cultivate, few to hill, but all to the harvest," Agustín Racacha remarked. In 1987, the Community gave in to some twenty disgruntled families who had long been waiting for their field assignments. The common fields were split up and assigned in household parcels. Pasa Qulqa became empty.

References

Acosta, Antonio. 1987. "La extirpación de las idolatrías en el Perú: origen y desarrollo de las campañas; a propósito de *Cultura andina y represión.*" *Revista Andina* 5(1): 171–195.

Adelaar, Willem F.H. 1982. *Léxico del quechua de Pacaraos.* Lima: Universidad Nacional Mayor de San Marcos, Centro de Investigación Lingüística Aplicada, Documento de Trabajo no. 45.

Arriaga, Pablo José de. 1968 [1621]. *The Extirpation of Idolatry in Peru,* translated by L. Clark Keating. Lexington: University of Kentucky Press.

Atran, Scott, and Joseph Henrich. 2010. "The Evolution of Religion: How Cognitive By-Products, Adaptive Learning Heuristics, Ritual Displays, and Group Competition Generate Deep Commitments to Prosocial Religions." *Biological Theory* 5(1): 1–13.

Boyer, Pascal. 2001. *Religion Explained: Evolutionary Origins of Religious Thought.* New York: Basic Books.

Boyer, Pascal, and Brian Bergstrom. 2008. "Evolutionary Perspectives on Religion." *Annual Review of Anthropology* 37: 111–130.

Cardich, Augusto. 1985. "The Fluctuating Upper Limits of Cultivation in the Central Andes and Their Impact on Peruvian Prehistory." *Advances in World Archaeology* 4: 292–333.

Cerrón-Palomino, Rodolfo. 1976. *Diccionario Quechua Junín-Huanca.* Lima: Ministerio de Educación and Instituto de Estudios Peruanos.

Chase, Zachary J. 2015. "What Is a Wak'a? When Is a Wak'a?" In *The Archaeology of Wak'as: Explorations of the Sacred in the Pre-Columbian Andes,* edited by Tamara L. Bray. Boulder, CO: University Press of Colorado. 75–126.

Duviols, Pierre. 1971. *La Lutte contre les réligions autochtones dans le Pérou colonial.* Lima: Institut Français d'Études Andines.

Duviols, Pierre. 1973. "Huari y Llacuaz. Agricultores y pastores. Un dualismo prehispánico de oposición y complementaridad." *Revista del Museo Nacional* 39: 153–191.

Duviols, Pierre. 1974. "Une petite chronique retrouvée: errores, ritos, supersticiones y ceremonias de los yndios de la provincia de Chinchaycocha y otras del Piru (1603)." *Journal de la Société des Américanistes* 68: 275–297.

Encarnación Rojas, Eulalia, and Narciso Robles Atachagua. 2011. *Breve Historia de San Cristóbal de Rapaz.* Lima: Gráfica Quinteros E.I.R.L.

Falcón Huayta, Victor. 2007. *Patrimonio de San Cristóbal de Rapaz, Provincia de Oyón: Khipu y Cajahuay (2005–2008)—Arqueología. Informe Final al Instituto Nacional de Cultura (RNA N° DF-0181).* Lima: Instituto Nacional de Cultura.

Flores Ochoa, Jorge A., ed. 1977. *Pastores de puna: Uywamichiq punarunakuna.* Lima: Instituto de Estudios Peruanos.

Gareis, Iris. 1989. "Extirpación de idolatrías e Inquisición en el Virreinato del Perú." *Boletín del Instituto Riva-Agüero* 16: 55–74.

Gose, Peter. 2008. *Invaders as Ancestors: On the Intercultural Making and Unmaking of Spanish Colonialism in the Andes.* Toronto: University of Toronto Press.

Gould, Steven Jay, and Richard C. Lewontin. 1979. "The Spandrels of San Marco and the Panglossian Paradigm: A Critique of the Adaptationist Programme." *Proceedings of the Royal Society of London.* Series B (205): 581–598.

Guthrie, Stewart. 1980. "A Cognitive Theory of Religion." *Current Anthropology* 21(2): 181–203.

Guthrie, Stewart. 1993. *Faces in the Clouds: A New Theory of Religion*. New York: Oxford University Press.

Híjar Soto, Donato Amador. 1984. "Los cjircas y otras deidades protectoras del área andina en el Perú." *Folklore Americano* 37(8): 103–108.

Isbell, Billie Jean. 1971–1972. "'No servimos más': Un estudio de los efectos de disipar un sistema de la autoridad tradicional en un pueblo ayacuchano." *Revista del Museo Nacional* 37: 285–298.

Jensen, Jeppe Sinding. 2009. "Religion as the Unintended Product of Brain Functions in the 'Standard Cognitive Science of Religion Model': On Pascal Boyer, *Religion Explained*, and Ilkka Pyysiäinen, *How Religion Works*." In *Contemporary Theories of Religion: A Critical Companion*, edited by Michael Stausberg. London: Routledge. 129–155.

La Serna, Miguel. 2012. *The Corner of the Living: Ayacucho on the Eve of the Shining Path Insurgency*. Chapel Hill, NC: University of North Carolina Press.

Larco, Laura. 2008. *Más allá de los encantos: documentos históricos y etnografía contemporánea sobre extirpación de idolatrías en Trujillo, siglos XVIII–XX*. Lima: Fondo Editorial de la Universidad Nacional Mayor de San Marcos and Instituto Francés de Estudios Andinos.

Lawson, E. Thomas, and Robert N. McCauley. 1990. *Rethinking Religion: Connecting Cognition and Culture*. Cambridge: Cambridge University Press.

Mayer, Enrique. 2002 [1985]. "Production Zones." In *The Articulated Peasant: Household Economies in the Andes*, edited by Enrique Mayer. Boulder, CO: Westview. 239–278.

Medina Susano, R. Clorinda. 1989. *Checras*. Lima: Consejo Nacional de Ciencia y Tecnología.

Mills, Kenneth. 1997. *Idolatry and Its Enemies: Colonial Andean Religion and Extirpation, 1640–1750*. Princeton, NJ: Princeton University Press.

Morris, Earl W., Leslie A. Brownrigg, Susan C. Bourque, and Henry F. Dobyns. 1968. *Coming Down the Mountain: The Social Worlds of Mayobamba*. Ithaca, NY: Andean Indian Community Research and Development Program, Department of Anthropology, Cornell University. Socio-Economic Development of Andean Communities, Report No. 10.

Murra, John V. 1972 [1562]. "El 'control vertical' de un máximo de pisos ecológicos en la economía de las sociedades andinas." In Iñigo Ortiz de Zuñiga: *Visita de la provincia de León de Huánuco en 1562. Vol. 2*, edited by John V. Murra. Huánuco: Universidad Hermilio Valdizán. Facultad de Letras y Educación. 427–476.

Parker, Gary J., and Amancio Chávez. 1976. *Diccionario Quechua Ancash-Huaylas*. Lima: Ministerio de Educación e IEP.

Rappaport, Roy A. 1999. *Ritual and Religion in the Making of Humanity*. New York: Cambridge University Press.

Rivera Andía, Juan Javier. 2005. "Killing What You Love: An Andean Cattle Branding Ritual and the Dilemmas of Modernity." *Journal of Anthropological Research* 61(2): 129–156.

Rivera Andía, Juan Javier. 2012. "A partir de los movimientos de un pájaro . . . La 'danza de la perdiz' en los rituales ganaderos de los Andes peruanos." *Revista Española de Antropología Americana* 42(1): 169–185.

Rostworowski, María, and Joyce Marcus. 1988. *Conflicts over Coca Fields in XVIth-Century Perú*. Ann Arbor, MI: University of Michigan Museum of Anthropology.

Salomon, Frank, and George Urioste, eds. and trans. 1991. *The Huarochirí Manuscript: A Testament of Ancient and Colonial Andean Religion*. Austin, TX: University of Texas Press.

Sherbondy, Jeanette. 1986. "Los Ceques: código de canales en el Cusco incaico." *Allpanchis* 20(27): 39–74.

Stevens, Wallace. 1954 [1942]. "Connossieur of Chaos." In "Parts of a World." *Collected Poems of Wallace Stevens*. New York: Alfred A. Knopf. 216.

Taylor, Gérald. 1999. *Ritos y tradiciones de Huarochirí*, 2nd ed. Lima, Perú: Instituto Francés de Estudios Andinos, Banco Central de Reserva del Perú and Universidad Particular Ricardo Palma.

Tooby, John, and Leda Cosmides. 1992. "The Psychological Foundations of Culture." In *The Adapted Mind: Evolutionary Psychology and the Generation of Culture*, edited by Jerome H. Barkow, Leda Cosmides, and John Tooby. New York: Oxford University Press. 19–136.

Turner, Léon. 2014. "Introduction: Pluralism and Complexity in the Evolutionary Cognitive Science of Religion." In *Evolution, Religion, and Cognitive Science: Critical and Constructive Essays*, edited by Fraser N. Watts and Léon Turner. Oxford: Oxford University Press. 1–20.

Weber, David John, Félix Cayco Zambrano, Teodoro Cayco Villar, and Marlene Ballena Dávila. 1998. *Rimaycuna: Quechua de Huánuco: Diccionario del quechua del Huallaga con índices castellano e inglés*. Lima: Instituto Lingüístico de Verano.

2

A LITTLE PALACE OF ANALOGIES

(and a revised structuralist view of cultural fundamentals)

Kaha Wayi's ritualism expresses attachment to earth, but it hardly resembles the sweet-tempered *pachamamismo* (Earth Mother devotion) popularized in tour books as Andean religion. The regime starts with an assumption that the agropastoral life is lived in a web of uneasy reciprocity. The network extends beyond people to include what is usually called inanimate nature: buildings, cliffs, pastures, stones, mountains, lakes. All are connected in nested hierarchies of seniority and power. Mountains have eminence among them; they are superhuman individuals—not gods, not spirits, not supernaturals, and not exactly persons either. Such beings, or objects that manifest them, were often called *huacas* in hispano-Quechua jargon of the colonial era. (*Wak'a* is a modern spelling.) This term was construed in Spanish as meaning "idol," and in the 17th century wak'a veneration suffered harsh Church campaigns against idolatry (Chapter 3).

Astride culture and nature: analogism?

In academe and the media, what used to be called idolatry now comes under the heading of "indigenous religion." Objects of veneration have been promoted to "gods" or "deities." But this terminological courtesy does not help either. The term "god(s)" tends to smuggle in premises of Christianity such as the primacy of belief (Chapter 7) and a nonmaterial essence. "Indigeneity" too looks more and more like a positional matter, dependent on who is speaking and why. Most Rapacinos don't use the word "indigenous" about themselves, because it sometimes carries a racial connotation and a suggestion of illiteracy. In this chapter we consider structuralism, a framework that seeks to minimize such extraneous pigeonholing of cultures. It asks us instead to concentrate on internal formal relations among the cultural categories that organize a given society's thinking, and to seek in these relations unspoken "deep" patterns of local, Pan-Amerindian, and eventually pan-human logic.

In 2005 Philippe Descola, a distinguished ethnographer of the Shuaran peoples in Amazonian Peru, published a new way to order the universe of cultures. Descola's scheme constitutes a major revision of the structuralist tradition to which he is heir as Claude Lévi-Strauss' successor at the Collège de France. The full exposition is *Beyond Nature and Culture*, a grand synthesis that vindicates the old-fashioned but still useful term ethnology (2013). (Ethnology means synthetic and comparative reading of ethnographies as a corpus.) His scheme closely involves ritual orientations but is not limited to them. Its objective is to more broadly characterize the varying premises and logics of different formal, categorical orientations to the world. It asks, all in all, what options are open to any group as it lays a basic unspoken grid to organize perceptions? Embracing the predominantly French venture of rationalizing cultural diversity down to a minimum number of variables, he posits only four ideal types. It is a supremely audacious summing-up of all that ethnology has learned.

This chapter only means to examine one quadrant of Descola's ethnological paradigm, and not to explain the whole fourfold model. In totality, the model daringly claims to provide theorized niches for *all* anthropologically known systems for organizing cognition. Our immediate purpose, however, is to see how Descola's notion of "analogy" clarifies Rapaz's view of the sociable universe.

The "classic" or Lévi-Straussian French structuralism which was Descola's point of departure pulled anthropology toward the "thought" pole of Bell's basic thought-action distinction (see the Introduction). Its cornerstone was the study of Amazonian peoples, emphasizing the unspoken minimal categories that lay beneath their explicit ritual, mythic, and artistic expressions.

In this vein, Lévi-Strauss often argued that societies founded their cognitive organization on an underlying antithesis between cultural and natural facts. Although structuralism of the 1960s–1980s remains a revered achievement, not all anthropologists with boots on the ground have been satisfied with that premise. "Nature versus culture" now seems a less basic and less omnipresent structure than Lévi-Strauss thought. Andean ethnographers are among the fieldworkers who called it into question. The distinction between cultural artifacts and parts of the nonhuman environment does not seem to have been salient in Rapaz's colonial rural tradition, nor is it now.[1]

Descola set about to renovate the idea of culture-as-structure by introducing different basic axes of contrast, and thereby created a new fourfold typology of fundamental orientations. One is the horizontal axis of physicality or "nature" (shown as rows in Table 2.1). This variable asks, do entities belong together as members of a single physical kind, with a common substance (e.g., matter)? Or are they physically diverse according to the most basic local criteria, being made of non-similar stuffs? In the cultures typed as "naturalism" (upper right), of which modern science is one, all entities belong to a single physicality: all things are made of one stuff, namely matter. By contrast, on the horizontal axis of "interiority" (mental life, awareness) the West considers consciousness not to be a property of entities in general. Only some things possess it.

TABLE 2.1 A simplified sketch of Phillipe Descola's scheme of "ontological routes"

	Similar in interiority (monoculturalism)	Dissimilar in interiority (multiculturalism)
Similar in physicality (mononaturalism)	**Totemism**	**Naturalism**
Dissimilar in physicality (multinaturalism)	**Animism**	**Analogism**

Source: Table adapted from Descola (2005, 2006, 2009) by Adrian Ivakhiv (2011), http://blog.uvm. edu/aivakhiv/2011/01/10/on-animism-multinaturalism-cosmopolitics/.

Descola bestows the time-honored label of "totemism" (upper left) on cultures which, like ours, attribute a common physicality to all things, but, unlike ours, equate similar substance with similar mentality. Each totemic category contains creatures grouped because they resemble each other in having similar substance and also in having similar interiority. For example, Nungar Australians recognize moieties (halves of society) called "Catcher" and "Watcher." Nungar consider that the crow belongs together with the human members of the "Catcher" moiety in a single physical category, so a Nungar person can say non-metaphorically that she is a crow. "Catchers" of seemingly different species "really" share such traits as "dark and leaden skin . . . vindictive, sullen and secretive" temperament. The cockatoo belongs to the opposite, "Watcher" moiety by virtue of "light brown skin, round faces and limbs, curly hair and . . . impulsive and passionate temperament." The bird shares these traits with "Watcher" people, who consider themselves non-metaphorical cockatoos (Descola 2006, 7).

In Descola's reading, totemism, like naturalism, is "mononatural": it perceives everything as existing within a single domain made of matter. But unlike naturalism, totemism attributes a characteristic cluster of interior as well as physical traits to each sort of entities in that domain. The totemists' world consists of a multitude of distinct but mutually known families of entities such as the cockatoo and crow families. Each family of entities groups together a set of human and nonhuman things that share "family resemblances." Many Native American societies developed totemic systems in which each "family" or totem contains both a human descent group (clan) and some nonhuman things with which it shares traits. For example, the Ho-Chunk (formerly Winnebago) population of Wisconsin includes a Bear Clan from whom the tribal police were (and to some degree still are) recruited because they share with their kin the bear's imposing strength.

The vertical, or cultural, axis is that of "interiority." It is represented by columns in Table 2.1. The upper left cell, totemism, as we have seen postulates beings who all have inward life and address each other by common codes and signs. That is, they share a culture. The totemist's world is therefore both mononatural and monocultural. In the upper right cell we find systems that consider all beings to be of one nature but to lack common signs or codes. Modern secular and scientific worldviews belong in this cell. The naturalist's world is, as it were, mononatural and multicultural. Such is the Western commonsense view.

The same contrast regarding "interiority" applies to the lower row of lifeworlds: those which construe entities as being of different "nature" or substance. On the left side of the lower row sit the Amazonian and many other cultures to which Descola has awarded the old word "animist," but in a new sense. Animists see beings as irreducibly diverse in their nature. The most basic animist nature is form or species. Jaguars possess a different basic nature from people. But jaguars share with other species a common interiority. Inside themselves, jaguars feel the same way people do; they experience themselves as persons. They experience beings of other species as other persons, differently "clothed" in substance, but sharing a similar inner life. Creatures can share codes such as speech, reciprocity, and sociability across species categories. Such is the multinatural but monocultural world of the Amazonian shaman or hunter as conceptualized by Viveiros.

And what of the fourth cell, referring to cultures that organize beings as diverse both in their nature or physicality, *and* in their interiority or cultural capacity? How can such a maximally diverse universe cohere at all?

This most puzzling multinatural-and-multicultural cell is the one where Descola locates Andean societies. Uru-, Aymara-, and Quechua-speaking groups such as (historic) Rapaz are classed together with many other agrarian or preindustrial complex societies: the Inka, the Nahua or Aztec states, inland West Africa, ancient China, and medieval Christendom, for example. To them he attributes "analogism."

Obviously it is a class of colossal importance for archaeology and for deep historiography. So it matters to Andeanists that Descola chooses as his exemplary case a modern highland Bolivian people known as the Chipaya (2013, 268–276). He takes as ethnographic baseline his colleague Nathan Wachtel's *El Regreso de los Antepasados* (2001 [1990]).

Chipaya ritual resembles that of Rapaz in fundamentals but it has proliferating geometric schemes for organizing time and space more complex than Rapaz's. In terms of Bell's functionalist typology of rituals, both Rapaz's and Chipaya's ceremonies tend to be "rites of exchange and communication" with nonhuman beings. Wallace would see their ceremonies as "rites of intensification" that stoke up vitality in the living surround.

By analogism, Descola means a cognitive tendency "that divides the whole collection of existing beings into a multiplicity of essences, forms, and substances separated by small distinctions" (2013, 201). Things and beings are never identical to each other in either physicality or interiority. He characterizes this prospect of infinite, irreducible diversity as "dizzying."

Yet it is not rare. Nor is it chaotic. Time after time, cultures have found ways to inhabit multiplicity by lining up innumerable substantially-and-subjectively different entities according to schemes of *analogy*: correspondence, hierarchy, inversion, homology, and so forth.

Common examples are systems of analogy between macrocosm/microcosm (e.g., astrology, whether Chinese, Indic, or Andean). As it is among zodiacal constellations, so it is among persons. Another recurring scheme connects body parts with plants or minerals that have analogous-seeming traits (e.g., medieval and

Chinese herbal lore): plants with heart-shaped flowers are "cordials" for the heart, and so forth. Many cultures analogize landforms to biological species. For example, in Andean folk geography, many villages have landmarks with such names as Snake Rock.

Macro-micro analogy is not the only logical framework in which "parts of a world" (Wallace Stevens' phrase) can be aligned. Analogism also generates structures for comparison such as dualisms of opposites, or complements: symmetries, inversions, or multilevel schemes. Some analogies posit properties such as yin/yang or hot/cold that sort out various levels of typology in parallel. Hierarchies are common schemata. Some cultures promote giant hierarchical analogisms like the medieval "great chain of being," or Rapaz's chains of ancestry from cosmic Lightning to politico-social Llacuaz alignments to local clans (*ayllu*). Kinship offers numerous analogical frames. Marriage and in-lawship form a model analogically likening the Huari-Llacuaz dynamic to the "circulating cosmology" that marries weather to land.

In Andean sacred culture one very common analogical template is the pattern of credit and equity: basic religious terms include "payment," "debt," "service," and so forth. They are analogically managed and apply in similar fashion to all levels of beings, from vermin to the mightiest snowcaps. The fact that Kaha Wayi's name derives from the Spanish word for treasury or community chest (*caja*) may or may not reflect a former use of the building, but it certainly reflects a central analogical structure for imagining relations among the world's parts.

By this analogical reading, Andean "religion" is a system of erudition, jurisprudence, and technique comparable with ancient Chinese or pre-Socratic Greek doctrines, rather than with shamanic animism, Christian theology, or natural science. Getting rid of these misplaced descriptors is a strong advantage of Descola's model.

But what about cultural *action*, as opposed to schematizing? How can a human way of *doing* things cohere in an infinitely subdivided, infinitely diverse universe?

For Descola, diverse beings (people and mountains, for example) do communicate but in a manner unlike those used in animism or shamanism. Analogism's signature action is sacrifice, a form emphasizing unlikeness between communicating beings. "Is such a world humming with conscious life . . . and intentionality really distinct from animism?" he asks himself. Yes, Descola says, insofar as every entity is a unique, unstable conglomeration of material and mental traits never interchangeable with any other. They don't share their substance or their culture; they connect to each other rather because they are logically related within analogical schemes. Moreover, each one fits into potentially uncountable schemes and relationships. It is all very hard to work out.

Communication by sacrifice is partial, anxious, uncertain (2013, 212–213). It is as if the ritualist translates a half-known tongue. The sacrificial gift is given in hope, not in knowledge, of a favorable relationship. This is certainly true of Rapaz ritualists, who seem burdened with doubt and frustration as they try to get predictable results by manipulating a few only partial correspondences (such as local human/mountain debts and credits, or local/geographical hierarchies and so forth). They feel they inhabit a universe full of incompletely understood relationships, some of them dangerous. When a ritualist wrangles with a mountain through ritual gestures and words, he must first implore the mountain to "hear us, old one; understand us, care about us." And he receives the mountain's reply in sparks, bubbles, and clouds, which are always understood to be *not* language but some montane analogue of language, which even an expert ritualist's effort cannot securely grasp.

A sacred house, but not for saints

Let's take an ethnographic look at Rapaz practice, trying on analogism as we go. Outsiders think it's remarkable that a non-Christian temple of the mountains stands literally on the same block with a Catholic church, peacefully and in plain view. It seems especially striking when we remember that this very village suffered intense Catholic persecution against mountain cults (which we'll sketch in Chapter 3).

Rapacinos, however, don't see anything remarkable about it. Is this because in some way Rapaz has been somehow isolated from pressures against Native American traditions? Hardly. Most Rapacinos are Catholics, all are Christians, and their town has the usual religious and political institutions typical of rural Latin America.

Rather, Rapacinos think the Kaha Wayi-Pasa Qulqa complex should be protected and kept separate from religion because the Church and the old sacred precinct address different sets of functions. Descola might say they manage separate relationships organized by different ranges of analogues. Analogism may be "dizzying" but it makes room for everything.

Normally people do not refer to the work of Kaha Wayi as religion, nor speak of the mountains as gods or even as spirits. Kaha Wayi is a matter of *"costumbre"* or unwritten customary law, not *"religión"* or *"culto."* The Trinity, Holy Family, and saints fit into a separate analogical structure, with a separate set of analogies connecting its parts and implying separate duties among people. These facts defy the commonplace equation of "indigenous religion" with syncretism. Kaha Wayi contains no Catholic symbolism: no saint images, no cross shapes, no written sacred words. Once, while at work in Kaha Wayi, I offered to make a donation for the patron Santa Rosa's festival. The response was that my gift would be welcome, but one shouldn't talk about such matters in Kaha Wayi.

The precinct is sacred in an old-fashioned anthropological sense: it is forbidden space that (to its adherents) radiates power. Its beautifully built flagstone walls and two padlocked gates are jealously controlled. Only one key exists. The "vice" or kamachikuq holds it at all times. By older customary law (now revised as Chapter 5 describes), nobody but the ritualist and balternos and their wives can enter.

The architecture of Kaha Wayi and Pasa Qulqa

The ritual-administrative precinct of traditional governance (see Figure 2.1) occupies an area of 346.17 square meters, close to the eastern edge of the village, on the same block as the famous painted church. One side of it lies along the boundary between the two traditional moieties, Allauca and Lamash, but it is considered to belong to neither. The precinct is surrounded on two sides by a recently rebuilt fieldstone wall with one large gate and a small lateral entrance. The other two sides are rammed-earth walls backing onto private residences. The precinct contains two buildings: Kaha Wayi, the "khipu house" (lower left in Figure 2.1) and the storehouse Pasa Qulqa (upper left in Figure 2.1). The two are roughly aligned, facing each other along a northeast-southwest axis, which forms an angle to the street grid. The walled plaza is unpaved and empty save for two electric utility posts, but excavation showed signs of heavy use both recent and historic.

The name Kaha Wayi consists of a Spanish root, *caja*, "chest, treasury," and a Quechua one, *wayi*, cognate to *wasi* in southern Quechua and meaning "house." Some call it the *tambo* or "way station," a hispano-Quechua term common in the colony. Others say Chawpi Ula, "Central Place."

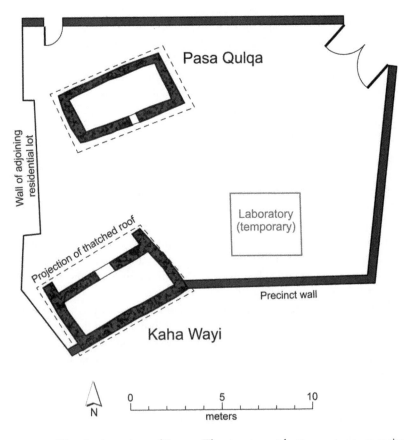

FIGURE 2.1 The ritual precinct of Rapaz. The structure at bottom, a temporary site laboratory, has been removed.

FIGURE 2.2 Kaha Wayi, the "Khipu House," in 2004 before architectural conservation. The Church cupola is visible behind it. Photo by the author.

Kaha Wayi, the "khipu house," (see Figure 2.2) is rectangular, with walls of irregular stone and earth mortar, and with adobe gables. A single northwest-facing door gives access to the main chamber, while a smaller opening in the southwestern gable 2.8 meters over the inside floor level opens into the now-empty attic. The end walls project past the main façade to form two buttresses. A low stone bench of a type common in regional prehispanic architecture runs along the base of the façade. The bench afforded seating for novices whose low rank allowed hearing but precluded seeing the rituals within Kaha Wayi. The main entry, a Dutch door, allowed sound and the ritually valued smoke of incense to reach these persons while precluding entry. Long eaves supported by extended sidewalls provide shelter over the bench.

The floor of the main chamber is compacted earth. Thick trunks of *quenual* (Polylepis racemosa) sustain the upper floor, 17 centimeters thick. This floor's upper surface was finished with a layer of smoothed clayey earth while its lower surface was covered with close-joined canes or *chacleado* and formed the ceiling of the lower chamber.

All around the interior of Kaha Wayi's main or lower chamber run adobe benches about 30 centimeters high, for the officers and ritualist. A niche near the ceiling on the northwest wall holds candles and remains of flowers.

Today, all Kaha Wayi's furnishings are highly sacred. The collection of khipus was in 2003 and 2004 draped in seeming disorder over a stick, which was in its turn hung from the cane ceiling. (This hanging rack lay parallel to the southeast or rear wall.)

FIGURE 2.3 The altar inside Kaha Wayi during a night session of the balternos or inner-cabinet officers. Each receives coca for his coca bag or *away walqi*. Photo by the author.

Even more important in the eyes of Rapacinos is the altar or offering table which stands near the center of the chamber (see Figure 2.3). Covered with two cloths, it permanently holds three small gourds for liquid maize offerings (*jurka*), a woven coca bag (*away walqi*), and a small lime gourd for seasoning coca. A large pile of coca leaf obscures most of the surface. From the ceiling hang 26 diverse objects dedicated as past offerings. A large broken pot on the floor serves as a censer for burning llama fat. Dry plant remains rest under the altar, while additional ritual pots sit under the khipu rack. In later pages of this chapter we will see these things in use.

Attachments and fights with cerros (mountains) and qucha (lakes)

Kaha Wayi is above all a center of communication with parts of the environment: the *awkin* mountains, weather, water, wind, organisms including animal and plant pests, and perhaps ancestors in an attenuated sense. It is the point through which communications can pass and equity can be established via demands and offerings. If Kaha Wayi is the "central place," its altar table is the center of the center. The actual point around which all else is arrayed is marked by a blob of llama fat, about the size of a grape, stuck to the underside of the tabletop, and said to be its life. It is annually renewed. The altar comes into action when it is activated or warmed up by offering, invocation, and group social energy (*voluntad*). Then it passes human offerings, words, and thoughts to their analogical destinations and relays the replies.

The Spanish word *cerro*, "hill, mountain," often means a mountain considered as a superhuman being. This hispanicism is one of many cases in which Spanish words have been adopted into Quechua as terms for sacred transactions, somewhat as Latin words are used in Catholicism to denote sacred usage. Most Central-Peruvian communities associate the Quechua term *jirka* with the mountain as superhuman being (Híjar Soto 1983, 103–106). Rapacinos know this usage but also use *jirka* to mean a herding location at high elevation.

Mountains are owners of weather and rain and send it at their pleasure. Analogically, wild creatures are their family and pets. Mountains hold dear all the creatures living on soil that they moisten, so these have to be named analogically. For example, it would be disrespectful to call a puma a puma, though *puma* is a proper Quechua word. Instead one says "his/her cat," because the puma is analogically the mountain's pet. Mountains have feelings much like those of humans, including possessiveness and anger. Mountains' sense of right and wrong is a moral-political system analogous to human community. It includes an ethic of deference to rank and an ethic of reciprocity, including vengeance. We humans incur debts when we use the mountain's water and when we take any of his progeny, even worms. Mountains' pride, anger, and jealousy make them hard to deal with. They talk to each other. By a further analogy, mountains of a given landscape are political beings; though rivalrous and unequal, they work together as a "council" and stand to each other in civic hierarchy as "president" (the highest mountain) and other ranks.

Again by analogy, mountains have different personalities as well as different but overlapping social networks, just as people do. They are social beings and don't like being neglected. Humans must not fail to give a sign when in sight of them. If a person offends a mountain, the mountain punishes him with the disease called *espanto* ("fright") or with bad luck. But there is nothing wrong with a human's defending his interest by interacting manipulatively with mountains. In speaking to mountains, persuasion, affection, pathos, guilt-tripping, stern admonition, and even anger are all acceptable rhetoric. The role of *awkin* is more like that of a lawyer than that of a magically empowered priest or ethical prophet.

Deglaciation is painfully obvious in the era of global climate change; some mountains that were snowcaps only two decades ago today are bare rock. One lamented case is Mount Chururu, whose flanks nourish Rapaz's communal herds. Rapacinos say one reason people address mountains as "old man" (*awkin*) is because they have white heads. As Mariscotti de Görlitz heard in the Andean south 35 years ago, "The loss of snow is the loss of their gift . . . The loss of snow is the loss of their greatness" (1978, 79). Scientists no less than agropastoralists see deglaciation as the source of concrete dangers such as lake-outburst landslides (Carey 2010). Rapacinos tend to see loss of ice, like bad weather in general, as a disturbance in equitable relations; I repeatedly heard deglaciation and global warming blamed on greedy extraction of coal and metal without proper reciprocity (foreigners being especially to blame). The underlying analogy likens water reserves on landforms to wealth in society.

The list of sacred places that Rapaz addresses in ritual varies somewhat depending on whom one asks, and where. The scheme is not a dogma, but a body of roughly cohering know-how. Different people take part in differently oriented invocations. Which mountains one has transactions with partly depends on where one's house, relatives, lands, and herds are. The most constantly invoked in Rapaz at all-community level are:

Yara Wayna (mountain)

Qumpir Wayna (mountain)

Saqsar or Susur Wayna (mountain)

Chururu (mountain)

Piluqayán or Pilawqayán (spring)

Tukapia (spring)

Chuqichuku (mountain)

Qisunki (mountain)

Most dominant mountains are male. But as analogism would predict, myths that explain landscape are often marriage myths. Chakwas Grande, "Big Old Lady," and Chuqichuku, "Silver Helmet," are "like a couple." Yara Wayna's name is interpreted as "young man calling out," because he and his mates call out to three small female hills, which seem to be climbing up the cordillera toward them, at Pilaw Qayan. If they had reached the Waynas, their fertility would have given Rapaz a warm zone of fruit and corn. But a jealous monolith called Zambo Rumi, or "Mulatto Stone," beguiled them with his flute, and there the girls remain, petrified, halfway to their mates.[2] In Chapter 3, extensive, world-organizing, logical networks based on analogies between genealogy and landscape will become visible.

A cordillera is a seen as a hierarchical system analogous to a segmentary polity. When one needs help from afar one might invoke a mountain one cannot see, such as the overlord mountains Waqrunchu and Yerupajá. These are distant giants of the cordillera more than 6,000 meters high. Should a Rapacino get ill in a faraway place, he can ask nearby mountains to relay the news that Rapaz is sending an offering and a request. Likewise, the devotees of Qisunki, who live farther down the Checras River, have to propitiate Rapaz's "young" hills the Waynas, because the Waynas have the earliest rain. Qisunki is asked to "coordinate" with the Waynas to make rain arrive downvalley in a sequence helpful to farming. Mountains are not omniscient like gods; just like people, they know what is near them, or else what they are told.

The varicolored high lakes (*qucha*) of the puna are treasured and propitiated almost as often as mountains. Mountains are spoken of as owning the lakes that their runoff feeds. Every Rapacino has truly impressive knowledge of hydrology.

One woman effortlessly spun off twenty lake names and their watercourses.[3] Most lakes are important because they feed Rapaz irrigation, but the large lake of Punrún, though outside Rapaz's boundaries, also gets major ritual attention. A mountain gains special rank if his slopes nourish a whole chain of lakes. For this reason, the "ornery" mountain Chuqichuku is revered despite his unfriendliness. As one might expect in an analogical system, artificial reservoirs are called by the same term as lakes, and they too need the favor of natural water-beings. Analogies among liquid systems, rather than distinctions between artificial and natural ones, rule terminology.

Artesian springs are treasured. They form important nodes of sacred geography and ritual practice. The underground currents that surface at springs are felt to be conduits through which the mountains not only supply water but also supply information and listen to people. I heard a spring compared to a long-distance telephone booth. Sparkles of spring water are likened to sparks popping from sacrificial fire. Two springs close to Rapaz village have permanent shrines and are frequently consulted by the ritualist. Only when those spots fail does he feel required to make the sacrificial ascent to entreat mountaintops or lakes face to face.

Works and nights at Kaha Wayi

The actual doings inside Kaha Wayi could be taken as a concert of analogies played out together, harmonically, in well-practiced formats. We could consider Kaha Wayi a palace of analogies, putting season and climate into articulation with agriculture and political authority.

Raywan Entrego, *or rebooting the year in Kaha Wayi*

It is New Year 2004. As Andean villages have done since the days of Viceroy Toledo (who imposed colonial laws of "Indian" government, 1569–1581), Rapacinos gather on January 2 for a town meeting to audit the performance of outgoing officers, install new ones, update the rolls and plan the coming year's agenda.[4] In previous publications I have called this kind of meeting by its Huarochirí provincial name, Huayrona (Salomon 2004). Although Rapacinos don't use that word, their town meeting is a Huayrona in form. Near the end of the meeting comes a customary sequence for installing the new members of the inner cabinet or Agropastoral Committee.[5] At the climactic time, the outgoing and incoming balternos come forward from opposite directions in formal regalia (brown ponchos, flowered hats, and coca bags) to embrace and toast each other straight from the bottle, "chest to chest" (*pecho a pecho*). The town crier or *fiscalejo* comes with them, announcing each new officer.

As afternoon shadows lengthen, the "vice" and his balternos are excused from the assembly. They troop off quietly to Kaha Wayi. The archaeologist Víctor Falcón Huayta and I were allowed to walk along after them. It was exciting to be brought in on a confidential *rimanakuy* or inner-cabinet meeting in the company of the khipus, the ritualist awkin, and the balternos.

There are moments when it's hard for an ethnographer to draw the line between witnessing and intruding. I have never ceased to feel doubt about this night, now twelve years in the past. Not that I meant to transcribe confidential judgments or invocations spoken in privacy to the cerros—as if I could transcribe Rapaz's unfamiliar Quechua fast enough! Nonetheless, just by being there in the ancient chamber, improperly dressed, without regalia, ignorant, and armed with a blinding camera flash, we did disrupt a solemn event. For the sake of creating a record that people may someday value, I think it was worth doing. But I would never do it again.

When the old and new "teams" of balterno file into Kaha Wayi they greet the ritualist or awkin, at that time Melecio Montes. It's important that the awkin have the "vice's" trust because the former will direct everything that happens in Kaha Wayi. Beside these leaders, three *comisiones* ("delegations") have to be formed: two officers representing each of the three rotation sectors in use as explained in Chapter 1. All outgoing officers attend as witnesses to the first part of the meeting, to be sure the balternos give the Community accurate information about the condition of the growing crops. Outgoing balternos sit on the bench by the khipus and incoming ones on the door side. Into the 1970s these plant ceremonies were symbolically directed to stone plant talismans called *papa ilan*, the lifestone of potatoes (Chapter 4), but now only live tuber specimens are used.

Now begins *raywan entrego* ("handover of sacred food"). "Handover" refers to transfer of agronomic, administrative, and ritual crop responsibilities from outgoing officers to incoming ones.

During the inaugural round of coca-taking (*boleo, chajcheo*), the new balternos receive their patrol assignments of field sectors and paddocks. Then each of the three delegations is charged to visit one of the field sectors under cultivation. Each delegation consists of one outgoing and one incoming officer and may include one comunero as witness. The delegations set out on foot while there is still good daylight. They look for damage by animals, infestations of fungus, insect plagues, bad drainage, and above all for adequate growth (for at New Year the plants should be in an early-to-middle stage of maturation).

While the delegates are away, the ritualist asks the mountains for permission to dismantle the past year's altar setting (*mesa*) and set up (*armar*) a new one. For this purpose, the incoming officers have brought a mass of coca, plus the resinous herb *kunuk*, tobacco, and llama fat. Removing the dessicated altar offerings from last year, the ritualist packs up everything: coca, kunuk, tobacco, liquor, llama fat, ashes from incense, chewed coca, and withered branches. The cleaning of the altar culminates with removing the hidden "navel" (*pupu*) at the center of the altar table's underside. The ritualist then cleans the table with kunuk water and patiently reassembles it, replacing the pupu, the altarcloths, and the offerings, diligently sucking coca all the while.

By this time, in the waning afternoon, the delegations are returning. It is time to "fill" and activate the new altar.

January being a crucial rainy month for crop growth, it's a good vibe if the delegations come back wet. They return to Kaha Wayi with large, flourishing green

FIGURE 2.4 Delegations return to Kaha Wayi with *raywanes* or crop samples from each agricultural sector.

plants carried by the outgoing officers (see Figure 2.4). These are plant ambassadors: the *raywanes*, or crop talismans, one of each species and each species representing one sector in use. It is Kaha Wayi's duty to honor and keep them all year.

Standing before the altar with a raywan, each outgoing officer reports agronomically on the state of his sector: size and health of plants, moisture, parasites, etc. There is a political as well as a technical reason for the detailed reporting. The incoming officers need to have the field conditions clearly attested on their first day, lest they be blamed for something that happened before they took office.

The succeeding round of coca-sucking and invocations is presided by the outgoing officers. The ritualist puts the new mesa into action by calling its completion to the attention of the mountains, all the while continuing to consume prodigious amounts of coca. Others are expected to follow suit. By about 8:00 p.m. the reporting of raywanes is finished. If the "vice" or kamachikuq approves the reports, all the outgoing officers are dismissed. The group now sits in flickering murk. A single candle glimmers from a recess in the stone wall.

Now that the ritualist is alone with his new officers, the crops, and the mountains, the raywanes pass to their place of honor: they are placed under the altar, replacing last year's dry stalks. They have become the vivifying essence of the current crop. As they receive the benison of invocations to the mountains and partake of sacrifices, they are felt to radiate botanical vitality.

Incoming officers distribute the second round of coca leaf, tobacco, and drinks. As the ritualist fires up the incense mixture of llama fat and kunuk, oily smoke fills the chamber. "The smoke warms up the mesa so the mountain will smell it," says ritualist Melecio Montes. "The mountain asks for it."

Anxiously the ritualist checks and rechecks the orange embers, looking for sparks that can be taken as replies to his murmured requests for rain and plant health. One balterno is appointed a helper to the awkin, and he distributes more ritual goods so Melecio, the ritualist, can concentrate on his "work" with the altar's three small *poronguitos* (gourd bowls). They are called *qucha*, "lake," and may be analogues of the lakes of the heights. When he activates (*calza*) the altar by offerings and words, the liquid "payment" in them "feeds" the regional water system.

Melecio has brought three colors of fine-ground corn: white, black, and red. In a can he stirs each colored meal with water, making a thick liquid that serves only as food for mountains. The left bowl (from his viewpoint) is called Ñawingucha, for red corn. The middle one, Jurka, receives black corn, and the right, Tinki, receives white corn, or in a year of scarcity brown *kuti* corn. The awkin also pours a portion into his own long gourd, which he reserves for sacrifice (*tinka*). With all the invocations this takes hours. It must be accompanied by many rounds of patient coca-taking and by long murmured speeches to all the mountains, name by name, in Quechua, with occasional short paraphrases in Spanish. Every once in a while the ritualist scrutinizes the bowls to watch for bubbles or turbulence, which would bring news of water coming from the cordillera.

When the moment for sacrifice comes, the ritualist raises his gourd and makes the final invocation. He goes outside into the starry night alone. There he talks in privacy directly with the cerros. He gives each a part of his liquefied corn reserve, and when he returns, pours the rest into the altar vessels. These liquids stay there indefinitely. As the level in each vessel falls, it is said that the mountains are drinking through the altar.

Each invocation has a simple verbal formula: "Cerro X, Cerro Y, Cerro Z, forgive our errors [n.b., not sins], talk to us, converse with us, so that there will be good rain, so the plants will grow well. We ask for good rain, good weather, we ask that there should be no hail, no drought, that the plants should not get sick. We ask that it should be for the best, all for the best." A good fifteen or more mountains must be called. Other beings can be interpolated, among which we heard Pasa Simin "Mouth of Seasons" and "Qulqa Pasa," that is, the storehouse Pasa Qulqa itself.

There is more to invocation than those simple recitations. "Talking with them is a matter of art and strategy, because each has his own personality and his own attitude," said Vice-President Víctor Gallardo. "You have to be especially careful to pay the mountains that are *chúcaro* ('ornery'), the ones that haven't made a deal with humanity."

Late rounds of coca, after midnight, circulate in a mood of frowzy, tired-but-stoked mental intensity. Some heads bow low. Eyelids droop and flutter in a stoned way. Remarks are few and subdued, consisting of murmured comments on any spark or sound that might be a reply from the cerros. When at last the ritualist pronounces the "work" complete, everyone must exit inconspicuously from the small side door of the precinct and go home unnoticed. The ritualist stays until late bagging and saving the remains of the "work," then locks up.

On January 3, 2004, it was past 2:00 a.m. when Víctor and I stepped from the smoky fug inside Kaha Wayi out under the Milky Way. We were trembling from cold, sore in the bones from sitting on lumpy stones, buzzed from too much coca, awed, and exhausted.

"A replacement for death": the order of the altar in Kaha Wayi

Centuries of clandestinity have transformed the many other ritual mesas described in ethnographies into portable, temporary arrays. What makes the Rapaz variant temple-like, and makes its officiant priest-like, is that Kaha Wayi's mesa is permanent, with immovable furniture and a house around it. It does not promote magical virtuosity or "shamanic" performance (as the word is all too loosely applied). Most popular mesas are performed ad hoc for clients, but the work of Kaha Wayi forms part of civic routine. Rapaz's customary law of contracting and paying a ritualist for the collectivity institutionalizes this.

A mesa is the place for *qarakuna*, serving the cerros coca, tobacco, liquor, a pair of cuyes, a sheep. The term is a Quechua verb meaning "to give for consumption, to feed." The thing offered is called *pago* "payment," *derecho* "right," or *cumplimiento* "fulfillment"—that is, something owed to the mountain.

When humans perform *qarakuna*, mountains eat, smoke, take coca, experience pleasant sociability, and thereby incur a debt to people. But this ethos also includes negative reciprocity. The hunger of mountains is a frightening fact. If people sacrifice stingily, the mountain in his hunger may attack people and eat them. Wasting illnesses are interpreted as repossession; the patient's flesh is being garnished. Formally paying the derecho can (hopefully) effect a cure or preserve life. "Qarakuna is a replacement for death," one man said. "With the liquid *jurka*, white, black and brown, one calls upon the mountain. First you call the mountain, then you show him: *kaymi derechuwayki* 'This is your rightful gift.' It's proper to offer three qarakuna. On the third, [the mountain] will accept." Kaha Wayi is sometimes called *qarakuna wayi*—"feeding house."

Coca leaf in Rapaz, as all over highland Peru and Bolivia, is never taken casually or alone. (Using coca alone might be a sign of witchcraft or mental illness.) It belongs strictly to ritual protocol. Coca time is time for peaceful, thoughtful sociability. It pulls a group together and focuses it. To consume coca one picks up one leaf, strips out the hard vein, and puts the leaf in one's cheek with a bit of *ichku* (mineral lime) or *llipta* (alkaline ash powder). After a while, the stuffed cheek bulges out. One should strive for a state of heightened vitality and focus (not easy to maintain because rounds of liquor also circulate simultaneously). To take more and more coca while performing qarakuna is meritorious, even if you get to the point of hurting your mouth. Of a distended cheek, participants say approvingly "his mouth is like a girl's breast." If somebody isn't *boleando* enough, the ritualist says "work harder."

The altar itself receives a share of each in coca round, thus being recognized as a person. Like every participant, the altar has a coca bag (*away walqi*) of its own—a very sacred object. It is as if the altar itself were the commander of the meeting, with all deference due first to it.

For any meeting with the mountains, one also needs llama fat (*llama wira*). Before ritual use, one has to clean it and soften it with the warmth of one's hands. When ready it is white and gooey, thicker than peanut butter and cohesive enough to roll into a ball, with no odor or taste. Today, as in Inka times, llama fat is esteemed as the very substance of life.

One sacrifices llama wira by putting small masses of it into *shanla*, or red-hot embers. Shanla too is a standard supply that a ritualist's assistant must carry even for long ritual journeys, always alight on a potsherd. Mixed with kunuk twigs, llama fat produces an oily cloud of resinous smoke: "It stinks so nice." Combustion is the actual medium of contact with cerros, and the ritualist watches it intently. When embers pop and sparkle, people feel reassured that the mountain is enjoying the ritual and "talking" to them. Flickering in the dark, the oily red embers reminded me of LED lights on a modem: they show that a message is flowing, but you have to perceive more than their flicker to understand and answer. That is the job of the ritualist.

The ritualist as advocate, priest, and hero

The ritualist of Kaha Wayi has resonant titles: *awkin*, *bendelhombre*, or *pasa kamaq*. The last of these titles, meaning "one who sets season/weather/time in order," is archaeologically suggestive because it exactly matches the name of the great Inka and pre-Inka shrine complex Pachacámac south of Lima. In the 1608 Quechua manuscript of Huarochirí, *pacha camac pacha cuyuchic*, "world-maker and world-shaker," was an epithet of the earthquake-causing divinity once worshiped there (Salomon and Urioste 1991, 100, 107, 108, 113). Could it be that the Rapaz officiant's modern title echoes the central logic of what was once the Andean world's most renowned sacred precinct (Makowski 2015)? One man tried to get the Pasa Kamaq idea across to me by saying, "It's like he's the Agropastoral Committee's own Superman."

The term *awkin* fits well with Descola's analogical ideal-type. For every awkin relationship in one domain there are analogous ones in other domains. Awkin is a respectful term for an old man or progenitor, alluding more to seniority in rank than to biological age. Like many focalized Andean concepts (*pasa* or space/time, Quechua *ayllu* or kindred, and *llahta* or settlement), awkin is a relational and scalable rather than categorical term. One's grandfather is one's awkin; likewise, the living as a group speak of ancient ancestors as awkin (Morris et al. 1968, 244–246); similarly the ritualist is awkin to the balternos; and so too the ritualist addresses a mountain as awkin. The great snowcaps are awkin to smaller hills. Always, the point is not mere length of endurance but generativity: the old have produced the existing world. Awkin might best be considered as a cardinal term in a generalized analogy using the idealized descent group as organizer of many domains.

Because he holds Rapaz's welfare in his hands, an awkin ritualist is often referred to as *bendelhombre*, from Spanish *bien del hombre* meaning "human well-being." Like the word awkin, bendelhombre is a scalable, relational term. Inside Kaha Wayi or out in the landscape, the man called bendelhombre addresses his own superiors the mountains with the same epithet bendelhombre.

Andean readers will recognize the title *awkin* from José María Arguedas' unforgettable 1956 ethnography *Puquio* about his hometown in the southern region of Ayacucho. Being a bilingual native son, Arguedas was able to follow not only the words but the thoughts of Puquio's traditional officers—locally called *aukis*—as they approached the mountain's inner self. Arguedas was a bilingual literary genius as well as an ethnographer. Nobody has brought us closer to the "heart of the mountain" than he did when he translated an invocation:

> Pukullu ukupi
> Verde siwar qenti
> Chaupituta hora
> Waqaqmasillay
> Rogaykaysiway
> Adoraykaysillaway
> Ama hina kaychu
> Orqopa sonqonpi
>   *Wiñasqaykita (1956, 207)*

> Inside ruin walls,
> Hummingbird, green emerald,
> At the midnight hour
> My companion in crying,
> Help me to plead
> Help me to adore
> Don't say no,
> You who grew
> In the heart of the mountain.

Numerous other ethnographies detail Andean mountain rites (such as Allen 1988; Arnold and Yapita 1996, 2001; Bolin 2010; Gose 1994; Montoya 1987, 473–501; Rösing 1995, 1996; Valderrama and Escalante 1988; and many more). Most of what an awkin does partakes of these far-flung practices.

Rapaz's awkin is contracted annually, to control protocol and sacrifice inside Kaha Wayi, and to speak for the village in the actual presence of the mountains, lakes, or weather. He is a civic functionary or priest and not an autonomous figure such as a seer, healer, or shaman. His contract follows normal legalistic forms, albeit somewhat cursorily, and provides a small salary as well as reimbursing documented expenses for ritual materials like coca, llama fat, etc. Contract disputes are not unknown.

The ritualists's duties, unlike a Catholic priest's, involve no unique magic or skill. What he knows, others know, albeit with less authority. His ways of practicing qaray are the same ones households practice on a smaller, private scale for their own fields and animals. The awkin's high place in analogical hierarchy is owed to his standing as negotiator or advocate on behalf of the social whole—the "transcendent collective" in Bloch's terminology (Chapter 5). By performing feats of sacrifice and austerity he demonstrates to the mountains that they can trust and deal with Rapaz. If they don't, he must challenge the mountains and even humiliate them—whatever it takes to make them comply.[6] Because this requires mortal daring, the ideal bendelhombre is a hero and champion of his people.

In 2003, four or five men were advanced enough in ritual to be eligible for the awkin-bendelhombre role. Traditionally, the contract is prized, and those who get it try to pass it to a son if any shows aptitude. A person who is not the son of a ritualist may ask for apprenticeship, but such a request is a delicate, confidential matter. If the master is willing, he will appoint the novice as his helper. The unwritten prerequisites are descent from a knowledgeable family, physical strength, maturity, dominant or authoritative personality, ability to hold liquor, memory, power of concentration, and intuition verging on visionary perception. A prospective bendelhombre needs to have intimate knowledge of mountains, lakes, etc., but he need not be a sociable or obliging person. Some ritualists have been standoffish men with reputations for being *recio*, "harsh."

Throughout the year, if rains are late, or water becomes scarce, or if hail and freezing weather threaten crops, the "old man" (as the ritualist is casually called in Spanish), together with his apprentice must take action.

His first resource is to call the powers from inside Kaha Wayi, using the altar as an operable maquette of the landscape. For this purpose, the three gourd bowls on the altar are "like three lakes," as a ritualist explained, equivalent to the lakes of the high puna where the mountains store their water. The ritualist activates (*calza*) this model of the landscape and thereby communicates with the cordillera through invocations and "feeding." If in-house action fails, the Community resorts in fixed sequence to mesas at Pasa Qulqa, at the spring Tukapia, and at the cave of Pilaw Qayán. As a final resort, the Awkin may climb the mountains themselves.

Melecio gave an example of his address to the remote mountain Wamaliano, exemplifying stern bargaining: "The mountains' character is harsh. You have to be unafraid . . . I say 'Wamaliano, please understand me: don't leave the poor comunero in hunger. Always listen and obey. Understand what I'm talking about. Don't make us suffer.'" Like a well-connected lawyer petitioning the central government to make local powers obey, an adroit bendelhombre speaking at the communication-relay spring Tukapia can send his message to the highest peaks.

If nearer connections fail, he climbs up to the lakes and snows to confront the mountains directly. He knows what place is responsible for a given problem because he studies the movements of clouds carefully. Before setting out, the bendelhombre and his assistant hide out fasting and celibate in Kaha Wayi, taking large amounts of coca. They eat only a little corn mush and sleep only in short furtive naps. Purified, the awkin and his apprentice set out at dawn for the heights, taking sacrificial animals such as black guinea pigs, as well as the usual mesa supplies. As they travel higher and higher, the master and his helper pause at each spring to perform a mesa calzada; they are passing through successive "gateways" to the cerros. Climbing while fasting and camping unsheltered is the heroic manner of the office.

At the stony beaches of high lakes such as Punrún the ritualist performs qaray, "gift-feeding," and presents his case. He watches ripples and cloud for a reply. If no favorable cloud appears, or if clouds wander away, he may express anger by slinging stones into the lake and insulting the cerros. He defies the mountain to hurl hailstones or lightning in combat. He must stand fast through the storm and dominate it as one does when breaking a rebellious animal, finally bringing it back as tamed rain. Comuneros of Rapaz consider themselves talented for such ritual—perhaps a Llacuaz memory—and retain a certain clientele among officials of lower-lying villages like Tongos, Puñún, or Tulpay when water is even scarcer.

If drought still persists, the Agropastoral Committee sends its bendelhombre all the way to the Pacific coast to bring back sea water and prime the celestial pumps. Riding the bus as if on routine business, he stealthily approaches the Pacific beach and collects seawater in a bottle. On return he pours some sea water into altar vessels. Pouring marine and puna water into the altar bowls simultaneously is called "uniting the waters" (*unir las aguas*), a powerful stimulant to rain. "Ocean water with water from Raracocha lake? A flash flood!"

Once rain is guided into Rapaz, it has to be "accustomed" so it won't wander away. At the first rainfall, the balternos would catch water in a jar and seal it to be stored in Kaha Wayi. "That would be so you could venerate it, so the rain wouldn't just go away for no reason." On the other hand, as the season advances, rain might become excessive. In that case, "They'd say, *partikur*, that is, fold over one corner of it [the altar cloth] so the rain doesn't get out of hand. So there won't be flash floods or washouts."

"Lady Storehouse" and the work of female officers

Face to face with Kaha Wayi stands the now-empty but still revered communal storehouse, Pasa Qulqa. *Qulqa* is cognate to southern Quechua *qullka*, "storehouse," a word well known to archaeologists who find arrays of storage cells near Inka ruins. The substantive *pasa*, cognate to *pacha*, means "time, season, weather." Asked to translate the name, villagers render Pasa Qulqa as *depósito del tiempo* ("storehouse of time" or "of weather"), or else *depósito estacional* ("seasonal storehouse"). Pasa Qulqa is also called Misya Qulqa, "Lady Storehouse,"[7] or Chawpi Qulqa, "Central Storehouse," or "the Tambo" (an Inka and colonial word for a way station).[8] *Qarakuna*, "Gift-Feeding Place," is another informal name for it—or her.

A dominant analogy of femaleness and maleness governs Pasa Qulqa's and Kaha Wayi's individual attributes and their respective political-ritual-administrative roles. They stand to each other in a somewhat huari-llacuaz way: to Pasa Qulqa's

FIGURE 2.5   Pasa Qulqa, the old community storehouse, after architectural
        conservation, 2005.

Huari-like depth, plenty, productivity stability, and femaleness, Kaha Wayi presents
Llacuaz-like orientation to heights, adversarial relations, dynamism, and maleness.

Pasa Qulqa (see Figure 2.5) is a robust all-stone building designed to sustain
great weights. It resembles Kaha Wayi in overall shape and size but differs in having
no adobe parts. Pasa Qulqa's exterior shows traces of having formerly been plas-
tered with earthen mortar and lime. It is rectangular, with three levels (Figure 2.6).
The foundations are 42–56 centimeters thick and about a meter deep. The walls
are of like thickness, 2.86–3.25 meters tall. Around all four walls runs a projecting
cornice of flat stones at 2.86 meters high. This feature is also common in local Late
Intermediate villages, whose ruins are plentiful. (The prehispanic village of Rapaz
was only a few meters away, at the prow of the promontory on which Rapaz sits,
but it was destroyed in the construction of the current soccer field.) Its masonry is
less than regular but stones are consistently placed flattest side outward. There are
no exterior buttresses or benches.

Two of Pasa Qulqa's three openings are on the southeastern side, facing Kaha
Wayi. The lower of the two southeastern openings gives access to a floor today 60
centimeters below ground level, with a ceiling height of 1.3 meters. Heavy trunks
of *quenual* wood sustain the middle floor, which retains its finish of smoothed earth
reinforced with stone. Access to the middle floor is through the higher of the
southeastern openings, now at chest height from the ground. The middle floor had

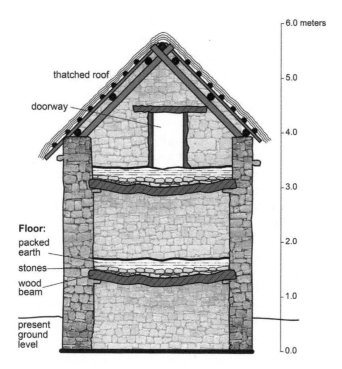

FIGURE 2.6   Pasa Qulqa, south–north section, 1:100 scale, by Humberto Maraví.

1.25 meters of headroom. Both openings had double stone lintels and thick stone thresholds. The top floor was built like the middle one, but it has collapsed. Access to it was through an opening in the southwest gable at 2.73 meters over present ground level and required climbing an exterior stairway or ladder. It is usual for prehispanic storage buildings to have small openings with obstructed access, as does Pasa Qulqa, perhaps for security reasons. Full particulars are on record from the archaeological viewpoint in Falcón Huayta (2007) and from the architectural viewpoint in Las Casas (2005).

Pasa Qulqa's bottom level: animals, sacrifices, skins, and legends

Pasa Qulqa's semi-subterranean lower level is identified in oral tradition with animal goods and animal sacrifice. This matches 17th-century testimonies in idolatry trials, one of which, in 1656, prosecuted a couple for maintaining "*chaguayes* which are cellars underneath the colcas" for purposes of sacrificial veneration (Duviols 1973, 179).[9] In 2005, Víctor Falcón Huayta studied Pasa Qulqa archaeologically, opening meter-square pits inside Pasa Qulqa and uncovering past use floors. He found animal remains in the upper and lower use strata. Patricia Maita Agurto analyzed them zoologically (2006). She found a minimum of 32 individual animals, of which 13 (40.6%) were cattle and the remaining 59.4%, in descending order of frequency, were sheep, llama or alpaca, goats, dog, deer, or undetermined. The cattle, camelids, sheep, and goat bones showed enough butchery cuts to convince her that they were cooking remains. Maita judges that at least some of these cattle and sheep were eaten inside the precinct. She considers animal sacrifice a possible explanation.

Many Rapacinos assert that in the bottom of Pasa Qulqa there existed a "lake" (*qucha*, a scalable word that can refer to bodies of water as big as the ocean or as small as puddles), or *pozo*, "well." Judging by practices in nearby villages, this probably refers to a large ceramic urn. It is usual for contained or still water to have female associations in contrast to the male associations of falling or rushing water.

Here special miraculous animals were kept, including a purportedly tame vicuña (vicuñas being untamable) and a pair of "red ducks" whose behavior predicted weather. With its "little grass and little pasture" the bottom of "Lady Storehouse" seems to have been envisioned (like Kaha Wayi's altar) as an operative miniature of the landscape, but one emphasizing tame qualities—an elaborate analogical complement to the temple. One got auguries of weather on the pastures by stirring the water of Pasa Qulqa's "lake" or "well" and observing bubbles. We found no physical remains of such a body of water, but similar practices are known in nearby modern villages, where the domesticated "lake" is an oversize ceramic pot.

Vivid memories express the animal mystique of Pasa Qulqa's bottom chamber. The ritualist Melecio Montes recalls that there were vicuña skins and deer. Encarnación Rojas and Robles Atachagua, native Rapacinos, explain that it was a place to sacrifice animals, including male vicuñas, for the *chaco*, or surround hunt season, hence its epithet Qarakuna, "feeding place" (2011, 41).

In former times, all the men from Pucará, Huaychao, and similar very high, very steep terraced mountaintop sites, used to come to Pasa Qulqa and there they would make a *maltón* [young reproductive male] llama go inside, and sacrifice it so they wouldn't suffer so much up there with the weather. In that way they rapidly got good winter weather [for pasture grasses]. That is what the lower floor of Pasa Qulqa is for.

I asked, did they voluntarily sacrifice their own animals? "No, no! They came to harvest [i.e. work as fieldhands or transporters in Rapaz' harvest]. By way of robbery, at night, on the sly, quietly, they took [llamas] and there they killed them and threw them down there in that lake, without the owner knowing." I repeatedly heard reminiscences that in Huari-Llacuaz tinged encounters like this, society winked at a certain amount of stealing, perhaps a sign of the antagonistic interdependences characteristic of "vertical" society.

Pasa Qulqa's upper levels: food reserves, plant talismans, seed tubers, and fertility ritual

Pasa Qulqa's middle and top levels stored the plant products of the common sector. As the harvest of common fields was unloaded in the precinct patio, they were divided into three parts. *Semilla*, "seed," consisted of some 400–700 kilograms of the best tubers that would be saved to plant the upcoming cycle. They were carefully stored on straw beds in the top sector and ritually praised as the "babies" that would grow into future crops (see Chapter 4). *Reserva*, "expendable stores," were stored in the middle floor. They included a much larger amount of food. The reserve supported feeding of guests, officers traveling as emissaries, households in urgent need, work crews on community tasks, and whatever festivities Kaha Wayi might authorize. Any food left over after these expenses became *reparto*, or "shares," for distribution to households, called *winaychaniy* (perhaps "deemed as my increase" (Adelaar 1977, 275)). A few of the most fruitful-looking and interesting tubers or cobs were set aside as *pirwa* ("granary") or *chukrush*. Hanging in the seed chamber, these trophy tubers (or cobs) would decorate and safeguard the crop.

Female authorities: the consorts of the kamachikuq (vice-president) and bendelhombre (ritualist)

Among the analogies that organize Rapaz, perhaps the most pervasive is the one likening male and female gender to production and distribution, respectively. It is very much the kind of thing Descola's model predicts, and it matters greatly to Andean studies for two reasons. One is that it bears on a longstanding contro-versy about whether the ritual complementarity of men and women reflects actual relations of power, or whether it is just an ideological notion. The other is that archaeological literature about "redistributive" functions of the Andean polity (still controversial after half a century) has not clarified what, if anything, redistribution has to do with gender (Feinman 2014).

A thick vein of collective memory, often with overtones of nostalgia, concerns female officers who formerly ruled the storehouse. Up to an uncertain but recent time—the political decline of the generation that died out in the 1990s—all the offices of the inner ritual-administrative cabinet were held by couples rather than household-heading men, and wives were at least nominally part of the quorum. On the balterno side, the female head was the *ispinsira* or *espensera* (the latter pro-nunciation prevailing in Spanish). The term derives from *despensera*, "steward," with Spanish feminine inflection. On the ritualist side, the bendelhombre's wife or *chakwas* ("old lady," again a seniority term) enjoyed authority. Inside Kaha Wayi, male voices dominated the rimanakuy (conversation). But it was otherwise at "Kaha Wayi's consort" (*compañera*), the storehouse Pasa Qulqa.

Elisa Falcón Racacha, a widow noted for her elegantly traditional dress, was born in 1933. In youth, she saw the espensera in full style but never held the title. She entered Kaha Wayi accompanying her husband when he held offices, and there she saw the espensera co-conducting rimanakuy (political discussion) with her husband. As first lady, the espensera wore a *vincha* (diadem) of silver, bulky earrings (*sarsillus*), and a long stickpin (locally called *kasha* or *brocha*, not the usual Andean word *tupu*). As Alicia Gallardo said, this first lady of the village would come out in splendor:

pure jewelry, all silver. My grandmothers had those jewels. They had some tremendous stickpins of silver that was completely white. The clasps of their necklaces too, their rings and earrings. Everything pure jewelry. And they were really pretty with their hair in little braids, everything neatly arranged. In those times there weren't fabric skirts. Everything was homespun, called *cordellate*. The skirts down to the floor. They didn't use socks, every step was in *llanques* [moccasins]. And their blouses were of the style called *polka* . . .

And while they were taking coca, they didn't touch their husbands, three or four days until at last it rained . . . The only thing they could ingest was kunuk water and ground corn made into liquid mush, like baby food, that's all. They'd smoke tobacco too. The espensera did all this in Kaha Wayi. She was like a *patrona* [sponsoring or commanding woman].

The espensera danced in bare feet and should look robust. Her *manta* or short cloak "should be blue outside with red inside. She wore wide *polleras* [multi-layered bell-shaped skirts]. "If she didn't bulk herself up that way, the potato harvest would be meager."

The espensera had to be present at Kaha Wayi and Pasa Qulqa when the crops were brought home "to perform the cult for each crop: oca, ulluco, mashua, potatoes. In November (potato-planting season), in the plaza at Kaha Wayi, she gave every comunero three or four handfuls of tubers. Not because of scarcity, but as a sign" of her benison on planting and as an earnest of the harvest. Teodora Falcón, another veteran of the old ritual order, emphasizes the espensera's grandeur:

> She used to wear five or six, up to ten underskirts, a lot of clothing, to make her figure big and pompous . . . She took coca with the bosses [i.e., balternos] in Kaha Wayi. In her lap she gathered the best potatoes, which she kept for seed. She'd lift her skirt to receive them, like this. With jewels and flowers, but barefoot.
>
> She was like the owner of the community storehouse [i.e., Pasa Qulqa]. She guarded Raywan Mama. Raywan Mama wasn't just in Kaha Wayi. She also had her own house. The espensera used to anoint the raywan plants with llama fat, so they'd grow strong. They actually did grow tall in her house and gave the fields force to grow. She was powerful, she was splendid, the espensera!

"Every *faena*," Irene Condor Luya remembers, "they [women with their balterno husbands] would go down to Kaha Wayi, as if going to the office." (A *faena* is an obligatory community work day.) Comuneros gathered in Kaha Wayi's forecourt with flowers in their hats. "They would go to the field *tinyando* [singing ritual songs], hacking, chopping, scraping everywhere. The Mayordomo would pull roots, he'd grab branches, and throw them, singing *ayayha*, *ayau*, singing *way-taraw*, *way-taraw* in a high voice, with those branches."

The espensera was responsible for weaving two authorized, decorated standard bags used to measure the product of the communal fields at origin and destination.

Two men with the title of *alqasaku*, "bag-lifter," were named by the kamachikuq to do the weighing.[10] Though these men wore festive flowers, they were really security officers: they had to make sure food got from the field to Pasa Qulqa without pilferage. The espensera presided over the count as the harvest arrived and directed the work of laying them away in the middle and upper floors of Pasa Qulqa.

Pasa Qulqa as "mother" of the commons

Pasa Qulqa filled up in harvest time and gradually emptied out through the hungry season of winter. She fed and protected the community, as old songs have it, "like a mother." The espensera and the awkin bendelhombre's wife, the "old lady" *chakwas*, had to preside together whenever "lady storehouse" was opened.

During the interval between harvests, the espensera was to release contents of the three floors as authorized by Kaha Wayi. This would normally include big subsidies for festivals and smaller ones for hospitality, viands of travelers on official missions, or sale as community revenue. At sowing, the espensera shared out seed tubers *wiya wiya* ("belly belly") to comuneros. As the year advanced, she would be expected to look out for scarcity. In January, the hungriest season, she would hand out "old lady potatoes" (wrinkled tubers) for relief of hunger, measuring by *milqa*, meaning the amount a woman can lift in the lap of her apron.

This system is said to have lasted with at least some of its pomp until about 1964–1965, the time when Rapaz reconquered its usurped lands and gained the means for a more commercial, more modernist, and more male-dominated cooperativism. The last vice-president to enforce Pasa Qulqa's old laws, and the last to prefer the Quechua title kamachikuq, was Mauro Huaman, who held office in those years. As USAID support for a newly launched commercial cooperative arrived, and as peasant communities like Rapaz won legal recourse over lands formerly occupied by encroaching estates, communal institutions of self-sufficiency including Pasa Qulqa became less important. Community officers of the 1960s are remembered as murmuring "We don't need any of those customs any more" (ACCSCR/R inv. 17). This shift apparently had the side effect of demoting joint male-female authority in favor of male-centered "constitutional" political habits.

The communal redistribution regime in agriculture was partly disbanded. Kaha Wayi retained power over cultivable land and it has never been privatized. But the reserved common fields were phased out and assigned to landless households as family usufruct parcels. In this way, the male part of the hierarchy concerned with production endured, but not the female part concerned with communal-level consumption.

Nonetheless, the memory of "Lady Storehouse" and her female hierarchy remained strong through the period of masculinization. Teodora Falcón, widow of the renowned awkin Lauro Montes and a spellbinding talker in either of her languages, loves to recount her time as the chakwas. She says that when Lauro roamed in search of weather, "I remained behind in Kaha Wayi, sucking on coca, just staying there chajchando, burning incense in Kaha Wayi so rain would arrive."

That's why we used to sing, why we sang with the small drum [*tinya*] when he made rain arrive, saying "*mayllay ururun, kayllay ururu*" as we used to sing there. [This song is analyzed in Chapter 4.] A-ha, there we sang, and there we took coca only, pure coca. We didn't drink alcohol, none, nor use tobacco, none. Chewing coca with llama fat, that's all, making little tiny balls of it like this and mixing it in with the coca. Not lime either. And neither food. Nothing with salt or with onions or broth, nothing like that. Only corn mush with kunuk, and kunuk water. Or chamomile without sugar. And nothing between man and woman. No, no, no. Each alone, alone, alone, in a sacred state, a sacred state. The mountain would receive you that way: clean, sacred, sacred.

Kaha Wayi was the same. Only in that state would it receive us, lest something bad happen. In years past, if anybody entered Kaha Wayi without taking coca, people would think or say, "I hope they die, I hope they get castrated."[11] All this to make rain arrive. And when we took coca, when we were incensing with kunuk, then clouds began to gather little by little, clouding, clouding, clouding over, and then serenely, serenely, serenely clouding. By 4:00 p.m., the rain arrived BUNNN!!! [thunder] T'T'T'T'T'!!!! [lightning].

Kamatsikuj, Mayordomo and all the officers had to go in Kaha Wayi with their wives. Equally both had to chajchar [consume coca], each in line. After chajcheo, when they finished the hour—because it's by hours [long rounds]—when they finish the hour, they could go. Just one would stay behind.

That would be the one called "old man" [i.e., ritualist]. And he'd ask [as each one bowed out], "How many times did you chajchar?" We had to hand in our used coca leaves. One, two, three, or any number of wads for the hours we served. That ball of coca, that ball . . . comes the rain and the hail: "BUNNN!!" "lulululutatatat! [thunderbolt, rain and hail rattling on roof]! Yes, water, we received water!"

When the rain came, we received it in a new vessel. We would gather it in a new vessel and put flowers in. Carnations. [Gesture of holding out a bowl:] Here's the rain falling, into this new dish. And from this new dish, when it was full, we'd save the water in little gourd bottles. Then we'd set it out. Then again we'd pour from it. When it fills up there, [the storm] calms. And there's the pretty rain. So nice, the rain. It was a lot of work!

The whole series of sessions and chajcheos took about five months. Indeed, a lot of work. If the work was more than a chakwas could handle, she had the option of hiring a *chakwansita* or female deputy to help her sing and sacrifice.

What does a bendelhombre know? "Analogical" erudition and monotheism

In Chapter 3 we will consider the attack on Andean ritualism during a period of persecution by Catholic clergy. Does Descola's scheme shed any light on this conflict?

Descola thinks of Abrahamic religion as an analogical worldview with a peculiar feature: an ultimate, apical correspondence at the top, which constitutes an analogy between One (God) and Everything (the world).

> The miracle of monotheism is to have fused all these particularities [i.e., analogical cultic connections] into one polyvalent God, unattached to any particular place or any segmentary membership: an operation so extraordinary that it did not take Catholicism, with its cult of the saints, long to restore the functional distribution peculiar to analogism.
>
> *2013, 275*

Leaving aside the huge question of whether "miracle" is a historically or philosophically sound way to describe monotheism and its offspring, we can accept for the moment Descola's suggestion about its peculiarity. Thinking analogically about monotheism might help explain the transatlantic religious wrangle of which Peruvian extirpation of idolatry was a part. In Peru, the Catholic approach to Andean ritualism passed through a relatively mild and diverse missionary phase from 1532 to 1569, then a more coercive stage of "reduction" or resettlement in villages, which enforced compulsory religious indoctrination up to about 1608, and after 1608 several regional waves of punitive repression against Andean cult.

It's easy for anyone born in the sphere of the monotheisms to understand the doctrinal objections to analogistic cults ("idolatry"). From the viewpoint of Abrahamic doctrines, an analogical system without an apex, and with many independently aggrandized lower nodes, seemed a perverse refusal to make sense. Pagan analogism seems to run in the wrong direction—not to approach the apex, but on the contrary to scatter in search of godlets no bigger than ourselves or our resources or vested interests, all of them easily possessed by demons. Only Satan could have rendered people so obtuse.

Certain branches of Catholicism (the Las Casian tendency and some neoplatonistic variants such as that of Garcilaso Inca de la Vega) were willing to treat practices like Kaha Wayi as errors, not sins. One could teach by dialogue with natives' partial or mistaken understandings of divinity. When some early padres perceived likenesses between Greco-Roman polytheism and huaca cult, they were exercising an insight similar to Descola's. They thought dialogue could work by reorienting the respective analogical systems toward their apices. But for more powerful Catholic movements, as for many Abrahamic-derived doctrines today, "idolatry" was a fatally inflammatory word.

Monotheism has as its apex a topmost analogy that collapses analogy itself: an analogy between the One and the All. Monotheistic, religiosity demands a rare singleness of mind. To the degree that Catholicism in the 16th and 17th centuries emphasized monotheism, it demanded views toward this apex, the ineffable summit of all analogies. At least theoretically, Tridentine doctrine required synthetic perception of Unity in Trinity as a fundament for "true" cognition. Extirpation had as its complement a great and popular literature of devotionalism, in Amerindian languages among others, aimed at intensifying, if not monotheism, at least awareness of God-imbued persons (saints) who pointed toward the divine apex. Extirpators of idolatry were above all concerned to forestall the decay of rural Christianity into wak'a by-products.

What extirpation fundamentally objected to was the *finality* of pluralism in "pagan" worldviews: the correct perception that they are multiple or they are nothing. One of Christendom's many nightmares was pagan knowledge, ever proliferating in wild fractals of categorical patterning, an expansive "archaic" erudition pulling away from centrality and governable cult.

Notes

1 By drawing mountains with stony yet vaguely human shapes, Felipe Guaman Poma de Ayala toward 1615 overturned an earlier European habit of illustrating Amerindian "idols" as anthropomorphic statues on the Golden Calf model. Instead he tried to convey the Andean idea of a land feature that is also a person (Trever 2011). The beings 17th-century extirpators of idolatry in central Peru tried to destroy were often objects that seem to lie astride the distinction between humanly made and natural things. Rapaz today sets enormous value on certain stones with few iconic qualities but person-like identities as animals. The village of Puñún near Rapaz had a Kaha Wayi-like structure of its own housing a naturally shaped but polished stone called Raywanta or Raywa (the "goddess" of food) who received morning corn offerings in pots that were tossed and left broken.

2 Encarnación Rojas heard another variant specifying that the young ladies were on their way from Casta to Cajatambo, that is, northward along the western cordillera face (2011, 13–14).

3 Cochaquillo, Chaupi Cocha, Churamachay, Chalcó, Anqarayuq, Suerococha Grande and Suerococha Chica, Huytuqucha, Hanka Kuta, Qinwayuq, Wasaqucha, Morococha, Lutacocha, Hawi, Brava Machay, Taho Verde, Uchkumachay, Chiuwriq, Ilaqucha, Punrún.

4 Formerly January 1, but the Municipality has taken over that day for its own civic pomp.

5 The new members are chosen in October and inducted privately overnight on January 1–2. Each outgoing member goes out at midnight and conducts his replacement to the "vice's" house. About 10 p.m. the old and new "teams" go to the Community office to don regalia and coca bags. They turn in their old staffs or receive new ones. They pass the wee hours together drinking hot punch and break up after breakfast.

6 An interesting example is documented in the middle Checras, where people address the prehispanic dead as awkin: "In late July, it is vital to the dehydration technique for preserving potatoes to freeze those tubers that have been buried in the beds of running streams. In this season, frosts and hailstorms normally occur in the highest pastures, notably in Chaupes, the site of a prehistoric ruin. There sacks of potatoes being prepared as chuno or trusco are frozen while their owners pass the night dancing, singing and playing guitars. If no frost occurs after a reasonable delay, a group of men, often led by the President of the Indigenous Community, roll away the stone door of a secret burial cave above the Poq Poq spring and remove the complete skeleton of a gentil [prehispanic human] to Chaupes, where they scatter the bones. They taunt the bones, abuse them, and announce to the pagan that he will remain scattered and far from his sanctuary until a frost occurs. The committee then stomps off to leave the pagan to work his magic. As soon as a frost occurs, the committeemen return the bones to the cave, singing in a lively procession from Chaupes thanking the gentile and begging his pardon" (Morris et al. 1968, 246).

7 *Misya* is not found in Quechua I dictionaries. It is an old-fashioned, often rural Spanish term of respectful address to senior women, preserved more in Chile and Argentina

than in the northerly republics. Misya may be one of many now-obsolete Spanish words retained in Quechua ritual lexicon.

8 It is not known whether a *tambo* or way station ever occupied the Kaha Wayi–Pasa Qulqa precinct. This is a matter that future archaeologists should investigate.

9 "tenían unas [*sara mamas* o talismanes de maíz] en unos chaguayes que son sotteranos que están debajo de las colcas a las cuales hacían sacrificios aparte y las tenían en gran veneración."

10 *Alqa* meaning "pintado" or "varicolored" might refer to the decorated measuring sack (Adelaar 1982, 18).

11 In Quechua, the verb *niy* covers both thinking and saying, as discussed in Chapter 4.

References

ACCSCR/R inventory no. 17. 1960–1968. Un Libro de Actas Depositado. No.76. 298 fos.

Adelaar, Willem F.H. 1977. *Tarma Quechua: Grammar, Texts, Dictionary*. Lisse, Netherlands: Peter de Ridder Press.

Adelaar, Willem F.H. 1982. *Léxico del quechua de Pacaraos*. Lima: Universidad Nacional Mayor de San Marcos, Centro de Investigación Lingüística Aplicada, Documento de Trabajo no. 45.

Allen, Catherine J. 1988. *The Hold Life Has: Coca and Cultural Identity in an Andean Community*. Washington, DC: Smithsonian Institution Press.

Arguedas, José María. 1956. "Puquio, una cultura en proceso de cambio." *Revista del Museo Nacional* 25: 184–232.

Arnold, Denise Y., and Juan de Dios Yapita, eds. 1996. *Madre Melliza y sus crías. Ispall mama wawampi. Antología de la papa*. La Paz, Bolivia: HISBOL, ILCA.

Arnold, Denise Y., and Juan de Dios Yapita. 2001. *River of Fleece, River of Song: Singing to the Animals, an Andean Poetics of Creation*. Bonn: Verlag Anton Saurwein. Bonner Amerikanistische Schriften.

Bolin, Inge. 2010. *Rituals of Respect: The Secret of Survival in the High Peruvian Andes*. Austin, TX: University of Texas Press.

Carey, Mark. 2010. *In the Shadow of Melting Glaciers: Climate Change and Andean Society*. Oxford and New York: Oxford University Press.

Descola, Philippe. 2006. "Beyond Nature and Culture." *Proceedings of the British Academy* 139: 137–155.

Descola, Philippe. 2013 [2005]. *Beyond Nature and Culture*, translated by Janet Lloyd. Chicago, IL: University of Chicago Press.

Duviols, Pierre. 1973. "Huari y Llacuaz. Agricultores y pastores. Un dualismo prehispánico de oposición y complementaridad." *Revista del Museo Nacional* 39: 153–191.

Encarnación Rojas, Eulalia, and Narciso Robles Atachagua. 2011. *Breve Historia de San Cristóbal de Rapaz*. Lima: Gráfica Quinteros E.I.R.L.

Falcón Huayta, Victor. 2007. *Patrimonio de San Cristóbal de Rapaz, Provincia de Oyón: Khipu y Cajahuay (2005–2008)—Arqueología. Informe Final al Instituto Nacional de Cultura (RNA N° DF-0181)*. Lima: Instituto Nacional de Cultura.

Feinman, Gary M. 2014. Review of *Merchants, Markets, and Exchange in the Pre-Columbian World*, edited by Kenneth Hirth and Joanne Pillsbury. *Latin American Antiquity* 25(2): 234–236.

Gose, Peter. 1994. *Deathly Waters and Hungry Mountains: Agrarian Ritual and Class Formation in an Andean Town*. Toronto: University of Toronto Press.

Híjar Soto, Donato Amador. 1984. "Los cjircas y otras deidades protectoras del área andina en el Perú." *Folklore Americano* 37(8): 103–108.

Las Casas, Gino. 2005. *Propuesta de intervención para la conservación y restauración de las estructuras Kaha Wayi y Pasa Qullqa: San Cristóbal de Rapaz.* Unpublished report to Instituto Nacional de Cultura.

Maita Agurto, Patricia. 2006. "Fauna arqueológica de Passa [*sic*] Qullqa." Unpublished report.

Makowski, Krzysztof. 2015. "Pachacamac—Old Wak'a or Inka Syncretic Deity? Imperial Transformation of the Sacred Landscape in the Lower Ychsma (Lurín) Valley." In *The Archaeology of Wak'as*, edited by Tamara Bray. Boulder, CO: University Press of Colorado. 127–166.

Mariscotti de Görlitz, Ana María. 1978. *Pachamama Santa Tierra.* Berlin: Mann Verlag. Indiana, Beiheft.

Montoya, Rodrigo, Edwin Montoya, and Luis Montoya. 1987. *La Sangre de los cerros: Urqukunapa yawarnin. Antología de la poesía quechua que se canta en el Perú.* Lima: Centro Peruano de Estudios Sociales, Mosca Azul Editores, y Universidad Nacional Mayor de San Marcos.

Morris, Earl W., Leslie A. Brownrigg, Susan C. Bourque, and Henry F. Dobyns. 1968. *Coming Down the Mountain: The Social Worlds of Mayobamba.* Ithaca, NY: Andean Indian Community Research and Development Program, Department of Anthropology, Cornell University. Socio-Economic Development of Andean Communities, Report No. 10.

Rösing, Ina. 1995. "Paraman Purina—Going For Rain: 'Mute Anthropology' Versus 'Speaking Anthropology': Lessons From an Andean Collective Scarcity Ritual in the Quechua-Speaking Kallawaya and Aymara-Speaking Altiplano Region (Andes, Bolivia)." *Anthropos* 90(1/3): 69–88.

Rösing, Ina. 1996. *Rituales para llamar la lluvia: Rituales colectivos de la región kallawaya en los andes bolivianos.* Cochabamba, Bolivia: Los Amigos del Libro.

Salomon, Frank. 2004. *The Cord Keepers: Khipus and Culture in a Peruvian Village.* Durham, NC: Duke University Press.

Salomon, Frank, and George Urioste, eds. and trans. 1991 [1608?]. *The Huarochirí Manuscript: A Testament of Ancient and Colonial Andean Religion.* Austin, TX: University of Texas Press.

Trever, Lisa. 2011. "Idols, Mountains, and Metaphysics in Guaman Poma's Pictures of Huacas." *RES: Anthropology and Aesthetics* 59/60: 39–59.

Valderrama Fernández, Ricardo, and Carmen Escalante Gutiérrez. 1988. *Del Tata Mallku a la Mama Pacha: riego, sociedad y ritos en los Andes peruanos.* Lima: DESCO, Centro de Estudios y Promoción del Desarrollo.

Wachtel, Nathan. 2001 [1990]. *El regreso de los antepasados: Los indios urus de Bolivia, del siglo XX al XVI. Ensayo de historia regresiva,* translated by Laura Ciezar. México DF: Fondo de Cultura Económica.

3

CHILDREN OF THE MUMMY
LIBIAC CANCHARCO

(and ideas about the sacralization of society)

For something like five hundred to a thousand generations, humanity in the Americas went its own way.[1] So America when compared with other continents would seem a "natural laboratory" of human diversity. Working far away from all the other places where states and empires grew, pre-Columbian societies developed peculiar and original complexities. In some ways the deep history of the Andes shows "roads not taken" by other peoples.

But in other ways, including religious ones, Native Americans hit on practices also found in lots of other societies. In this chapter we will consider one of those practices: the veneration of mummified ancestors and of mountains considered as the ancestors of ancestors. Andean mortuary culture (culture focused on death and the dead) is a spectacular area of archaeology, rich in unique artistic invention. At the same time, though, these inventions can be taken up as an important pristine case within a worldwide ethnological discussion. Why have so many peoples independently invented ways for the dead to be forever present? And if present, why sacred? And if sacred, what does the exaltation of the departed suggest about religiosity itself?

Rapaz is one among hundreds of Andean places where mummies (*malki*) once were the focus of elaborate devotions. In this predominantly historical chapter we will look at some historic particulars of Rapaz ancestor veneration, putting it into relation with the still-productive vein of theory derived from Emil Durkheim and his early 20th-century disciples. First, we will consider the era of the Spanish invasion of Peru, 1532 onward, including the question of whether Kaha Wayi and Pasa Qulqa already existed at that time. Second, we will consider Rapaz-area mummy cult and priesthood as it was affected by Church persecution after the last pre-Columbian generation had already died (that is, from 1614 to the later 1670s). Third, we will sketch the possible meanings of popular "idolatries" in the last phase of colonial rule.

The historical context: when Spain set out to rule Andaxes

Three years after invading and toppling the Inka state, Spanish witnesses saw the last performance of the rituals for imperial mummies. Celebrants "made obeisance to all the embalmed bodies of the dead lords . . . as if they were alive." Nobles and functionaries of the empire shared drinks with mummies, toasted and saluted them, and thus dramatized political society as an everlasting thing (Molina 2011 [c.1576], 63).

At that time the Inka ceremonial center in Cuzco was already being destroyed. A Spanish lawyer sleuthed out the cherished mummies of Peru's past emperors, abducted them from their hideaways, and set them up as exhibits for the eyes of Spaniards in Lima, where they were finally lost. The Inka state's supreme religious cults, especially the gold-clad Cuzco solar temple with its priesthood, was looted. Cuzco ceased to house a pantheon of coopted sacred beings from other ethnic groups. Because Christians easily found and wrecked these topmost structures of Andean religion, there would never again be a countrywide church-like hierarchy of Andean priests. Spanish authorities became zealous to snuff out forms of "Indian" (*yndio*) sacred leadership, including Christian leadership. People of native blood were for a long time barred from becoming Catholic priests, lest Andean loyalties dilute the doctrine of the new Archbishopric.

One consequence of decapitating imperial Andean religious structures was to dislodge the unifying Inka ideology of kinship and descent. The Inka state had formerly promoted a ritual system of sacrifice, marriage, and alliance unifying Peru's many ethnic groups. Now, innumerable cults were suddenly detached from the all-empire circuit of sacrifices and delegations (the *Qhapaq Hucha*; Duviols 1976). Local habits and adaptations gained importance. Local or ethnic ancestor cults would furnish ritual-political structures to *curacazgos* (colonial ethnic polities) for a good century. Mummy veneration took place in "old towns" (ruined pre-Columbian villages), in funerary caves, or at stone houses of the dead. Leaders of these ceremonies retained unofficial power and wealth—even while their followers also took part in Catholic masses, indoctrination, and festivals. Up to about 1600, rural people probably did not think of these adaptations as resistance but simply as practical adaptation to a new regime. Rapaz was a typical example.

Rapaz stood in a province Spaniards named Andaxes (later, Andajes) after an ethnic group in historic Cajatambo Province. Rapacinos could have been among the earlier Americans to see the Spanish seaborne invaders. Miguel de Estete, a soldier in the Pizarro brothers' 1532 invasion of Peru, says 23 Spaniards marched through Cajatambo and Oyón Provinces only four months after this very first landfall. At an unknown date in the 1560s, another early Spaniard, Juan Serrano, heard Andax people wondering aloud why anyone would want to be a Christian:

> Report on what I, Juan Serrano, have seen, understood and heard about the Indians of Peru in the Provincies of Andas [Andaxes] and Caxatambo and the Atabillos. It is the following:

When I, Juan Serrano, talked with them to say they should be Christians and telling them this many times, they would say, why would they want to be Christians? And when I said, in order to serve God and not steal nor take their neighbor's wife away nor talk badly about anybody nor kill and many other things such as the holy commandments of the law order us, they would reply, that they do not want to be Christians because the Christians were stealing and taking away their wives and daughters against their will, and that they didn't see in us any good sign nor any good deed. And they gave many more reasons, in which they did not lie, but rather in everything they said about Christians, told the truth.

I saw that many of them are people of lively understanding. In my judgment they are close to the faith, because they only believe in the sun and in other things which [illegible] and if they were taught the doctrine they would believe in our holy faith.

For among them there is very great order and reason [*cuenta y razon*] and in the time when there were no Christians in the land, they kept account and reason of the people suitable for war and of the babies who were born and of those who died and of everything, sheep and lambs of the land [i.e., llamas and alpacas]. And they had their towers which they call storehouses [*depositos*] where they had a lot of corn from one year to the next . . .

In Peru every valley has its own language. Guayna Caba [Inka] ordered that there should be a general language which is the one used in the province of Cuzco and, and that in their court no other should be spoken. It was ordered by the said Guayna Caba that it should be practiced and known for more than one thousand five hundred leagues that he governed, and that the Indian who didn't know it should die for it. And so this is the one that Christians today talk with the Indians, because the Christians know no other of theirs.[2]

Serrano's account of native skepticism about Christianity may imply that he sympathized with the "Las Casian" critique of colonial coercion. Or he could have been siding (perhaps insincerely) with crown-sponsored functionaries who were trying to curb destructive exploitation by colonial opportunists. Serrano speaks of the worship of the sun in present tense, so in 1560, 28 years after the invasion, Andaxes perhaps still practiced the solar worship promoted by Inkas (Noriega 2010, 68, 73). But this rather standard description might also be influenced by early chroniclers of the conquest of Cuzco.

Not until the 1570s did Viceroy Francisco de Toledo reorganize the new Viceroyalty into the durable shape we now remember as colonial Peru. Rapaz village begins to show signs of colonial political economy in that decade. By 1573 Hernando de Montenegro had "a valuable sugar mill" at Santiago de Andahuasi, down-valley from Rapaz. Near where the Checras River joins the Huaura, he built the *obraje* of San Juan de Churín. Obrajes were low-tech industrial sites powered by the coerced labor of the *mita*, a Spanish forced labor levy (Pereyra

1984–1985, 44). The ruins of an obraje are still visible on the path Rapacinos take to their pastures on Lot 29.

Rapaz was relatively sheltered from Toledan statecraft because smaller and higher villages in Cajatambo seem to have been among those less affected by forcible "reduction" or resettlement in supervised tributary villages. By 1573 *doctrinas* (missionary congregations) had been created at Churín, Andajes, and Cochamarca. But apparently Christianization lagged in the upstream area. Captain Pedro de Arana found that the Andajes "population . . . seems not to have been substantially removed from their ancient settlements." Just two villages had saint's names.

Only some three decades later does a "reduced" village of Rapaz figure in reports. Even then, it hardly conformed to the Toledan model: the new settlement stood contiguous with its prehispanic precursor. Usually Toledan administrators worked hard to get people away from "old towns" where non-Christian cult was anchored (Pereyra 1984–1985, 54, 213). Rapaz's pre-Columbian center lies under part of modern Rapaz, covered over by the current soccer field.

The Viceroyalty in Lima considered that this kind of situation meant insufficient Christianization.

> In 1583, the secretary Cristóbal de Miranda stated emphatically that the 11,843 people who inhabited the repartimiento of Andajes had not yet been resettled "even though . . . in the general inspection they were ordered to be reduced to four towns." Reductions began to exist toward 1600. Father Hernando de Avendaño mentions a large number of colonial towns in this region in his inspection summaries of 1614.
>
> *Pereyra 1984–1985, 59*

The upshot is that for some 80 years—one long lifetime, or the upbringing of three generations—Rapacinos and their peers lived under compulsory Christianity yet dwelled cheek-by-jowl with their prehispanic shrines and tombs. Unlike most villages, Rapaz was "reduced" right in its old location. So there is room to ask whether the Kaha Wayi-Pasa Qulqa complex might not in some part conserve a prehispanic institution that, unusually, survived physically through the colonial transition.

The uncertain antiquity of Kaha Wayi and Pasa Qulqa

Two archaeologists first brought Kaha Wayi and its historico-cultural setting into scholarly view: the Pole Andrzej Krzanowski and his Peruvian counterpart Arturo Ruiz Estrada. Krzanowski began scouting upper Huaura archaeological sites on his own in 1972. In 1978, 1985, and 1987 he formed and led the Polish Scientific Expedition to the Andes, an unusual initiative at a time when Soviet-bloc governments rarely let social scientists perform independent overseas research (1977, 1978). In his first days crashing through the cactuses to inspect ruins, Krzanowski heard about the Rapaz khipu legacy, but, he writes, "In that period I didn't believe that this could be real. Campesinos told me lots of things about buried treasures and marvelous ruins, many of which could not be verified."

Meanwhile, Arturo Ruiz Estrada, a Quechua-speaking, Lima-based professor of archaeology and early surveyor of archaeological sites in the upper Huaura, independently heard about the Rapaz legacy from a rural schoolteacher. He followed up on this remarkable news with an excursion on horseback (Rapaz still being roadless), which yielded the first published photos of the Rapaz patrimony (1981). Ruiz joined forces with the Poles, working as their field advisor. He was not only Kaha Wayi's first scientific visitor but also the first to interview people who guarded it (Montes 1996).

Archaeologists, like Rapacinos, notice likeness between Pasa Qulqa and nearby prehispanic ruins. Without even leaving Rapaz one can overlook two hilltop villages probably constructed in the Late Intermediate period (that is, the three or four centuries prior to Inka conquest). One only has to go as far as Pinchulín ruin, adjoining Rapaz's modern cemetery, to see prehispanic constructions resembling Pasa Qulqa (see Figures 3.1, 3.2). They have the same salient cornice and double-linteled square window seen in Pasa Qulqa. Straight down below Rapaz on a bluff overlooking the Checras River stands a Late Intermediate fortified village ruin called Rapazmarca, whose structures include a tower-like building (storehouse?) that resembles Pasa Qulqa in its cornice and gables (see Figure 3.3) (Noriega 2006).

FIGURE 3.1   The double stone lintel of this building aperture in the Late Intermediate ruined village of Pinchulín resembles that of Pasa Qulqa. Photo by the author.

FIGURE 3.2 Double lintel of the middle-floor aperture in Pasa Qulqa. Photo by the author.

FIGURE 3.3 Building in the ruined Late Intermediate village of Rapazmarka, with gable and cornice resembling those of Pasa Qulqa. Photo by the author.

The archaeologist Aldo Noriega, studying remains in Rapaz's neighboring municipality of Oyón, found what he suspects to be the headquarters that Inkas constructed to supervise the upper Checras-Huaura when they conquered it toward 1500. He also found an Inka road that runs up the cordillera and over toward Pumpu, the major Inka stronghold in the old homeland of Llacuaces (Noriega 2000, 2009).

Not much is known about relations between the Inkas and their "Andax" subjects. Perhaps their earliest ethnic noble we know of, one who may have reached adulthood under the Inka, was one Tumay Guarox (AGI/S Lima, 566 L.4 F.218, 1541). In oral tradition, modern Rapacinos recall their original "native lords" as four men called Chaguas who headed four lineages. Chagua is a regionally common naming element. The Qahatrawa (today Cajachagua) kindred, they say, dwelt on the puna, sheared vicuñas, and never felt cold. The Aqachawas, or Raqachawas (today Racachas) were warriors and dwellers in the river margin. The Ninanchawas were political lords. The Mananchawas are folk-etymologyzed as "those who say no"—resistant people.

Although little-known, these legendary lineages are not completely without archival support. Encarnación Rojas found in an unidentified notarial copybook at the National Archive papers about a 1759 pasture dispute involving "Don Juan Ticse Mayanchagua . . . [and] Don Antonio Ninachagua" as native lords of Rapaz (2011, 28). The colonial categorization of Rapaz as a *pachaca* or "hundred" of the Inka census hierarchy may be a genuine pre-Columbian trace.

But what can be said concretely about the physical age of the Rapaz precinct's structures?

The archaeologist Víctor Falcón Huayta, then working at the Lima's National Museum of Archaeology, Anthropology, and History, joined our Rapaz Project in 2004–2005. He carried out a series of excavations within the Kaha Wayi-Pasa Qulqa precinct. They extended to the interior of Pasa Qulqa but not that of Kaha Wayi because the Community forbade it. In 2008, University of Wisconsin graduate student Raymundo "Tony" Chapa collaborated with him. Not being an archaeologist myself, I offer only translated extracts of their joint conclusions:

> The cultural floor which was excavated to make the foundations of Pasa Qulqa is of Late Intermediate origin. The site seems to be a periphery of the precolumbian population concentrated in Quisquis (where Rapaz's soccer field now exists). The foundations may have been set immediately before or just after the [Spanish] conquest.
>
> Pasa Qulqa's architectural form partly fits Late Intermediate design: stone eaves, protruding cornice, and double stone lintel. But the two-shed roof seems based on another model: Inka construction, or else Spanish. Late Intermediate style of the region uses one-shed roofs.
>
> Inka presence is indicated by ceramic fragments. Not enough area was excavated to eliminate nor confirm the previous existence of Inka architecture. Krzanowski did not find Inka constructions inside spaces built in the Late

Intermediate. In previously studied sites [of this region] Inka constructions in almost all cases were made in imperial Inka style, not as hybrids within local construction.

One can think of this place as an example of transitional archaeology from the early colony. It is possible that the complex represents a remodeling of the architecture of power, responding to the new pre-Toledan colonial situation [that is, the earliest phase of Spanish rule, 1532–1569]. It lacks the Hispanicized regularity of *reducciones* or resettlement villages. The oldest residential houses in the village are sited irregularly with respect to the current street grid, another sign of a possible pre-Toledan pattern.

All the samples collected [in Pasa Qulqa] from layer C, the yellowish earliest surface, and Floor 1 (the last surface) are of relatively uniform kind. Apparently, for about 300 years following the initial construction of Pasa Qulqa, no new layers accumulated. The material laid down after this period, i.e. at the end of the colonial era and beginning of the Republic, shows two slim lenses of burning activity, corresponding to dates toward the end of the colony. These activities include an act of burning in a hole, which later was cleaned. The still-burning embers and the remains of a small mammal were then deposited in a small hole dug half a meter in front of the burned patch. This procedure is similar to the sacrifices carried out in Pasa Qulqa today.

Kaha Wayi seemingly shows more modern traits, such as: eaves built of adobe bricks, the construction of the interior ceiling with logs that penetrate the walls to the exterior, the dimensions of the main door, the built-in bench on the facade, and the projecting buttress walls which extend the end walls to frame the facade. These traits exist in structures datable to the 17th century, one of them being Rapaz's own church.

Falcón and Chapa 2008

Falcón Huayta in his report to the Instituto Nacional de Cultura drew an overall conclusion:

Kaha Wayi-Pasa Qulqa as a dyad remained in action through the whole colonial era [1532–1825] and until the early decades of the 20th century. The "archaic" traits of Pasa Qulqa are due to a conscious conservative attitude on the part of Rapacinos themselves. They maintained precolonial architectural characteristics associated with the building's function, that is, the storage of communal foodstuffs and seed, in a building traditionally reserved for the access of women. In this way a coherent link was established between the Qulqa, agricultural products, fertility, and women—a synthesis corresponding to Andean world view and as supported by an agropastoral productive system.

2007

Extirpators and the assault on Andean ancestor veneration

It was not in the wars of Spanish conquest but in the mid-colonial era a century afterward that Andean peoples felt the full repressive force of early-modern Christianity. During the early decades of Spanish rule some clerical factions had favored patient dialogue with unconverted peoples in hope of engaging their "natural" religiosity. Later, a 17th-century upsurge in demonological thinking inclined theologians to thunder against New World indigenous rites as not merely pagan but diabolical. Campaigns against indigenous sacred culture had to do with papal decisions to tighten and standardize parish structure lest America, like Europe during the Reformation, fractionate over rival claims to religious authority. Some mid-colonial bishops afflicted by nightmares over the atrocious Thirty Years' War of 1618–1648 feared indigenous ritual leaders might become dangerous "heretics" liable to subversion by Spain's Protestant enemies.

By the middle of the 17th century there was nothing tentative nor experimental about Andean Christianity. Christian images, says Ana Sánchez, had already saturated popular thinking. Yet at the same time, mummy veneration and the organization of ritual around pre-Columbian *ayllu* or corporate descent groups were still staples of rural religiosity. After a century of severe depopulation caused by epidemics and by flight to escape forced labor or tribute, rural highlanders implored their ancestors to restore abundance. Andean sacred traditions excelled in practical magic, while Christianity complemented them with "the sumptuous forms of the Baroque." Doctrine was vague but vividly lived out. Rural clergy found their own local alliances, and sometimes opposed the intervention of *visitadores* (religious inspector-judges) because they had already made deals with local nobles that involved tolerating precolumbian-derived ritual in exchange for seasonal "gifts" and services.

Into this scene came newly militant clergy who proposed uniformity, regulation, and precise dogma. In the big picture, Andean repressive campaigns form part of a more general movement throughout both Protestant and Catholic Christendom against informality, diversity, and archaism. The essence of both reformation and counter-reformation was to be "a new order: one credo and one only" (Sánchez 1991, vii, xi, xiii, xliv).

Juan Carlos Estenssoro Fuchs argues that what looked to the clergy of Lima like "idolatry" was not native Andean paganism at all but, on the contrary, popular Christianity as it had evolved in a lifetime of cohabitation with Andean cults (1998). Scandalized churchmen asked how *yndios* could possibly have clung to ancient ancestor cult and "false gods" long after they had gained revelation and scripture, unless by the inducements of the Devil? The eclectic religiosity of country people was recategorized from traditional muddle to Satanic lore. Canon lawyers devised a new repressive apparatus: an institution independent of the Inquisition but parallel to it, with special judges and courts trained to sniff out indigenous heterodoxy. They called this project extirpation of idolatries. It became an expanding career path for Lima's fiercely competitive corps of clergymen.

Rapaz and all Andajes Provinces suffered extirpation in waves. The pioneer extirpator Hernando de Avendaño attacked idols in ten Huaura basin villages including Rapaz in 1614, followed by a lull. Archbishop Bartolomé Lobo Guerrero authorized a party that to some degree affected the Huaura basin near the end of his rule in 1622, followed by another lull. Then, throughout the long tenure of his successor Archbishop Pedro de Villagómez (1642–1671), Jesuits and other clerics mounted a more determined assault on rural ritual. This series of campaigns lashed the region for three decades. And finally, after some forty years of relative calm, Pedro de Celís in 1724–1725 loosed on the Checras-Huaura region one last round of persecution.

In the pages that follow we will not retell the whole well-studied history of extirpation,[3] but only track a few suspects related to Kaha Wayi, Pasa Qulqa, and the Rapaz tradition of ritual-cum-social authority. We will focus in on the cult of the dead and the divinity of food—topics selected because they exemplify central themes in one foundational kind of theory about religiosity.

Caution is in order: 17th-century evidence was extracted by coercion, even torture. Translation problems and dogmatic bias distorted testimony. For example, Spaniards from earliest times to the 18th century sometimes referred to Andean ritual buildings as "synagogues" or "mosques." Extirpators made mirroring errors, projecting characteristics of their own organization onto their objects of scrutiny. For example, they tended to see centralized hierarchy, dogma, witchcraft, diabolical "parody" of the Mass, and conspiracy where we would see pragmatism, diversity, and local politicking. Yet despite the extirpators' misperceptions of American ritualism, extirpation trials do preserve amazingly detailed and vivid information about Andean cults—mostly from the mouths of unhappy Quechua-speaking *yndios* coerced into denouncing their kin and neighbors.

Rapaz 1614: Hernando de Avendaño burns Libiac Cancharco, Rapaz's llacuaz progenitor

Rapaz was one of the first places to take a hard blow from the extirpators. It lay on the path of Hernando de Avendaño during his first experiments in repressive field research. In 1613, Archbishop Lobo Guerrero called on the young vicar Avendaño to investigate the Provinces of "Checras, Andaxez, Cochamarca, Churín, and of Andax, Cauxa [modern Caujul], Cajatambo and its district including Atavillos, Ananpiscas y de Lurinpiscas y Pacarao, and of the Valley of Quintay," that is, a swath of the western slope north of Lima (Guibovich 1993, 175). Local curates considered it an area in vulnerable condition: "some poor and elderly people suffer from thirst and hunger and sell their ponchos to buy water and food, and they put up with it because they are still in their rituals and idolatries" (Tineo Morón 2016, 21–22). Sick and elderly people were among the ones religious investigators were most likely to question because they were knowledgeable but easily intimidated.

In February of 1614 Avendaño hiked up to Checras. On an elevation over Rapaz Avendaño soon made a spectacular find. In his own words:

the body of a very ancient chief [curaca] named Liviacancharco, which was
found in a very rugged wilderness about one league from the town of San
Cristóbal de Rapaz, in a cave, under an awning, with his *huama* or golden
diadem on his head, dressed with seven very fine *cumbi* [luxury-grade] shirts,
which the Indians said the ancient Inka kings had sent him. This body and
that of a majordomo of his, named Chuchu Michuy, who was at another
place, were carried as is to Lima so the Viceroy and the Archbishop might
see them. On [Avendaño's] returning to the Andajes a solemn *auto da fe* was
held convening all the towns in the province, and these bodies were burned
along with many other *huacas*.

Guibovich 1993, 230;
Duviols 1973, 168; translation by the author[4]

The lavishly dressed mummy Liviacancharco, or Libiac Cancharco, embodied the
imagined essence of llacuaz identity. His seven gift shirts testify to seven occasions
when the Inka had recognized him as one of the empire's official shrines. The first
part of his name (*lliwya-*) had the sense of "sparkling" or "resplendent." The second
(*kancharkariy*) denoted something that "throws off rays" or "lightning" (González
Holguín 1989 [1608], 62, 214). In calling themselves the offspring of Flashing
Lightning, the Llacuaz-descended people of the Rapaz area identified themselves
as people of the heights, lightning strikes being in fact much more common at
higher altitudes. Such grand mummies as Libiac Cancharco stood at the apices of
pyramidal lines of descent; each was seen as a common ancestor and patron to all
ayllus (descent groups) who saw themselves as related through him.

Mummy caves (*machay*) high in the cliffs of the central Andes were power
resources, not just emblems. Processions bringing apical ancestors gifts and asking
their favor in the form of good weather or fertility were prime occasions for reun-
ion and sharing among far-flung agropastoralists. Ethnic lords' standing inhered in
upholding great mummies' primordial heroism—and on lords' political ability to
protect them against theft by rival groups or Christian persecutors. Specialized, lavishly paid priests acted as oracles, who decided in the ancient hero's name appeals
about marriages, production, and politics (Curátola Petrocchi 2008).

Libiac Cancharco meant the world to Rapacinos, for in their eyes custody of his
mummy established them as a foremost group. Libiac Cancharco was said to have
descended mysteriously from the heavens at Raco Mountain, "progenitor of all llacuaces" according to Duviols. Raco Mountain is close to Rapaz, a few kilometers'
hike up and over the cordillera crest. Raco is part of the cordillera that divides the
Lake Junín high plain from the west slope. So in the Andean geographic idiom
of myth, it makes sense that Raco, through Libiac Cancharco, led the conquer-
ors westward and downward. The anonymous 1603 treatise "Errors, Superstitious
Rites, and Ceremonies of the Indians of the Province of Chinchaycocha"
(published by Duviols in 1974) affords a wealth of mythic and geographic data about
those lightning-ancestor's mythic kindred, as well as about Flashing Lightning's
central importance to branches of the "Yaro" or Llacuaz expansion.

Libiac Cancharco was mummified and worshipped where his heroic trajectory had ended (Duviols 1973, 166–167). Over a substantial area, that place was believed to be Rapaz. Of course, the Rapaz version was not the only version of his story. As is normal in segmented societies, social segments (ayllus, in this case) each told a proprietary variant of one charter myth, without any single version being authoritative. Innumerable villages of Huari-Llacuaz constitution had mummies, heroes, and myths on the theme of Libiac. Sometimes the tradition that a locally celebrated mummy was a child or grandchild of Libiac Cancharco was a way of saying that the political system constituted a westward or down-valley extension of early llacuaz "conquests." Places with Libiac mummy-heroes felt themselves to be mutually connected and culturally similar, even if nobody knew the exact genealogical connection.

So it was important when Avendaño arrested 298 people for adhering to Libiac Cancharco of Rapaz. Much to Avendaño's disgust, at the 1614 "exhibition" he staged in Checras, *ayllus* (descent groups) lined up for punishment in the plaza carrying their ancestors' dried bodies. In enduring their punishments, they still hoped to connect their own lines of ancestry one last time with their condemned forefather. Andean people often showed themselves more concerned with the integrity of the everlasting lineage than the salvation of their individual souls. For them, repositioning the dead in or near churches was a way to reorient whole ancestral lines toward Christendom (Gose 2008, 156). In 1623 Avendaño wrote an executive summary of his extirpations in the Mercedarians' parish of Rapaz and sixty other localities, boasting that he found 12,130 people guilty of idolatry. Of these, Rapacinos formed 2.5%.[5]

But the clerics did not succeed in erasing Flashing Lightning's cult, even after they had kidnapped and desecrated his mummy. As a young man in the 1950s the archaeologist Cardich saw rites in honor of Libiac Cancharco still performed at Cerro Raco (2000, 71, 80). Certain Central Peruvian mask dancers still perform today as stand-ins for long-lost mummies (Barraza 2009).

During the forty or so years after Avendaños's raids upon initially defenseless villages, wak'a politics underwent some important changes. Not that prosecutions become any less harsh; Bernardo de Noboa, Extirpator from 1659–1663, was aggressive even by standards of his time. He freely resorted to torture, leaving trial records that transcribe the screams of the victims. But the accused increasingly learned to avail themselves of "Protectors of Indians," a type of court-appointed counsel unavailable to earlier victims. In 1659 such a lawyer counseled villagers to derail extirpators by handing over as idols "the first stones they might happen to run into" (Espinoza Soriano 1981, 120). Also, this was a time of rising prosperity for native lords or kurakas (Medina Susano 1989, 81–87). Checras-area nobles spent a lot and borrowed even more to gain control of church-building, which was crucial to the padres' careers. They thereby gained leverage on curates. Rapaz's enormous "painted church" (known for its late-colonial murals) is an example. Such local lords were in a position to shelter their friends. And since selected sons of Indian nobles were getting Spanish and Latin education in Lima, some bicultural operatives could play both sides of the street.

Yet this is not to say the destruction of the ancestors had no effect. In *Invaders as Ancestors*, Peter Gose published a thesis (which the archaeologist Guillermo Cock had foreshadowed in a footnote; 1980, 243) that mid-colonial repression did effectively destroy a central component of Andean piety (2008). That component was ancestor mummy veneration. A few mummy cults managed to survive into the late colony. But being the most portable, flammable, and conspicuously pagan part of Andean ritual, mummies in huge numbers were reduced to ash—sacred ashes that received grief-laden invocations of their own.

When extirpators burned malkis before the horrified eyes of their descendants, they made it impossible to reproduce instituted social relations in the time-honored way. Gose argues that a new way of affiliating social groups to everlasting facts came into being. According to Gose, sacrificial devotions to mountains—that is, "Andean religion" as we know it—is not an ancient tradition but an adaptation to the mid-colonial destruction of most malkis and the radical disruption of ancestry-structured practices.

The Kaha Wayi-Pasa Qulqa complex has some of the characteristics Gose would see as post-extirpation normality. Among them are a resolutely detailed focus on geography, rather than genealogy, as the main paradigm of power. When people speak ritually to "the Old Ones," they mean geographic powers and not the ancient dead in the earth. No longer does anyone identify mummies as his own ancestors, nor did I hear anyone speak of any mummy (for mummies still do turn up occasionally) as a named ancestor. On the contrary, when they find mummies and ancient funeral structures or caves, people propitiate them more with dread than love. Like most rural Andean people, Rapacinos fear that the old *malkis* may hate and hurt modern humans who have taken over the earth that once was theirs. No longer are particular mummified ancestors used as benchmarks for tracing relationships among the living. Instead, it is the mountains who are Rapaz's overlords—not because they have particular kin relationships with named groups, but because they globally "own" the land and the climate.

But why must the dead exist forever? A classic sociological view of death

Anthropologists are forever fascinated by the fact that humans, unlike most other creatures, take care of their dead and especially by the fact that care of the dead (mortuary) is always ritualized. It is omnipresent, stereotyped, elaborated in form, and carefully set apart from the free-form practicality of daily life. Why should care of the dead, of all things, be a pan-human core of culture and ritualism?

Anthropology's modern debates about mortuary culture originate in the brilliant circle of Émile Durkheim and his students before the First World War. Durkheim, disturbed in youth by what he saw as the French people's crumbling solidarity during their 1871 defeat at German hands, problematized solidarity itself: what makes a society hold together at all? He called his new positivistic inquiry *sociologie*, but his interests reached far into ethnology's fundamental questions and attached great importance to then-novel reports on the lives of "primitive" peoples. We will lightly sketch first the specialness of the dead via a Durkheim-derived theory, then glance at more far-reaching Durkheimian argument about what we humans are doing when we pay homage to sacred powers generally.

World War I cut short the life of Robert Hertz (1881–1915). But at only 26 years of age Durkheim's stellar disciple published an essay still vital to ethnology (1960 [1907]). Hertz leapt beyond commonsense individualist notions of why we focus on death (fear of mortality, speculation about an afterlife, and so forth) to produce a powerful general explanation that also explains many recurring particularities. Mummy cult like Rapaz's figures among such recurrent inventions. Hertz demanded the characteristic Durkheimian intellectual move: he requires us to flip our perceptions from the individual's viewpoint to that of the collective.

Of course, Durkheim and his students understood perfectly well that society does not have a separable physical body, nor a bounded biological entity. Least of all is Durkheim attributing to society an over-self or group mind. A society is a thing in a class by itself: it is a life-resembling arrangement of lives. This web or constellation has consequences and needs of its own, not reducible to the wishes of men and women who are its material medium. Durkheim sometimes speaks *as if* this sociological entity had an über-mind of its own, and that is what he means by the "viewpoint of society." One must never lose sight of the fact that the social organism is a metaphor. Durkheim speaks of society's viewpoint somewhat as we might speak of an ecosystem's viewpoint.

Society is organism-like in the way that it acts as a system, not the kind of entity that it is. The organic metaphor serves to start us discovering the needs and powers of the collective. For example, a given society's sheer scale (small and "tribal" versus large and industrial) compels people to connect with each other in some ways and not others. Solidarity in a small tribe of people who all know each other must be a different phenomenon from solidarity among the people of the French Republic, most of whom are unknown to each other. Such effects are not the sum of individual choices; they have a logic of their own over and above human wishes. They are "social facts." Invisibly sovereign social facts are what sociology (including ethnology) set about to discover. Early sociological topics were the law of reciprocity, the social (not psychological) causes of suicide, and the reason why death commands piety.

The collective, or society (any society), is then an organism-like totality composed of individuals and their relationships. Durkheim proposed that this invisible, bodiless thing, society, might be studied somewhat as we study gravity. Sense experience does directly show us what gravity is, but by measuring gravity's effects we indirectly identify its properties and begin to formulate a theory about it. Likewise society, though invisible, exerts its own orderly and measurable force on people. However much the person experiences himself as a unique sovereign will, he is not freely shaping his life because his thoughts are reworkings of "collective representations." Collective representations do not arise from personal thinking but from the totality of uncounted minds interacting over time as they do society's work. A "collective consciousness" is not a majority opinion, a personal belief, nor an explicit proposition. It is the shared system of unspoken notions that unreflectively organize our movements as social beings. They are prior to and constitutive of thinking. Through these non-individual components of selfhood, society installs within the person a replica of itself: shared morality and potentials for solidarity.

And because society is made of persons and solidary relations, the death of a member is an injury to society. This last was the problem Durkheim's stellar student Robert Hertz took up. In proposing to reveal the nature of death as a social fact, Hertz takes the organic metaphor to a daring extreme. Wanting to make us perceive, so to speak, society's point of view on mortality rather than the individual's, he seeks to put into words the "collective consciousness" of mortality. If society could speak its posture to death, it might say:

> Death does not confine itself to ending the visible bodily life of an individual: it also destroys the social being grafted upon the physical individual, and to whom the collective consciousness attributed great dignity and importance. The society of which that individual was a member formed him by means of true rites of consecration and has put to work energies proportionate to the social status of the deceased: his destruction is tantamount to a sacrilege . . .
>
> Thus, when a man dies, society loses in him much more than a unit; it is stricken in the very principle of its life, in the faith it has in itself . . . But this exclusion is not final. In the same way as *the collective consciousness does not believe in the necessity of death*, so it refuses to consider it irrevocable. Because it believes in itself a healthy society cannot admit that an individual who was part of its own substance, and on whom it has set its mark, shall be lost forever. *The last word must remain with life.*
>
> *Hertz 1960 [1907], 77–78, emphasis added*

"Above all else," D.J. Davies paraphrases, for Durkheimians "society is concerned with itself and with its continuity through those constituent individuals who are, as it were, bearers of 'society'" (2000, 98). When a Durkheimian says "society is concerned," he means that *if* the collective as a whole were the sort of being that has a separate mind, that mind's concern would be for maintaining "the things of its own proper experience," its own interests and strength, namely, an arrangement of persons (Durkheim 1967 [1912], 483). Society does not let simply a part of itself (a person) disappear. That would disorganize the web of relations around its lost human component, making room for entropy. Instead, society—and Hertz means any society, anywhere—socializes death in such terms that "the last word must remain with life."

And so, everywhere and in myriad ways, a dead person becomes a new kind of person. Societies act as if under the compulsion to counteract people's physical decomposition by *replacing* the ruined body and *relocating* its proxy in a socially viable standing. Once the lost man or woman has been processed into something other than a disappearing biological mess, it becomes possible for others to reconnect around him as if no insult to society had occurred. On the contrary, social order may even be enhanced, because his proxy may even become a personage more long-lived and influential than he ever was: a great ancestor, like Libiac Cancharco. Hertz' ethnological examples center on "primitive" peoples of island Southeast Asia, but he also summarizes practices ranging from mummification to endocannibalism (ritual eating of the beloved dead) and even mentions the swanky new graves in Père Lachaise Cemetery in Paris.

At first glance, the gamut of mortuary practice appears great. At one extreme people annihilate the corpse and at the other they make it last forever. But Hertz's thesis is that these proceedings are really all one. All obey a two-stage program: first the "release" of the doomed bodily person and then the "reintegration" of a proxy purified of mortal damage. Hertz chooses as prototype double burial, in which the deceased is allowed to rot until soft tissue is gone and the survivors have exhausted their mourning. This is the "wet" phase of the dead person's transition. After a time, the dead one is reconstituted as a "dry" being by rescuing his bones and installing them as a different, non-mortal kind of person. Now he deserves pomp and reverence: he is an ancestor, and his survivors no longer mourn but celebrate him. Society acquires a "double" in the mortuary zone, a society of immortals that anchors and guarantees normality. "Poignantly, death resembles birth in transferring an individual from one domain to another . . . surrounded by mystical qualities" (Davies 2000, 99).

Hertz's essay goes on to explain mortuary diversity. Some societies minimize the biological remains of the dead by cannibalistically recycling them into their own flesh. They thereby become in their own flesh their ancestors' monuments and reincarnations. Ancient Peru was among societies that go to the opposite extreme. They preserved bodies indefinitely, building around them ideal and ritual patterns of behavior. From Peru's *malki* mummies we can gain some light about what ritualism and sacredness are.

Ancestor cult doesn't just occur in random societies. Andean peoples were typical of the kind of societies that generate pompous ancestor cult. These are societies depending on tightly circumscribed inherited resource bases of land and water, as in the irrigation states of Egypt and China. In a society like that, everyone literally owes his livelihood to those who made room for him by dying. A Quechua myth collected in Peru's Huarochirí Province as early as 1608 expresses the idea: in primordial times people did not die but multiplied, overcrowding the land to the point of cannibalism and starvation. They had to accept death as the precondition of life. Societies that see their social reproduction as a matter of inheriting limited resources tend to attribute success to the repetition of an ancestor-focused program. In every generation one marries a spouse descended from close, known ancestors. One defends territory in in the ancestors' names so land and water can pass only to people with similar genealogical claims.

Ritual uniting ancient and current generations does more than just repair the damage done by one kinsman's death. In placing a relative among "dry" ancestors like the ancient Libiac Cancharco, performers renew the very order of relations that makes life possible. The making and visiting of a hard, "dry" ancestor results in the retention, with improved stability, of relations traced from her or him. These relationships form a matrix on which the living can view social doings as determined, regular, and intelligible. Planting, harvesting, marriages, and political successions had to be decided with the oracular advice of the relevant mummies. A certain kind of society regenerates itself through this powerful "collective representation"; that is mortuary's function.

Since the 1990s, mortuary anthropology has revised Hertz's essentially conservative, functionalist view of what mortuary achieves. Like anthropologists in general, ritual studies researchers have been looking for ways to retain powerful Durkheimian insights while also making room for human agency and change.

However true it may be that the making and care of ancestor focuses all minds on ideas of continuity, the actual work of attaching people to the ancestral core (where shall our late grandmother sit?), of voicing malkis' wishes in oracles, and of deciding what distant relatives may join the cult always involves politically freighted actions. The consequences change society.

Mummy priests in Peru became wealthy and politically active, not only by receiving fees but by administering the endowments of specific mummies. The incessant making and modifying of tombs must have involved negotiated decisions among kinfolk, not necessarily unanimous. Certainly mummy shrines' rank and form kept changing long after their consecration. In one case, far into the 18th century, well after extirpation came and went, the insurgent Andagua kuraka Gregorio Taco was still attracting followers by promising access to his potent ancestors (Salomon 1987). What once looked like "disturbance" in Andean tombs has been reinterpreted by recent archaeologists as incessant reopening and remodeling of the dead, even forced appropriation (Shimada and Fitzsimmons 2015). Ritualism? Yes, apparently. But even Hertz's admirers today recognize that faced with unpremeditated changes, society alters its putatively immortal self as well as reproducing its current self.

The extirpators and the assault on Mama Raywana, "Mother of Food," in the 17th century

Hertz's *Death* covers only one of the functions that seem to be associated everywhere with religiosity. To get a broader idea about what religion in general was to Durkheimians, we need to glance at the master's overarching theory as formulated in 1912 in *The Elementary Forms of the Religious Life*. We'll bring along Raywana, Peru's beloved food mother.

Chapter 2 described Raywan Entrego, the ritual in which Rapaz's outgoing and incoming agricultural offices present young plants called Raywanes to Kaha Wayi and the mountains. Raywan Entrego is simultaneously an administrative routine, an agronomic inspection, and a sacred propitiation. But what does Raywan as a concept include? Raywana's story is one point at which we can see how extirpation cut into mid-colonial Andean practices, changing but not ending them.

Mama Raywana is the name of a beloved mythical being, often called goddess of food. Annually the lady Raywana steps out as the star of the harvest. She comes attended by "a line of dancers each carrying various foodstuffs, such as corn, potatoes, squash, and always a stuffed bird."[6] A male or female dancer in rich female dress impersonates the womanly, glamorous "mother of the crop." Sometimes Raywana wears a crown decorated with little birds. Men dancing alongside flirt with her (Cardich 2000, 69–108; Domínguez Condezo 1982, 29–33). Raywana and her myth are common in ethnographies and folklore studies over a huge swath of central Peru (Huánuco, Cerro de Pasco, and Ancash; Domínguez Condezo 2003, 92–95). In costuming, pink is her insignia color. Rapacinos call their pink-fleshed favorite potato variety *papa Raywana*.

Some myths pair Mama Raywana with Libiac Cancharco as wak'a of cultivators and herders, respectively—even where cultivators and herders are the same people in different parts of their work life (Cardich 2000, 95).

In primordial times, Mother Raywana was the owner of food. She saw humans burning and wasting food, so she took back all edible plants, leaving them to starve. Hearing the cries of famished people, some birds took pity. Flycatchers threw fleas into Mama Raywana's eyes, and while she was blinded, they snatched her baby daughter Conopa. (Conopa is a term for crop fetishes or talismans, such as the *ila* of plants mentioned in Chapter 2.) Some say that by kidnapping baby Conopa, humans blackmailed Raywana into returning the crops. Others say Conopa himself gave people the ability to farm.

So Raywana is loved as the abundant mother of food, but she is a mother with a potential grudge.[7] By using tubers or seed, humans have stolen her babies. Harvesting metaphorically inflicts the same theft of offspring on every cultivated plant. Plants' mother must therefore be treated with tact as well as love. In marrying Raywana (that is, becoming cultivators), people acquire a wife who gives much and demands much—a wife who may have mixed feelings (Tello 1960, 152; Rostworowski 1983, 53–56, 65–71; Domínguez Condezo 1982; Jiménez Borja 1973, 33).

In Huánuco (over the cordillera crest from Rapaz), Raywana's festival includes an act called "giving birth" (*wachay*). It expresses fully the idea of agriculture as marriage to a superhuman female. Near the end of the festival, pregnant Raywana (the dancer) goes to sleep in a hut while her attendants seek out a midwife to help her. Meanwhile, other dancers circle around her birthing hut. An elder in the role of Awkin, her mountain-father, takes coca for an augury of good birth. At last Raywana emerges from her birthing hut "making corn, potato, and olluco dance between her hands." But who, spectators ask, are the fathers of her food-children? She names as fathers the various young men standing nearby. If a man acknowledges one of the crops as his child, he receives a crop token from the hand of the awkin. These crop-gifts have amulet-like power of fertility. The ritual "father" becomes responsible to care for it, increase it, and assure abundant production for the community.

So if Raywana is mother of food, and being a farmer implies being a father of food, then a farming man has the mountain-awkis as his in-laws. The work of the bendelhombre and the work of Kaha Wayi would then take on an aspect of approaching one's parents-in-law. The cultivator, in turn, becomes an awkin ("old man") in relation to food; crops are his and Raywana's children.

Farming societies in many places play with ideas of farming as sex. These ideas are great fun, often performed for ribald laughs. But in colonial Peru they got a lot of people in trouble when during the middle wave of extirpation, the 1650s, prosecutors latched onto information about Raywana. She was at that time adored over a wide region. In at least one place, Mangas, she had an ancient house and "colca" of her own (Duviols 2003, 604). In 1724–1725, the last big wave of extirpation led by Pedro de Celís found Raywana in a sacred complex for the common-field planting. The description sounds much like today's Kaha Wayi complex. Raywana paraded with the leadership in the canal-cleaning festival and at the common planting (García Cabrera 1994, 521, 523, 525).

All religions are true: the Durkheimian perspective

How might this look in Durkheimian perspective? Raywana is food. She is a sacred symbol of campesino life, whom people take into themselves as nourishment. This nourishment becomes their very bodies. Consuming it together becomes a sign of solidarity: we are what we eat, and we all eat the same local sustenance. The notion that dining together ("commensality") makes us an emergent collective entity is common in almost all societies and is greatly elaborated in sacred ritual.

Exalting the superhuman as transcendently edible of course rings a bell for those who know Christian communion. Is it a fluke that other kinds of worship also entail the ingestion of sacred beings? Durkheim thought one "elementary" case of association between eating and divinity laid bare the very crux of religiosity.

Durkheim was deeply impressed by ethnographic reports that primitive Australians such as the desert-foraging "Arunta" people (today called Arrernte) carried on an intricate round of ritual that organized society in discrete sacred categories. If ritualism and the sacred are central to societies so tiny and mobile, so archaic, then surely (Durkheim thought) they must be basic attributes inherent to human society and not just "add-ons" deriving from social complexity. And if ritualism was a feature of all societies, it must manifest a fundamental property of society as such. Durkheim purported to find in "primitive" or "elementary" examples the principle which underlies the vast surface diversity of sacred practices.

In doing ritual deeds, people everywhere gather around things which are special, like the altar table of Kaha Wayi. These inspire respect or awe and are not to be used in ordinary ways. Gathering around them inspires feelings that an overarching, invisible force is present. Ritual actions such as the long nighttime invocations in Kaha Wayi, a Mass, or the Australian clan feast cause people to feel and celebrate a power that sustains us and judges us, a power that we depend on and exalt.

Durkheim believed the key sacred symbol among Australians was the totem: the plant or animal that members of each clan recognized as its "crest" or emblem. For its totem, for its visible essence, members felt affection and reverence. They were bound to protect it from harm, so it would protect them. Each totem concentrated in one sign the reality, dignity, and well-being of its people as a society.

Yet at a certain festival called the Intichiuma, each clan gathered and, working itself up to an "effervescence" of group feeling and excitement, would sacrifice and eat the totem. Durkheim's understanding of the Intichiuma rests on what now seems a shaky reading of Aboriginal ethnography, and yet his interpretation of it has inspired many subsequent theorists.

When Australians felt that their festivities around the totem brought them into the presence of an invisible, sustaining, and fateful power, they were not mistaken. On the contrary, Durkheim wrote, religious "effervescence" around a symbol is a valid perception of something real that cannot be perceived any other way. We do in fact live by virtue of an invisible, bodiless, nonhuman entity that makes, sustains, and can break us. That being is society. When people celebrated the creature emblematic of their clan society and then ingested it, they were symbolically exalting and then introducing into themselves their overarching commonality in the form of a communal substance. When Intichiuma celebrants ingested the essence of their clans, they were experiencing society's power to "penetrate and organize itself within us." When people worshipped the totem they were realizing society itself.

The social whole is different from the additive sum of its human parts. It endows people with a legacy of "collective representations" they could never create as individuals—languages, laws, moral sentiments, categories of cognition, rules of reasoning, and technical know-how. Yet the social whole has no viable existence except as instantiated in people. It needs them: their loyalty, their solidarity with each other, their commitment to do the things that make social life—our only life!—possible. Eating Raywana's food-babies realizes agrarian life.

The Durkheimian vein of theorizing is open to many critiques above and beyond its dubious reading of Australian data. For one thing, functional theory is good at explaining how institutions can reproduce themselves but not at explaining why they change. Although Durkheim was hugely concerned with the breach between traditional and modern society, he was better at discerning the strangeness of modernity than explaining why modernity happened. For another, Durkheimian theory tends to assume "the social" as a bond affecting all members alike, but in fact not all individuals stand in similar relations to society. Their interests can conflict. And, like most functionalist theories, it contains a thread of circular reasoning.

Yet the Durkheimian vein has proven fertile of fresh argument for over a century. Compared to many social-scientific explanations, it stands out for one striking implication: a Durkheimian may deny every specific belief about the sacred and yet hold that all religions are true.

Kaha Wayi taking a new shape: "little houses" of cult and the charlatan Quiñones

In this closing section we return to summarize what little is known about how the Kaha Wayi-Pasa Qulqa complex assumed its current form. In 1681 Diego de Rocha, who knew the Checras area, said that rural people still gathered in prehispanic "old towns" for civic governance:

> In these Indians' ancient pre-Christian towns there is a public place elevated in a spherical shape [*sic*, meaning circular?], fenced with very tightly set stones and planed flat. This place they call Cayan. From there it was announced what they should attend to. Today court orders are proclaimed there, and they give notice of rentals and other obligations of subjects, and there the officers (*principales*) and camachicos get together to set their quota charges (*prorratas*) and decisions, and to hear as a matter of justice whatever needs to be ventilated about these things.
>
> *Rocha 1891 [1681], 31–32*

These *cayanes* or ritual-governmental plaza groups have been studied by Guillermo Cock. Each *cayan* had a *colca* or storehouse and *chaguay* (cellar) where sacrifice accompanied storage, as at Pasa Qulqa. Chaguay, like Pasa Qulqa today, had feminine attributes. Other enduring features include a hearth, birds, animal fat, colored corn, gourds, special-purpose ceramics, magic musical instruments, skins, and offerings dressed in textiles. These familiar ritual goods lasted through at least the first two waves of extirpation (Cock 1980, 225, 238).[8]

But as far as I know, no prehispanic cayan as such is still in service. Rather, at some apparently late colonial time, central-Andean rural people seem to have shifted their centers of storage, traditional governance, and sacred work from prehispanic "old towns," or cayan-type plaza groups, to facilities more integrated with villages— that is, to infrastructures more compatible with the officially promulgated Toledan village plan. This seems to be the process that gave rise to the Rapaz precinct and to the "collcas" which form the modern space of civic government in many villages.

An Archbishop of Lima in 1724–1725 decided to revive extirpation after some four decades of near-dormancy. He gave the commission of Visiting Judge to D. Pedro de Celís, curate of Checras and Paccho, who had been agitating about idolatry in his parish. The resulting short-lived but intensive persecutions aimed specifically at the sub-region of which Rapaz forms part, including especially Pachangara and Andajes. He went after holy beings we have already discussed, such as Libiac and Raiguana. But there are significant differences between early and late wak'a activities.

One 1724–1725 theme is the finding of "little houses or synagogues" containing objects for manipulating nature. This accusation differs from middle 17th-century descriptions of ritual places, which were usually labeled as caves, "collca," "chaguayes," or "cayanes" rather than "houses."

Celís found in Concepción de Oyón a weather-controlling building that resembled Kaha Wayi: "In this town a very small house which was closed has been conserved since the time of paganism." It might even have been Kaha Wayi itself (since modern Rapaz is situated within the limits of old Concepción de Oyón). In Andajes Maria Pasquala said that "in the old town site called Poac Guaranga which is the same as Eight Thousand they worshiped in a little house of the ancients having a basement and mummies a stone idol with all the features of a man called Misay Guanca" (García Cabrera 1994, 499, 516, 526–528).

Weather control in "little houses" was done by manipulating liquids, a practice which continues in Kaha Wayi. In Pachangara, a certain Martín Phelipe specialized in this kind of magic: he used a vat called Tinlla Cocha[9] that was filled with chicha and agitated so as to form a rainbow (*tumanku*).

> In his house this deponent used to have a big vat called Tinllacocha, which the whole town held in great veneration . . . when they filled it with chicha [corn beer] it would begin to make noise. And then they would dress it (*rebozar*) with llama hides, cloaks, tiaras, skirts, and women's stickpins, and many were needed, because it was very big. In this way the chicha that was inside it would turn different colors and then it would form a halo similar to a rainbow, which would last until everyone had drunk from the chicha. They thought it would engender in them great strength when they went out to till the common field, and so they would make a gesture as if going to sow, so that it would bring forth a lot of fruit.
>
> *García Cabrera 1994, 503–504*

The magical vat resembles the magical "lake" formerly held in the basement of Pasa Qulqa, and the practice of seeking signs in agitated water also matches modern practice.

Modern Kaha Wayi, like late-colonial "little houses," contained weather-controlling musical instruments. In Rapaz the now-lost instruments were called "the magic orchestra." In 1724 something similar was inspected: "several trumpets . . . to expel the pest, others waters, others for going to the *mita plasa* [public recruitment of forced labor], others for their recreations and seedtimes." Celís burned "four fifes, of which one served to expel smallpox from the town, another to expel water when they pressed upon flat places, another to attract winds and diseases, and each one was played with a different tune (*tañido*)" (García Cabrera 1994, 492, 501, 503, 505, 515).[10] "Flutes" were different from the big conch trumpets used to signal from town to town and call guests to rituals.[11] In Oyón an elderly lady showed the investigators "in the little house or synagogue . . . an infinity of filthy things . . . some of the bronze flutes which were in the said little house or synagogue were used to serve to expel the wind and others to attract it." The woman was recorded as 84 years of age, so she would have been in her teens during the previous surge of extirpation (García Cabrera 1994, 499–500).

Other rites took place outdoors, almost identical to modern ritual mountain-climbing, the "search for weather," and canal-cleaning ritual. "They enchant (*conjuran*) cloudbanks or storms, or stone the waters when it rains, with a drum and dressed in the style of their prechristian age."[12] He was told in Naván that "They would go to the intake of the canal where the men gave it five shots from their slings . . . giving to understand that they would have plenty of water that year, and they used to carry unfermented corn beer to the canal intake" (García Cabrera 1994, 194, 489).[13]

Indeed, the cults of *jirka* in 1724–1725 concern some of the same mountains venerated today. One Sebastian Ripai gave the judges to understand that certain paired stones served in worshiping "Llaruguaina," perhaps Yara Wayna mountain in Rapaz. "Llaruguaina," together with his wife Mamaguanca (Mama Wanka, "Mother Monolith") were known as "parents of the republic" (García Cabrera 1994, 492).[14] Rapaz's Qisunki Mountain figures under the name Quichunque (Griffiths 1996, 225).

Apparently storehouses distinct from "little houses" continued to exist. The female role in managing storage is mentioned toward 1725 in Andajes, where "two women always went who used to guard the goods of the commons" (García Cabrera 1994, 526–527).[15]

In sum, the ritual resources of Rapaz about 1725 seem to have already assumed pretty much the same forms they have today. But one tendency in late-colonial Rapaz seems strange today.

In the late Spanish colonial era, assertive persons built sectarian followings or clienteles around the old wak'as. These leaders contended for power by combining pre-Christian rites with blackmail and magic. The extirpator Celís' favorite enemy was one Pedro de la Cruz, alias Quiñones. Quiñones promoted a certain "little house" of ancient construction as an animal-sacrificing temple to uphold the welfare of common fields. He set himself up as a new priest of Libiac Cancharco. De la Cruz/Quiñones gathered influence across many communities, partly by providing magical help for prosperity or love.[16] His followers regarded him as a challenger to colonial village lords who had become unpopular because of their association with forced labor. His enemies saw him as a shady, unscrupulous manipulator of the poor. Troublemaker and subversive, or religious revivalist? Or both?

Quiñones reorganized and revitalized "an established cast of deities" in a new constellation of belief and power (Gose 2008, 23). His practice was more individualized and less communal than the pre-extirpation mummy-centered leadership. It consisted of a personal clientele. He worked within a colonial power structure, but not in the way state or church prescribed; Quiñones was the khipu master of a Spanish *obraje*, and by using a khipu to track his townsmen's labor compliance, he also spied out their secret private needs. He harnessed the sexuality/fertility of the living as well as piety toward the dead.

One set of accusers said he organized a group sexual rite of passage for teenagers. Called *mactación*, it allegedly included ritualized defloration and sacrifice of the resulting blood.[17] He seems, through a fog of church ideology, to resemble some of the sinister "cult leaders" of our time. Whatever Quiñones was up to, it seems to have been transitory, for the "little house" Kaha Wayi lived on to embody public and collective ritual rather than conflictive and exclusive counterculture.

Was Kaha Wayi-Pasa Qulqa worship and governance already taking modern form by the 1720s? Apart from Celís' campaign we have found no clear records of Andean ritual activity from the last colonial century or the first century of Peru's independence, so it is not yet possible to say. Rapaz's parish church has an unusually complete series of internal papers that never mention its neighbor Kaha Wayi. Denunciations of Indian diabolism lost their audience in the mid 18th century as natural-philosophical, rather than theological, explanations for America's peculiarities came into fashion among both clergy and civil elites. After the defeat of several widespread Andean rebellions in the 1780s, hereditary ethnic lords were pushed from political power, opening more political space for village councils, from which the balternos of Kaha Wayi inherit their constitution.

"The eighteenth-century community transformation meant a greater democratic margin in social relations and a wider margin of political autonomy," from which Kaha Wayi may have benefited (Thompson 2002, 279). It may even be that village institutions grew in autonomy under the remote and indifferent Republican state of the earlier 19th century. As we will see in Chapter 5, a few of Kaha Wayi's belongings attest to ritual activity during the independence era, including activity related to emerging creole armies and elites.

Notes

1 The dating of human settlement in South America remains controversial. Many archaeologists accept the Monte Verde remains in Chile as firm evidence of a 14,000-year BP human population in the south of the Andes. Discounting the 500 years since Spanish invasion, and using conventional modern demographic "family generation" of 25 years, this suggests 540 precolumbian generations. Assuming earlier motherhood (at 20 years), as was common among preindustrial Andeans, the number rises to 675. Given a less consensual starting line such as the Pikimachay Cave radiocarbon date of 22,000 BP, a similar estimate yields 860 to 1075 generations.

2 "/1r/ Rrelacion de lo que yo Juan Serrano tengo bisto y entendydo y oydo de los yndios del peru de las probincias de andas y caxatambo y de los atabillos es lo siguiente: hablando yo Juan Serrano con ellos sobre que fuesen christianos y diziendoselo muchas bezes di[tachado]zian que para que quieran ser christianos abiendoles yo dicho que para serbir a dios y no hurtar ny tomar la mujer de su proximo ny dezir mal de nadie ny matar y otras cosas segund que los santos mandamientos de la ley nos lo mandan/1v/ rrespondyan que no quieren ser christianos por que los christianos hurtaban y les tomaban a sus mujeres y hijas [tachado] contra su boluntad y que de nosotros no b[e]yan señal ny obra buena y para esto daban otras muchas rrazones de las quales no mentyan syno que en todo lo que se dize de los christianos dyzen verdad. Muchos bi dellos que son gente de bibo juicio y estan a my parecer cerca de la fe porque no crehen syno en el sol y en otras cosas que se [ilegible] y siendo doctrinados creherian en nuestra santa fe [tachado] porque entrellos ay muy gran cuenta y rrazon y tenyan en el tyempo que en la tierra no abia christianos su cuenta y rrazon de las personas que en la tierra abia de guerra y de las [tachado] criaturas que nacian y de los que moryan y de todo el ganado obejas y carneros de la tierra y tenyan sus torres que llaman depositos donde tenyan

mucho mayz de un año para otro / . . . ay en el peru en cada balle su lenga y mando guayna caba que ubiese una lengua general ques la que se usaba en la probincia del cuzco y que en su corte no se hablase otra la qual lengua se mando por el dicho guayna caba que se guardese y supiese por mas de myll y quynyentas leguas quel señoreaba y quel yndio que no la supiese que muriese por ello y ansy es la que los christianos el dya de oy hablan con los yndios por que nynguna otra entyenden los christianos." (AGI/S Indiferente General 1528 No. 42. Undated, early 1560s? Relacion de los indios de Andas, Caxatambo y Atabillos hecha por Juan Serrano.)

3 A compact introduction is available in Gareis (1989). Since Duviols' great 1971 monograph, which pioneered the field, other worthy syntheses have appeared, such as Cock (1980), Doyle (1988), Ramos and Urbano (1993), Mills (1997), and Brosseder (2015). Larco (2008) reveals a previously unstudied northern area of extirpation.

4 "el cuerpo de un curaca antiquísimo llamado Liviacancharco, que se halló en un monte muy áspero, como una legua del pueblo de San Cristóbal de Rapaz, en una cueva, debajo de un pabellón, con su huama o diadema de oro en la cabeza, vestido con siete camisetas muy finas de cumbi, que dicen que los indios se las enviaron presentadas los reyes ingas antiguos. Este cuerpo como se halló y otro de un mayordomo suyo llamado Chuchu Michuy . . . se llevaron a Lima para que los viese el señor virrey y el señor arzobispo y bolviéndoles a los Andajes se hizo un solemne auto convocando todos los pueblos de la provincia y se quemaron estos cuerpos con otras muchas huacas."

5 "estando en la dotrina de nuestra señora de villaharta [old name of Oyón?] que es de los religiosos de nuestro señor de la merced hizo la de la visita y escrutinia [*sic*] en las formas y por las diligençias que pareçe hizo en el pueblo de san xrispoval de rrapaz consta que hallo culpadas en la dicha idolatría dozientas y noventa y ocho personas a las quales por auto que proveyó en tres días del mes de setienbre del dicho año [1614] absolvió en presencia del padre presentado fray Alonso de espinosa cura de la dicha dotrina y de simon de vrique notario de la dicha visita" (Avendaño 1947 [1623], 227).

6 "una fila de bailarines portando cada uno diversos frutos, como choclos, papas, calabazas y siempre una ave disecada."

7 The linguist Weber documents this epithet in Huánuco: "payshi kaycan micuypa maman" "es la madre de la comida" (Weber et al. 1998, 454).

8 "El dicho don Alonso [Ricary] llebo al dicho Vicario a la colca donde se guardaba la ofrenda que se hac[ia] al ydolo Choquerunto y su muger Zaramama en la qual se hallo como quatro fanegas de maiz blanco y negro, y como dos fanegas de cocopa, dos cestillos de sebo de llama y unos mates a modo de xicaras manchadas de sangre, en que recogian la sangre para ofrecer a las guacas, de las llamas que mataban, muchos mates y potos con que bebian y comian cuando celebraban los dichos sacrificios. Y en la dicha colca habia un chaguay al modo de sotano, en el qual abia muchas zaramamas, cuies, coca, sebo, pellejos de llama, callanas de sebo, todo enterrado y 27 pesos y medio real en medios en dos taleguillas . . . los bestidos das zarasmamas . . . con las plumas del paxaro Hasto Tucto en una petaquilla con una guama, que parece que es lo que se ponen en la cabesa los yndios quando baylan a su ussanza antigua."

9 Perhaps this is an errant transcription of *tinya qucha*, "drum lake," referring to the small drum often used in ritual and discussed in Chapter 4? Or *tinshay* "to splash," as recorded in Junín (Cerrón-Palomino 1976, 133)?

10 "quatro pifanos el uno servia para echar las viruelas del pueblo, el otro para echar las aguas quando apretavan las llanuras otro para atraerlas otro para los vientos y pestes que cada una se tocava con diferent tañido."

11 "un caracol de una quarta de largo el qual lo tocavan para que los de los pueblos sercanos ocurrieran a un tiempo a sus sacrificios y se hoia de tres a a quatro leguas de distancia heredado de la gentilidad de familia en familia" (García Cabrera 1994, 515).

12 "conjuran nublados o tempestades o apedrean las aguas quando lluebe con tambo bestidos a uso de su gentilidad."

13 "hivan a boca de la sequia a donde daban los hombres sinco jondasos y que se seguian de en tres en tres dando a entender que tendrian mucho agua aquel año y que llevaban chicha cruda a la boca de la sequia."

14 "para su inteligencia era lo mesmo que padres de la republica."

15 "que ciempre hiban las dos mugeres que guardaban los vienes del comun y que tambien iban otras personas."

16 Churín, Maray, Sayán, Canín, Paccho, Moyobamba, Picoy, Guayllanín, Tongos, Puñún, Pachangara, Curay, Allaranga, Cochan, Guacracancha, and Turpay are mentioned. All these are in Rapaz's immediate area.

17 *Mactación* is an interesting word. It seems to be an interlingual pun fusing ecclesiastical and Andean meanings. In Catholic liturgy, *mactación* (cognate to Spanish *matar* "to kill") means death as an element of sacrifice to God. It is sometimes applied to the death of Jesus (Rueda and Moreno 1995, 521). For the sound-alike Quechua noun *macta* González Holguín in 1608 gave the gloss "Adolescent boy from nine to fourteen years" (1989, 334). We do not know if the Andean usage originated with the prosecutor Veramendi or if he took it from popular speech (AAL/L IyH old Leg 3 Exp. 10 = current Leg 11 exp. 7. 1724–25. Autos criminales contra Pedro de la Cruz alias Quiñones yndio y Francisco Bartolomé su Nieto por delitos de idolatría [Maray, Pachangara, y otros lugares] 1724–1725. 43 fo. f.30r).

References

AAL/L Idolatrías y hechicerías Leg. 3 Exp. 10 = current Leg 11 exp. 7. 1724–1725. Autos criminales contra Pedro de la Cruz alias Quiñones yndio y Francisco Bartolomé su Nieto por delitos de idolatría [Maray, Pachangara, y otros lugares] 1724–1725. 43 fo.

AGI/S Lima, 566 Leg.4 Fo.218. Real Provisión 16-08-1541. Real provision de D. Carlos y Doña Juana al gobernador de la provincial del Perú, por la que le mandan que, según la provisión dada sobre que no se quiten a los encomenderos los indios que tienen sin ser antes oidos y vencidos por fuero y derecho, no quiten al capitán Hernando de Montenegro, vecino de la ciudad de los Reyes, los que le fueron encomendados que son "en la provincia de los Atavillos el cacique Tuma y *Guarox señor del pueblo de Andox* [*sic*]" con los pueblos y principales sujetos a él.

AGI/S Indiferente General 1528 No. 42. Undated, early 1560s? Relacion de los indios de Andas, Caxatambo y Atabillos hecha por Juan Serrano. 1fo.

Avendaño, Fernando de. 1947 [1623]. "Testimonio de la visita y extirpación de idolatrías que hizo el Dr. D. Fernando de Avendaño." In *La iglesia de España en el Perú: Colección de documentos para la historia de la Iglesia en el Perú, que se encuentran en varios archivos*, edited by Emilio Lissón Chávez. Vol. 5. Sevilla: n.p. 225–234.

Barraza Lescano, Sergio. 2009. "Apuntes histórico-arqueológicos en torno a la danza del Huacón." *Antropologica* 32(27): 93–121.

Brosseder, Claudia. 2015. *The Power of Huacas: Change and Resistance in the Andean World of Colonial Peru*. Austin, TX: University of Texas Press.

Cardich, Augusto. 2000. "Dos divinidades relevantes del antiguo panteón centro-andino: Yana Raman o Libiac Cancharco y Rayguana." *Investigaciones sociales: Revista del Instituto de Investigaciones Histórico-Culturales* 4(5): 69–108.

Cerrón-Palomino, Rodolfo. 1976. *Diccionario Quechua Junín-Huanca*. Lima: Ministerio de Educación and Instituto de Estudios Peruanos.

Cock Carrasco, Guillermo Alberto. 1980. *El sacerdote andino y los bienes de las divinidades en los siglos XVII y XVIII*. Tesis de grado Bachiller, Pontificia Universidad Católica del Perú, Programa de Letras y Ciencias Humanas.

Curátola Petrocchi, Marco. 2008. "La Función de los oráculos en el imperio inca." In *Adivinación y oráculos en el mundo andino antiguo*, edited by Marco Curátola Petrocchi and Mariusz S. Ziółkowski. Lima: Pontificia Universidad Católica del Perú—Fondo Editorial and Instituto Francés de Estudios Andinos. 15–70.

Davies, Douglas J. 2000. "Robert Hertz: The Social Triumph over Death." *Mortality* 5(1): 97–102.

Domínguez Condezo, Víctor. 1982. "Raywana: La danza más antigua de Huánuco." *Boletín de Lima* 22(4): 29–33.

Domínguez Condezo, Víctor. 2003. "Jirkas Kechuas: Mitos andinos de Huánuco y Pasco." Lima: Editorial San Marcos.

Doyle, Mary. 1988. *The Ancestor Cult and Burial Ritual in Seventeenth and Eighteenth Century Central Peru*. PhD dissertation, Department of History, University of California at Los Angeles.

Durkheim, Émile. 1967 [1912]. *The Elementary Forms of the Religious Life*, translated by Joseph Ward Swain. New York: Free Press.

Duviols, Pierre. 1971. *La Lutte contre les réligions autochtones dans le Pérou colonial*. Lima: Institut Français d'Études Andines.

Duviols, Pierre. 1973. "Huari y Llacuaz: Agricultores y pastores: Un dualismo prehispánico de oposición y complementaridad." *Revista del Museo Nacional* 39: 153–191.

Duviols, Pierre. 1974. "Une petite chronique retrouvée: errores, ritos, supersticiones y ceremonias de los yndios de la provincia de Chinchaycocha y otras del Piru (1603)." *Journal de la Société des Américanistes* 68: 275–297.

Duviols, Pierre. 1976. "La Capacocha: mecanismo y función del sacrificio humano, su proyección, su papel en la política integracionista, y en la economía redistributiva del Tawantinsuyu." *Allpanchis* 9: 11–57.

Duviols, Pierre. 2003. *Procesos y visitas de idolatrías, Cajatambo, siglo XVII*. Lima: Pontificia Universidad Católica del Perú and Instituto Francés de Estudios Andinos.

Encarnación Rojas, Eulalia, and Narciso Robles Atachagua. 2011. *Breve Historia de San Cristóbal de Rapaz*. Lima: Gráfica Quinteros E.I.R.L.

Espinoza Soriano, Waldemar. 1981. "Un testimonio sobre los ídolos huacas, y dioses de Lampa y Cajatambo, siglos XVI–XVII. Supervivencias en Cajatambo." *Scientia et praxis* 15: 115–130.

Estenssoro Fuchs, Juan Carlos. 1998. *Del paganismo a la santidad: La incorporación de los indios del Perú al catolicismo. 1532–1750*. Lima: Instituto Francés de Estudios Andinos. Travaux de l'Institut Français d'Études Andines, tomo 156.

Falcón Huayta, Victor. 2007. *Patrimonio de San Cristóbal de Rapaz, Provincia de Oyón: Khipu y Cajahuay (2005–2008)—Arqueología. Informe Final al Instituto Nacional de Cultura (RNA N° DF-0181)*. Lima: Instituto Nacional de Cultura.

Falcón Huayta, Víctor, and Reymundo Chapa. 2008. Memoranda "Cotejo de fechas radiocarbónicas de Rapaz," 24 julio 2008. Unpublished project document.

García Cabrera, Juan Carlos. 1994. *Ofensas a Dios, pleitos e injurias: Causas de idolatrías y hechicerías, Cajatambo, siglos XVII–XIX*. Vol. 1. Cusco, Peru: Centro de Estudios Regionales Andinos, Bartolomé de Las Casas.

Gareis, Iris. 1989. "Extirpación de idolatrías e Inquisición en el Virreinato del Perú." *Boletín del Instituto Riva-Agüero* 16: 55–74.

González Holguín, Diego. 1989 [1608]. *Vocabulario de la lengua general de todo el Perú llamada lengua qquichua o del inca*. Lima: Universidad Nacional Mayor de San Marcos.

Gose, Peter. 2008. *Invaders as Ancestors: On the Intercultural Making and Unmaking of Spanish Colonialism in the Andes*. Toronto: University of Toronto Press.

Griffiths, Nicholas. 1996. *The Cross and the Serpent: Religious Repression and Resurgence in Colonial Peru*. Norman and London: University of Oklahoma Press.

Guibovich, Pedro. 1993. "La carrera de un visitador de idolatrías en el siglo XVII: Fernando de Avendaño (1580?–1655)." In *Catolicismo y extirpación de idolatría: Siglos XVI–XVIII*, edited by Enrique Urbano y Gabriela Ramos. Cusco, Peru: Centro de Estudios Regionales Andinos, Bartolomé de las Casas. 169–240.

Hertz, Robert. 1960 [1907]. *Death and the Right Hand*, translated by Rodney and Claudia Needham. Glencoe, IL: Free Press.

Jiménez Borja, Arturo. 1973. *Imagen del mundo aborigen*. Lima: n.p.

Krzanowski, Andrzej. 1977. "Archaeological Investigations in the Upper Huaura Basin (Central Peru), Part I." *Acta Archaeologica Carpathica* 17: 121–137.

Krzanowski, Andrzej. 1978. "Archaeological Investigations in the Upper Huaura Basin (Central Peru), Part II." *Acta Archaeologica Carpathica* 18: 201–226.

Larco, Laura. 2008. *Más allá de los encantos: Documentos históricos y etnografía contemporánea sobre extirpación de idolatrías en Trujillo, siglos XVIII–XX*. Lima: Fondo Editorial de la Universidad Nacional Mayor de San Marcos and Instituto Francés de Estudios Andinos.

Medina Susano, R. Clorinda. 1989. *Checras*. Lima: Consejo Nacional de Ciencia y Tecnología.

Mills, Kenneth R. 1997. *Idolatry and Its Enemies: Colonial Andean Religion and Extirpation, 1640–1750*. Princeton, NJ: Princeton University Press.

Molina, Cristóbal de. 2011[c.1576]. *Account of the Fables and Rites of the Incas*, translated by Brian Bauer, Vania Smith-Oka, and Gabriel E. Cantarutti. Austin, TX: University of Texas Press.

Montes, Valentín. 1996. *Rapaz desde el fondo de los siglos*. Lima: Librería Gráfica Miller S.R.L.

Noriega, Aldo. 2000. "La arquitectura prehispánica de la Provincia de Oyón." *Arkinka* 96: 86–97.

Noriega, Aldo. 2006. "Rapazmarca, un asentamiento con arquitectura multicultural en la región de Rapaz-Oyón." *Arkinka* 126: 78–83.

Noriega, Aldo. 2009. "Algunos comentarios acerca de las sociedades que habitaron los valles de Huaura y Checras antes de la llegada Inca." Unpublished ms.

Noriega, Aldo. 2010. "Las huancas de Checras: Un modelo arqueológico de la resistencia ideológica andina a la hispana." In *La prensa escrita y la difusión de las ideas de libertad*, edited by Mariano Lorenzo Melgar Valdivieso. Lima: Universidad Nacional Mayor de San Marcos, Fondo Editorial. 59–74.

Pereyra Plasencia, Hugo. 1984–1985. "Mita obrajera, idolatría y rebelión en San Juan de Churín (1663)." *Boletín del Instituto Riva-Agüero* 13: 209–244.

Ramos, Gabriela, and Henrique Urbano, eds. 1993. *Catolicismo y extirpación de idolatrías, siglos XVI–XVIII: Charcas, Chile, México, Perú*. Cusco, Peru: Centro de Estudios Regionales Andinos, Bartolomé de Las Casas.

Rocha, Diego Andrés. 1891 [1681]. *Tratado vnico, y singular del origen de los indios occidentales del Piru, Mexico, Santa Fé, y Chile: Por el Doctor Don Diego Andres Rocha*. Tomo II Colección de libros raros y curiosos que tratan de America. Tomo 4. Madrid: Imprenta de Tomás Minuesa.

Rostworowski, María. 1983. *Estructuras andinas del poder: Ideología religiosa política*. Lima: Instituto de Estudios Peruanos.

Rueda, Marco Vinicio, and Segundo Moreno Yánez. 1995. *Cosmos, hombre y sacralidad: Lecturas dirigidas de antropología religiosa*. Quito: Ediciones Abya-Yala.

Ruiz Estrada, Arturo. 1981. *Los quipus de Rapaz*. Huacho: Centro de Investigación de Ciencia y Tecnología de Huacho.

Salomon, Frank. 1987. "Ancestor Worship and Resistance to the State in a Colonial Quechua Society." In *Resistance, Rebellion, and Consciousness in the Andean World, 18th to 20th Centuries*, edited by Steve J. Stern. Madison, WI: University of Wisconsin Press. 148–165.

Sánchez, Ana. 1991. *Amancebados, hechiceros, y rebeldes (Chancay, siglo XVII)*. Cusco: Centro de Estudios Regionales Andinos, Bartolomé de las Casas.

Shimada, Izumi, and James L. Fitzsimmons, eds. 2015. *Living with the Dead in the Andes*. Tucson, AZ: University of Arizona Press.

Tello, Julio C. 1960. *Chavín, cultura matriz de la civilización andina: Con revisión de Toribio Mejía Xesspe*. Lima: Imprenta de la Universidad Nacional Mayor de San Marcos.

Thompson, Sinclair. 2002. *We Alone Will Rule: Andean Politics in the Age of Insurgency*. Madison, WI: University of Wisconsin Press.

Tineo Morón, Melecio. 2016. *Catálogo de la Serie Documental de Curatos del Archivo del Obispado de Huacho (1600–1979)*. Lima: Quellca.com.

Weber, David John, Félix Cayco Zambrano, Teodoro Cayco Villar, and Marlene Ballena Dávila. 1998. *Rimaycuna: Quechua de Huánuco: Diccionario del quechua del Huallaga con índices castellano e inglés*. Lima: Instituto Lingüístico de Verano.

4

SONGS FOR HERDS AND CROPS

(and thoughts about religious experience)

with Luis Andrade Ciudad[1]

When a Rapaz villager needs the favor of a mountain, lake, *ila* lifestone, or ancestor, he murmurs this Quechua invocation:

> Mana musyaq, mana yatraq
> "wawaa, tsurii" nimay.

My bilingual friend and neighbor Néstor Cóndor wrote it down thus in my notebook. He puzzled over it, then, very tentatively, suggested a Spanish gloss:

> Aunque no sepamos, ni anunciamos [el saber]
> Considérenos como tus hijos.

Putting this beautiful little Quechua couplet into English baffles me. Both lines make Quechua distinctions—about knowing, about parenthood—that lack English as well as Spanish equivalents. Moreover, Quechua's system of optional number marking makes the speaker of the sentence ambiguous between "I" and "we." In translating Néstor chose "we," perhaps just because he happened to be sitting with his wife.

> Though we cannot guess, though we cannot tell,
> Call us "my children," "my own."

The Quechua verbs in Néstor's invocation translated as "to guess" and "to tell" divide up the notion of knowledge in a way that escapes English. *Musyay* denotes the speculative, intuitive, or subjective aspect of knowing such as guessing and imagining, while *yatray* denotes the articulate, practical, speakable aspect of knowing. The *musyaq*/*yatraq* pair reminds us that parallel usage of similar-meaning words (sometimes called "thought rhyme" or "semantic parallelism") is a richly elaborated vein in Quechua poetics (and in many other languages); as Mannheim emphasized, it is an implied play of concepts (1998). In any language, poetic art plays with the specific properties of that language. And thought rhyme nowhere near exhausts the translation challenges of these seven words.[2]

Like Néstor's little invocation, ritual language is often poetic language. Some anthropological linguists have parsed out linguistic tendencies typical of sacred speech across many cultures. They include (for example) constrained choices of intonation, fixity of form, and specialized, archaistic vocabulary (Bloch 1989, 25). The liturgical core of language used in Kaha Wayi ritualism, namely a series of murmured invocations and petitions, does have these properties. But its relatively inaudible voicing in performance tells any listener that these are not words for public ears. I therefore think it is better not to publish utterances that seem to fall within the sense of cultural privacy.

In this chapter we will consider instead a wider area of ritual language that surrounds core liturgical language and amplifies it (Keane 1997, 52–55). It consists of songs for public functions (work days, celebrations) taking place under *balterno* authority. Coca-sharing, speeches of exhortation, displays of staff and flower insignia, "work crosses," and minute-taking delimit the ritual frame. We will look at ritual-linked songs in order of increasing emotional pitch, from cheerful outdoor work songs to verses of somber intensity in a closed all nighter. Each kind of verse intensifies a certain state of mind: murmured invocations in Kaha Wayi concentrate one on determined solemnity; field labor songs charge up bodily energy and solidarity; and night songs for the lifestones evoke loyalty and closeness to them.

Toward the end of the chapter, we will take up a question that almost everyone brings to Anthropology of Religion courses: what is all this intensity about anyway? Several theories try to explain the association between the programmed, highly structured quality of ritual on the one hand and on the other the exalted, excited, or altered states of mind that often go with it.

The family of theories that concentrate on religious experience as such is known as phenomenological theory, of which we will sketch older and newer variants. Phenomenological anthropology is quite different from other approaches because the subject is neither biological substrates, nor observable behaviors, nor shared institutions. It offers theories of experience. Phenomenological theories are no less psychological than cognitive theories, but unlike the latter they are concerned specifically with impressions inside the individual's head. They are about seeming not being: that is, about the way the world appears and feels to people who share a given religion as an inculcated subjectivity. Harder-headed social scientists may see subjectivities as mental gossamer, too subtle to grasp with responsible methods. Yet for ethnographers who take "the native's point of view" as their grail, it seems only realistic to consider religiosity as a matter of "lifeworlds," that is, worlds as known in personal consciousness.

Quechua, a vulnerable giant

We will be approaching ritual intensity via Rapaz ritual language and song and therefore via Quechua. For those unfamiliar with this giant among Amerindian languages, a short briefing should be useful.

In Rapaz, Quechua as a general-purpose language is almost gone. Nonetheless songs in the Kaha Wayi tradition are performed in Quechua or not at all. In 2007, the linguist Luis Andrade Ciudad joined me to study the local variety of Quechua and especially ritual songs connected to Kaha Wayi, Pasa Qulqa, and Santa Rosa's cycle (which includes a drama about the last Inkas). Santa Rosa is the Catholic patron saint of Rapaz.

Quechua is often misleadingly called the language of the Inkas. Inka rulers did speak one kind of Quechua, but the time when Quechua became their imperial administrative tongue forms a late, short chapter in Quechua's much longer story. Dialectologists today recognize two major branches of the Quechua family. The variety labeled as the Inka language belongs to the branch now called Quechua II, a widespread group of tongues found over vast stretches of both the southern Peruvian Andes into Bolivia and Argentina, and also, separately, a large stretch of northern Peru into Ecuador and Colombia, including parts of Amazonia.

In the space between these two Quechua II areas lies the central-Peruvian terrain called Quechua I.[3] Linguists think Quechua I had probably been in use in central Peru for a long time before Quechua II developed. As is typical of languages spoken over a long era within a limited territory, Quechua I shows a dense proliferation of local varieties (Cerrón-Palomino 1987).[4] After a detailed study in terms of sound system, morphology, syntax, and lexicon, Luis Andrade Ciudad concluded that the Quechua of Rapaz belongs to the variety called Yaru (Andrade 2011).

Yaru and Pacaraos Quechua, which have mutual resemblances, belong to the area where highlanders called themselves llacuaces (Chapter 1; Adelaar 1986, 3).[5]

With up to ten million speakers, the Quechua languages form a giant constellation among native American tongues. But it is a vulnerable giant, now suffering rapid attrition. Yaru Quechua, like nearly all Quechua I varieties, has become an endangered language. In Rapaz only people over about fifty use it in daily conversation. Most of these are women, particularly herdswomen who spend a lot of time in remote puna outposts. Rapaz parents stopped teaching Quechua to their children several decades ago, so most youngsters only know scattered phrases. This situation signals impending language death.

Two forces are swiftly eroding Central Quechua. The first is that schooling promotes Spanish and demotes Quechua. Even before Rapaz had a public school (that is, before 1970), privately contracted teachers urged parents to stop using Quechua at home. Peru adopted a government program for bilingual-bicultural education in the 1970s but the Ministry of Education has not applied it to Rapaz's school because the ministry does not consider the town sufficiently bilingual. Rapaz public school teachers who know and like Quechua are constrained by a curriculum that leaves it no room. The only public part Quechua plays in Rapaz schools is a pageant consisting of an infantile version of the "Encounter of the Inkas" (*Inka Tinkuy*), a folk drama played at the festival of Santa Rosa.

Because parents are anxious for their children to master the one language which will help in competing for urban jobs, they rarely resist anti-Quechua policies. On the contrary, many seem to have absorbed a mistaken notion that being bilingual will prevent children from acquiring good Spanish. One woman remembered, "My father used to say, 'If you just keep talking Quechua, I'm going to cut out your tongue.'"[6]

The second force undercutting Quechua is the denigration of central-Peruvian Quechua I relative to southern or Cuzco Quechua II. Patriotic intellectuals without training in linguistics have long exalted the so-called language of the Inkas as *qhapaq simi* (the "noble tongue"). They belittle all other dialects as deviations from what they consider to be Peru's classical language (Coronel-Molina 2008; Coronel-Molina 2015, 107–141). This premise is woven deep into patriotic cultural discourse and local indigenism (Niño-Murcia 1995).

Alicia Gallardo is a shopkeeper and native of Rapaz whose grandfather worked as a freelance teacher up to 1943. She recalls the effects:

> My mother used to say to me: "Your grandfather told me that around here people talk dialect, and you shouldn't learn it, because it's not good Quechua." [Alicia's grandfather said:] "You're wasting your time talking those dialects. Those dialects are no use. The real Quechua is in Cuzco."
>
> But my mom used to say, "Well, [I'll teach you] just so you'll know that Quechua does exist in Rapaz." And she would teach us to count: huk, ishkay, kima, trusku, pisqa, huqta, qantris, puwa, isqun, trunka. Only that far. And Mom didn't want us to talk any more than that, because it wasn't the real thing.
>
> One time I saw . . . television in Lima, and it said, "Tawa kanal Limamanta Pacha," right? And my Mom said to me, "See? It doesn't say *trusku* but instead *tawa* [four]. So our Quechua is mistaken. And it's not Quechua. And so don't practice it." And this is the reason why she didn't let us.[7]

What Alicia recalled is a classic example of a linguistic stigma or shibboleth. The TV broadcast she mentioned was a short-lived Quechua channel that the revolutionary nationalist government of Juan Velasco Alvarado sponsored at the end of the 1960s. Its name meant "Channel Four from Lima." The word for "four" happens to be a glaring indicator of regional speech, and hence of prestige. *Tawa* is the high-status southern word, as compared to central Peruvian *trusku*. Alicia's mother had been taught that the noble Inkas spoke using *tawa* (for example, in the name of their empire, Tawantinsuyu). So she supposed that people who say *trusku* are on the low side of a status distinction. Alicia and lots of others gave up on her family's Yaru language, thinking it would bring a stigma on them.

But in one respect, and one only, Rapaz goes against the tide of extinction: it conserves Yaru Quechua as the special language of ritual. The youngest ritualist of

FIGURE 4.1 From handwritten rehearsal books, young women learn Quechua songs of the *Pallas* or princesses for the pageant "Encounter of the Inkas." Photo by the author.

the village and heir apparent to the role of *bendelhombre*, Fidencio Alejo, was born around 1970. He prefers Spanish in conversation, but he is a rigid Quechua traditionalist when he conducts ceremony. His ritual Quechua is fluid, moving, and rich. Villagers of the adult generation generally respect his standard and have feelings of propriety about it. If anybody lets Spanish creep into a ritual song, listeners find fault. Just because Rapaz does associate Quechua with venerable authority and legitimacy, people judge severely their own Quechua competence. Even people who can produce viable discourse say "I can't really talk it properly; my grandparents are the ones who know."

Whether Yaru Quechua can stabilize in its ritual niche is hard to guess. Ritual stabilization has happened in societies that maintain Latin, Hebrew, Quranic Arabic, Pali, or Sanskrit for ceremonious purposes. But this usually happens in societies that have formal structures to inculcate ritual speech, such as memorization schooling or Holy Scriptures. Teodosio Falcón, a past *bendelhombre* (see Figure 6.1), feels frustrated that the village has no specific way to teach ritual lore. Quechua is not normally written, the exception being hand-copied rehearsal books from which young women learn the song of the *pallas* or Inka princesses for the pageant *Inka Tinkuy* ("Encounter of the Inkas") (see Figure 4.1). Younger adults sometimes say they feel guilty about neglecting their linguistic legacy, even as they take pride in the village's high levels of Spanish literacy. What follows, then, is partly an ethnography of living ritual, but it also contains elements of "salvage ethnography."

Tinyas ("drum songs") as poetry for making life flourish

Our emphasis here is on songs for animals and plants in connection with the regime of Kaha Wayi and Pasa Qulqa (Rivera Andía 2003). The next few examples are *tinyas*: songs that convey human praise and energy toward growing things. The *tinya* is a handheld, single-skinned drum. Men and women both sing tinya but with different voices. Men sing in a high tenor, while women sing in a piercing falsetto. Both sexes sing solo, for long stretches, with loud steady energy, their throats and faces tensed. Tinya verses typically end with a special whoop: *Wahii! Ahii! Wii hii hii!* in Quechua, or Spanish ¡*Dice!* We recorded and Luis Andrade transcribed eighteen tinyas. Tinyas are a genre well known in ethnomusicology under various regional names.[8]

Tinyas for green beauties: breaking earth, planting seed potato, and cultivating

In 2005, Teodosio Falcón Ugarte sang from deep memories of his ritualist days a tinya for the beginning of the farming year. Breaking ground with hoes and plows is felt to be a somewhat transgressive necessity because it injures earth. This song expresses feelings of love and unease toward Mama Raywana, the female avatar of food, who is here imagined as present in seed potatoes. From it we get a first general idea of the poetics of farming.

Raywansitala naqanam kananqa
   Pikuy tambuman tamboraytⁱanki
Raywansitala manam nilaysu
   Naqam kananqa tamboraytⁱanki
Pikuy tambola nikushqalampam   5
Chikus grandispa delantilantraw
Ama, mamala, "manam", nilaysu.
Ama, matala, "manam", nilaysu.
   Waylapa tikⁱaypam tushuraytⁱanki
   Tushulaykitraw añulaykitraw   10
Ururu mashtaypam mashtaparaykⁱanki
Ururu mashtaypam mashtaparaykⁱanki
   Kumuneerula traykyamunanpaq
   Kumuneerula presentamuptin.
Raywanitala, pirwanitala   15
   Kushuru mashtaypam, mashtaparaykⁱanki
   Waylapa tikipam, tikiparaykⁱanki
Viva, vivala, kamachikuqla
Viva, vivala, mayordoomula
   Aykya faneegata truranki   20
   Aykya faneegam pwestaraykⁱanki

Alqasakuqla, ama nisunsu
   Naqash nombreshqa; naqash rirqushqan.
Alqay manaqtaq ombresitula
   Mayor ombrela uryayk^{y}atrarin   25
   Mayor ombrela qutuyk^{y}atrarin.
Wawalantasun trurayt^{y}ulashun
Wawalantasun pwestayt^{y}ulashun
   Amay, ombrela, "manam", nilaysu
   Kamachikuqla mayordoomola.   30
Dosi-dosita trurayt^{y}ulanki
Dosi-dosita pwestayt^{y}ulanki
   Kuru shamuptin, hielo shamuptin
   Kuru shamuptin, hielo shamuptin
Kamachikuqtri, mayordomotri   35
   Defendilanqa altolaykita
Tsaymi defendin qahapalata.
Kamachikuqmi defendilanqa
   Productolanta alpay kurunpaq
   Wawachalanta qarayk^{y}unanpa(q).   40
Viva, vivala, mayordoomola
Viva, vivala, kamachikuqla
   Wawalaykipaq defendilankim
   Kurulapita defendilankim.
Altuy shamuqta defendilankim   45
Altuy puriqta defendilankim
   Qaqapatapish.

A rough English version might be:

   Oh, Raywana dear, now it's ready.
      Where the pickaxe pierces earth, you're being buried.
   Oh, Raywana dear, don't say no.
      Right now you're being buried
   Where the pickaxe pierces earth, as was said,   5
   In front of everyone, big and small.
   Don't say no then, little mother.
   Don't say no then, little plant.
      As waylapa grass flourishes, that's how you'll dance
      In your dance, in your year.   10
As *ururu* algae spread [afloat], so you'll spread out
As *ururu* algae spread [afloat], so you'll spread out
For the arrival of comunero,
At the arrival of comunero.
Oh Raywana dear, oh little storehouse   15
   Like *kushuru* algae spread [afloat], you'll spread out

Like waylapa grass growing, you'll grow out.
Hurray, hurray, for the kamachikuq
Hurray, hurray for the mayordomo.
    How many bushels you'll lay away for us,
    How many bushels you'll set apart for us.   20
Oh bag-lifter, don't you say no
They say you're already appointed, already seen.
Oh officer, man, don't you deny it,
    The man in charge is [already] mounding,   25
    The man in charge is [already] hilling.
We're going to lay her babies away,
We're going to set her babies apart.
    Don't say no, man,
    Oh kamachikuq, oh mayordomo.   30
A dozen dozens you'll store away then,
A dozen dozens you'll put aside safe
    Even if the worm comes, even if a freeze comes
    Even if the worm comes, even if a freeze comes.
Maybe the kamachikuq, maybe the mayordomo   35
    Will defend [the crop] from the [cold of the] heights;
    Yes, he's the one who'll defend it from frost.
Yes, it's kamachikuq who will defend [it],
Defend the crop from worms in the earth
For the sake of feeding his [own] little babies.   40
Hurray, hurray for the mayordomo
Hurray, hurray for the kamachikuq
For the sake of your babies you'll defend [the crop],
You'll defend [it] from the worm.
From the encroaching [ice of the] heights you'll defend it;   45
From the stalking freeze you'll defend it,
    And also from the frost.

In the first verses, the female and sensuous character of agriculture comes to the fore: the singer comforts Raywana, the food mother, about the brutality of chopping earth and burying seed tubers. He or she solaces Raywana by foretelling her future beauty, when she emerges and matures as leafy plants. The greenery of potato bushes will be like the green *huaylapa* of the heights, waving along the curved slopes. Then the muddy hillside mess of a newly sown field will give way to a landscape as beautiful as wild grass on the mountainside.

Starting in line 11 Raywana is comforted with a different simile: in the coming season her greenery will spread out into its field as algae spreads out over water on the high lakes. The two kinds of algae the poem evokes are further discussed below.

As the poem advances from line 17, its voice shifts toward human beings, calling on people not to shirk the service of Raywana, or the needs of a hungry village. This shift brings a more commanding tone.

The poem says, elliptically, that the original sin of agriculture expressed in the Raywana myth will be reenacted as the agricultural cycle advances. The song says to her that the harvest will not be mere infanticide because at harvest time the workers will tenderly store her "babies" (tubers) in Pasa Qulqa (line 27). Raywana's babies will feed human babies. Some, as seed tubers, will reincarnate Raywana in the coming year.

The last part of the song (lines 31–47) celebrates the balterno officers of agriculture (Chapter 2) and exhorts them to be ready for heroic labors in defense of the growing crop. To "defend" against worms, cold, and frost as the song promises includes both policing the fields and making long ascetic sacrifices in Kaha Wayi, or contending with the mountains and lakes.

Phrases equivalent to "don't say no" are addressed both to Raywana and to people called to duty. They remind us of the political tone of the supra-household sphere: everything depends on cooperation, but authority has limited power to enforce it. Saying no, lagging, or making excuses endangers the common good. This rhetoric is typical of many kinds of Rapaz ritual language, whether addressed to mountains, people, or biota: affectionate wheedling goes together with implied threats. Esthetic pleasure goes together with anxiety about possible moral faults.

The direction-shifting dynamic as the song curves from an environment-loving perspective to a socially disciplinary one is a typical tinya dynamic, also found, for example, in tinyas for bringing the harvest to Pasa Qulqa (Salomon, Las Casas, and Falcón 2015). All examples begin as songs addressed to a sacred being and then turn to address people: officers, a ritualist, or workers. The song seems to swoop down from sacred space into the gritty here-and-now of toil, bringing exalted feelings to bear on the task at hand. It effects a conveyance of human *voluntad* ("goodwill, commitment") at once to superhumans and to fellow humans.

Tinyas about algae, canal cleaning, and irrigation

Two elder ladies, Santa Flores Evangelista and Teodora Falcón Altamirana[9] (see Figure 4.2), love the old songs even though they have converted to Protestant Christianity. When Teodora was the wife of a famous bendelhombre, she attended innumerable rituals. They included many years' canal-cleaning or water festivals, now discontinued because PVC pipes make the job unnecessary. At an age probably over eighty, Teodora still has a lovely bright-toned soprano voice, which she usually employs in piercing Andean falsetto.

To understand her songs, you have to know how much Rapacinos like algae. Vegetables always being scarce near the top of the biosphere, the edible algae of the lake (Nostoc and possibly others) make garnishes for soups and stews. Rapacinos consider algae beautiful as well as tasty. The way floating algae moves on waves is compared to silky green clothing on a moving body.

When Teodora sings about Chinchaycocha Lake, she is carrying on a deep tradition. The Inkas subsidized what was already in their time an ancient Chinchaycocha cult (Duviols 1974, 292). In 1603 the unknown cleric who reported on the

FIGURE 4.2 Teodora Falcón Altamirana outside her house. Photo by the author.

region's "errors," and later the pioneer extirpator Albornoz (Chapter 3), both noted that highlanders revered Chinchaycocha because it was the mythic place where camelids first emerged into human life. The old-time *yndios* may not have been far off archaeologically, since the site of Telarmachay, considered the oldest clear hearth of camelid domestication, is close to Chinchaycocha.[10] Singing about or to Chinchaycocha might then express an extraordinarily deep mythohistoric memory: the most conservative readings of Telarmachay put domestication earlier than 2500 BCE (Pinto et al. 2010, 27).

This Chinchaycocha song belonged to the canal-cleaning contest discussed in Chapter 1. Teodora starts by invoking Lake Chinchaycocha as the place from which Rapaz's two springs flow. She calls the lake a bendelhombre, or being who blesses humanity with welfare (lines 1–2). In Chinchaycocha's presence she calls us to honor water (lines 3–4).

Chinchayqutrala,
   Bendelumbrela
Náqanam urala,
   náqanam diala

Oh Chinchaycocha,
   Oh blessing on people,
Right now is the hour,
   Right now is the day.

She means the day for dredging canals, which entails offerings to the lake. In the verses that follow she poses a series of questions and answers that effect the tinya swoop: they shift the center of attention from the sacred lake to the natural setting around it.

Teodora's poetic voice asks where three kinds of edible algae come from: *kushuru*, *ururu*, and *rasapa*. And what she discovers, with a note of happy surprise in her voice, is that the hitherto vague place algae comes from is right "here," on Chinchaycocha. What seemed scarce and distant is revealed to be close at hand, as deictically indicated by *kay* "this" (lines 6, 8, 12, and 14).

Maylay i-kúshurum?	5
Kaylay i-kúshuruy	
i-Maylay i-úrurum?	
Kaylay i-úruruy	
Chinchay-i-qutrala,	
táriray ómbrela	10
Tsaylay i-úrurum,	
kaylay i-úruruy	
Maylay i-rásapam?	
Kaylay i-rásapay	
Chinchay-i-qutra rásapam,	15
kaylay i-rásapay	

Where from kushuru?	5
This is my kushuru.	
Where from ururu?	
This is my ururu.	
Oh, Chinchaycocha –	
Find it, then, people:	10
That there is ururu,	
This is my ururu.	
Where from rasapa?	
This is my rasapa.	
Chinchaycocha rasapa,	15
This is my rasapa.	

The dominant line has two dactylic feet. Within each line, the third syllable of the first foot is a sound /i/ that has rhythmic effect but no verbal sense. Teodora's /i/ has an exaggeratedly abrupt glottis-opening onset and glottal-stop ending, making a clean *tick* of voice. It makes one think of a drummer clicking the rim of his trap on the off beat. In lines 5–8 above, and other places, the effect of this midline sound is to accentuate a swinging alternation pattern: "where?"—"here"—"where?"—"here." The strophes seem to jump back and forth between far and near in a way suggestive of dance—probably the brisk *huaylash* dance associated with water festivities.

Canal cleaning is done from the top of the system downward, first through main canals and then (in smaller crews) ramifying out along field-irrigating ditches. The next and final series of verses proceeds as if in such an imagined downstream motion. It praises the lake indirectly by saying how thirsty the workers feel as they get farther away from it. It is a song of longing for the moment of water release, when water will rush down from the top of the system into Rapaz's water taps and irrigation ditches.

In line 19 the "I" in Teodora's voice laments the lack of water (lines 19–20) and fears drying up (lines 21–22). Then there is a sudden dramatic resolution in lines 23–24. She answers herself affirming, as if it were a revelation, that water and food are everywhere around us.

> Maypim asequiala
>   Shalaamunkiqa
> Ay, nuqalaymi,
>   yaku-u-nayla   20
> Ay, nuqalaymi,
>   saki-i-kulay
> i-Maypim i-yákunay,
> i-maypim míchanay.

> Canal, coming along
> Through wherever—
> Ah poor me,
>   thirsting for water   20
> Ah poor me,
>   all drying up.
> —My water is everywhere!
> —My food is everywhere!

The final couplet is a triumphant cry of relief and pleasure, bursting forward, as if symbolizing the moment when water freshly released from the lake bursts forth at Rapaz's public water outlets. These first fruits of water were caught in a special bowl and taken to Kaha Wayi for blessing and preservation while people celebrated and tossed water playfully at each other. The dance was called *paqtsa*, "waterfall." This allusion completes the song's joyful transit from high to low, from sacred to human, and from lake to village.

Night songs of the animal powers

For a llacuaz-like people, of course, animals' rites matter at least as much as agricultural ritual songs. Teodora Falcón remembers:

> The widows sang tinyas, the *camporas* [wives of balternos], the herdswomen, the cowgirls. With their small drum they'd go along drumming, pom-pom-pom. They used to take the animals to town for inspection in the plaza, singing tinyas and decorating them with ribbons. Their [the animals'] talismans lived in Kaha Wayi and there they [the widows] sang for them.

The roundup (*marcación*, *señalakuy*, and other terms) relocated after Rapaz won back the great expanse called Lot 29 in 1963 and built up its expanding cooperative. Herds, especially cattle herds, became too big and too distant to bless and brand in town. Animal-specific rites and objects then came to live on the heights of Jankil, at the location whose songs we will discuss below.[11]

The lonely corral Jankil is way up near the cordillera crest. It was once a herding station of the Algolán estate. A little house next to it was built as lodging for estate herders. But now, on ritual nights, this little house called Jankil Wayi has become something like a herding counterpart or branch of Kaha Wayi. Jankil also has a bureaucratic name, *centro ganadero* ("livestock center"), and is reserved for communal herds only.[12] It serves the community's herd of sheep, another of cattle, and a third of alpacas. Each species has its turn at the wet-season roundup in February and again at the dry-season roundup in June or July.

The kamachikuq, or vice-president, today has as his counterpart the mayordomo or herd manager. Just as the kamachikuq commands a small corps of agricultural officers, the mayordomo has both senior and junior *pastores*, or designated herdsmen, at least one for each species in the communal herd. And just as the kamachikuq with his balterno corps is responsible for administering field rights and field use, the mayordomo is responsible for recording the numbers of animals according to their reproductive categories each winter and summer. He also administers the branding or earmarking of new animals, veterinary treatment and salt feeding, reproduction, and protection from predators or rustlers. (Security is no small matter; rustlers with military weapons commit homicides as well as stealing herd animals.)

Almost every Andean ethnography has something to say about the over-the-top festivities at roundup, of which North America's western rodeo circuit seems like a domesticated relative. In the nearby Chancay watershed, Alejandro Vivanco Guerra compiled a magnificently verse-rich ethnography of pastoralism circa 1960, recently rescued from obscurity by Juan Javier Rivera Andía (2012; see also Arnold and Yapita 2001 from Bolivia and Dransart 2001 from Chile). The classic high points of the roundup include athletic dance and song, the ritual feeding of animal effigies, cattle wrangling, care of the "loving stone" (*khuyaq rumi*) buried in the corral's center, and animal-human parties during which livestock wear garlands and people wear harness bells.

At roundup time people set aside in-town discipline and celebrate the carnal side of life. (The wet-season roundup occurs close to Carnival season and is sometimes called Carnival.) Branding day is the day for playful flirtation and wild, risky games. I once heard a teenager relish an upcoming roundup by saying "It'll be savage!" That day I saw a young and normally decorous woman wrangle a young bull to the ground, sit on his neck, grasp his horns in her hands and thump his head in the dirt while shouting outrageous sexual brags.

At nearby Mayobamba 45 years ago, an ethnographic crew witnessed a really rambunctious roundup.[13] Since their report has become almost forgotten, it deserves quoting:

After the branding and re-ribboning of the cattle and the distribution of the llama *pachamanca* [earth-baked meat feast] a dionysian chapter ensued as the woman in charge of the village cattle and village favorites were "branded." A group of men would run a person down, lasso her with braided leather ropes, and wrestle her to the ground, while a hot iron was prepared in the fire. The fiery brand was used to menace the victim, but burned off on a tied dog's fur before being pressed in mock marking on the personage's buttocks.

In revenge attack, some branded persons hunted down their branders and chased bystanders to stab at them with the awl-like knife used to punch holes in the cows' ears. The chase and scattering animated all villagers into a frenzy. The air was bacchanalian. Although shots of liquor had been toasted regularly along the rows of men and women in turn, only a few were notably intoxicated. The source of the frenzy which erupted was more the generated communal excitement of unusual and energetic emotional outlets.

So enlivened, the villagers adjourned to the square, driving the cows and llamas before them in the moonless night, chanting, dancing and drumming. In the obscurity, candles and a Petromax lamp were used to open the chapel, bring forth the Saint John image and seat him on his calves and baby llamas. Drunken men held the statue securely on each animal, and danced the terrified beasts in circles, threatening all in the ring of on-lookers with the nascent horns, except those in the safe grouping of chanting women and drum-beating men. After burlesque turns on about five of the calves and two llamas, St. John was retired to his litter at the church altar. The llamas were corralled and the cattle driven back to the community's alfalfa patch. Most people went home for supper although many men stayed on to drink in the community assembly hall.

Morris et al. 1968, 256–257

"Bacchanalian"—but that does not mean cattle festivities lack ritual proprieties. In Rapaz, each household attends carrying a white cloth, coca, tobacco, wine, a medium-sized Peruvian flag, and a leather lasso, whether the rite is for a family herd or a communal one.

A cycle takes three days. The corral area is prepared with a ritual array or mesa, ribbons, coca, tobacco, red and white carnations, candy, and treats including apples or oranges for the mountain power. One round of coca-taking is called *pasa cerro*, asking permission to tread on the mountains. A person who takes a lot of coca ("works a lot") will have good increase. Cows, camelids and sheep get a drink of liquor laced with "medicine" and a portion of coca. Bright multicolor tassels are tied into animals' ears as *unanchay*, "signals" of ownership. Irene Luya Condor explains that:

There is a mesa [a small underground chamber of ritual items] hidden under one stone of the corral wall: three *poronguitos* [small gourds] of white, black and *kuti* jurka [liquified corn of the same three colors used in Kaha Wayi], bottles of wine, pisco and anisado [liquors], and candy, all hidden. At the end, when the account was done and the new animals branded, and everyone had taken plenty of coca, the new mayordomo would dance around in the corral throwing candies to the animals.

An overtone of danger is never lacking. Herd rituals are journeys to the far edge of civilized life, therefore a close encounter with hungry and dangerous powers. This idea is closely bound with the ideal of Llacuaz valor and aggressiveness. Luis and I were cautioned several times about taking part in the roundup at Jankil. People said, "Be careful, people sometimes die in their sleep up there." When we failed to see the implied point, a franker warning came that bad characters can use the occasion for surreptitious human sacrifice. During roundup nights one must stay awake and exert coca-enhanced mental energy, willing oneself to stay in touch and in favor with the mountain power. If a person nods off at Jankil, a neighbor has an opportunity to "sell" the weakling to the mountain as a sacrifice (by passing his coca leaves over the victim). This betrayer will receive unnatural good luck with herds. The sleeper will soon die. Suspicious illnesses are sometimes explained this way, as is suspiciously sudden prosperity.

Ila or lifestones

Ever since the 17th century, *ila* for plants and herds have been described by outsiders as "amulets" or "talismans."[14] In colonial times these words denoted genuinely effective magical technology. Today, the same words have acquired belittling meanings: they suggest mere lucky charms. But *ila*, like the similarly "folklorized" Hopi word *kachina* and the Scandinavian word *troll*, was originally a term for awesome beings. In Quechua it still is.

Ilas are never made. They must be found by luck, usually at high elevations. There are greater and lesser ilas, from grape size up to brick size, and their powers vary. In central Peru, ilas are usually natural stones with animal-like or crop-like shapes. Others are fossil ammonites with ram's-horn shapes or horn-like stalactites. Ila-seeking is a constant quest. Sometimes one may be helped by animals who find them while nosing around for salt (Flores Ochoa 1977).

Ila are said to have voices. Sometimes one hears the bleat or moo of what seems to be a lost animal but turns out to be an ila that wants to be found. Ilas need to be tended in protective boxes, with cloth and ribbons, coca and gifts. If they don't feel well served, they make themselves get lost again. If buried together, they multiply. They "have their time" at roundup. Celebrants then take them out of their secret storage places and set them up near a main pasture or a corral. Ilas are sung to, given offerings, and finally returned to hiding or reburied. Putting sheep tails, ears, or offerings near them is called "sowing" them, suggesting that sacrifice is a form of cultivation in the animal realm. "Daring families keep their ilas in boxes in their homes. . . . Many villagers consider ilas to be unsafe, due to their power of sucking human blood to increase their efficacy . . . The death of a woman who spat and secreted blood, was attributed to the box of ilas in her house" (Morris et al. 1968, 136–137). Behavior around ilas reminded me of protocols for handling radioactivity.

Ilas have vivid personalities. People love but also fear important ones. Cattle ilas are overbearing, gigantic spirits in animal form, and humans have only fragile social bonds with them. Juan Mario Alejo Gallardo explained that:

> The ilas ask the mountains for rain and pasture grass, and also ask that the predators such as puma, fox, and condor shouldn't damage the animals. . . . there has to be a special place in the estancias, because ilas might eat children if they saw them. They're dangerous because they demand their service from people, they require it. It should be the Mayordomo [of the village] or the *patrón*-owner-father who calls on them. This duty goes from fathers to sons. The firstborn son should inherit it.

Mario then explains that Yanabotella is Rapaz's most powerful bull ila.

> Yanabotella was found in Kaha Wayi when they were building a wall for the house of Don Manuel [a neighbor adjacent to the precinct]. Yanabotella has a smooth shape, like cattle. Yanabotella had escaped mysteriously [from a previous sojourn with Rapacinos] because he was displeased with his pay- ment. The builders were preparing earth to make clay plaster, and they found him. The man in charge gathered him up, washed him, and performed his warming-up rite, his *qunupada* with llama fat. They guarded him with [the famous cow ila] Kintalera Ruywa.[15] People got happy and took coca in Kaha Wayi. That was 1985, when I joined the community.

Yanabotella is now the supreme ila at the Jankil livestock center. He comes out on roundup nights to reign with his consorts the great cow ilas Kintalera and Pariacata.

Up late with the ilas in Jankil

Fidencio Alejo, the heir-apparent to become bendelhombre, was in 2007 also the mayordomo of communal livestock. Despite warnings about surreptitious magical sacrifice, we accepted his invitation to join the community in celebrating the ilas at Jankil's summer roundup.

One afternoon all the herdsmen saddled their horses, prepared packsacks, and journeyed up to the tawny high pastures of Jankil, accompanied by only one woman, the cook. The train of horsemen filed along the vertiginous water canyon of Punguyuq, then trudged up past green terraces of an agricultural sec- tor into the upper pasturelands of Lot 29, finally arriving at windy Jankil, just below the cordillera pass over to Rancas. As the gilded late-afternoon light faded, frost hardened to crystal-patterned ice on the rivulets that wind through a water meadow. The cook doled out a rustic supper. Herdsmen crowded by starry twilight into the windowless little adobe house.

FIGURE 4.3 The ila Yanabotella in the cattle shrine box during the nighttime rites at Jankil. Photo by the author.

Pitch blackness descended on the interior. A single candle mounted on a bench glimmered in one corner. There Fidencio emplaced the prepared box containing the ilas. Luis and I peered over the heads of men as they settled down. Dimly at the far corner we could see by candlelight, animals of black rock tethered in a tiny garden of coca (see Figure 4.3). Their rounded shapes looked like the sculptor Henry Moore's animal forms. The two biggest ilas occupied the center of the shrine: the great bull Yanabotella, called "the boss who takes care of everyone," and the great cows Kintalera and Paria Kata. In each corner of the box corsages of red and white carnations nestled in cigarettes.

Dozens of cattlemen jostled as they found spots on the floor, then sat down cross-legged bumping shoulders. The interior became full, then jammed. As cold descended horse-blankets were folded into impromptu robes or sleeping bags. Quietly at the start, Fidencio signaled the beginning of the "turns" of "work," meaning coca-taking. Round after round we sucked coca, huddled in the murk and squirming for space. At the end of each round we handed in our "work" (used coca wads), then sipped from a kettle of hot Fanta mixed with white rum. Murmuring subsided to silence—but a wakeful silence.

It felt strange to be wedged into a crowd of silently, concentratedly thinking, semi-tipsy men in the dark. Coca time is time for quiet, for a buildup of "will" and concentration. Despite the roughneck air of the gathering I never doubted its sacred nature, so strongly did I feel the cowpokes around me cultivating an intense, shared, interior state of mind. As the night advanced all of us nestled body to body. The crowd became dense enough so that if one man tucked his knees the movement would ripple through the crowd. Packed-in bodily contact makes for abnormal sensitivity to neighbors' small motions and breathing. The crowd seemed a single close web of feelings.

Later when I asked about it, that state of mind was usually described as *voluntad* "will," a word that implies both willpower and goodwill. Willpower entails strong mental focus on addressing and persuading the ilas and on desirously visualizing their favor. Goodwill entails a swell of affection, longing, and generous loyalty to them. The desired state of mind is mostly inward; during long intervals of silence barely a murmur between friends would be tolerated. Everyone must be alert for signs that the ilas might give. The man with voluntad must be on edge, reaching out in his mind for signs, so that a tiny spark, sizzle, or moving candle shadow can arrive as the word of an ila. It is the ritualist's challenge to keep evoking crescendos of receptive, electrifying, but still silent voluntad through the long, cold night.

Fidencio's back stayed turned to us as he finished small tasks over the box of animal powers. He passed a package of gathered hoofprints over the llama-fat incense. He readied a length of red ribbon for lassoing Yanabotella. He prepared the ilas' elixir in reserved bottles ritually referred to as mountains, murmuring invocations. Formally he saluted the ilas on the part of the Rapaz Communal Enterprise and offered them gifts—"our *cariños*" or endearments.

Sometime around midnight, whispering died out and only breathing hung in the air. From the ila shrine came not a spark or a sound. I felt as if we were a crew of astronauts packed in a capsule hanging in the blackness of outer space.

Suddenly, to the thumping of the small drum, Fidencio loosed from his throat the tense, anguished tinya of the animals. (It is transcribed and translated in the next section.) His sudden cry reminded me of the flamenco song *saeta*, a devotional genre whose name derives from Latin *sagitta* "arrow."

Into the cold morning hours, coca kept making its rounds marking breaks from "turn" to "turn." At each turn Fidencio called out in song to the ilas and asked the mountains about the coming year of pasturage. Before the muzzles of the stone animals, llama fat smoldered in its offering bowl. Fidencio coaxed them to talk through combustion, urging forth "stars" (sparks), making the soft "tsk tsk tsk" sound herdsmen use to calm nervous animals. Between songs he murmured reassurances to Kintalera, Yanabotella, and Paria Kata that the men had plentiful good will.

"Give us three stars, give us four stars," he urged. Silence. Aside, to the assistants called his "service" he said, "They're jealous. Skittish. They're fidgeting, they're shoving." He grunted in frustration. The mesa was turning difficult. "Ah. Ah. Ay. Oah. . . . live peacefully, live, old chola," he reassures Kintalera.[16] Thicker and thicker the greasy, spicy smoke of offering hung in the air. Fidencio began to speak brusquely to the dark box, as one losing patience with unreasonable people. Tension ran through the room. The stone animals refused to reply. Fidencio let out a sigh, whispering, "They don't want to talk to us. They're being harsh, not showing good will." He coaxed the embers, asking for sparks: "stars, three stars, four stars."

After a tense time, the embers sparkled a little. Even in the blackness we could feel arms and shoulders starting to relax. After that, Fidencio's renderings of the ila songs took on more full-throated, less anguished tones, and finally expanded to a triumphal volume. As sparks became more frequent, Fidencio led the herdsmen away from tension toward satisfaction, now allowing those who wished to sing tinya join him in chorus. About three a.m., he felt the work was done, the ilas reassured. The crowd lay back, still in the dark. The reverent context gradually dissolved into a sociable one, with a few huaynos of romance sung before the exhausted cowpokes dropped into sleep.

The next morning, aching in hips and shoulders, we hauled ourselves off the floor to share a breakfast of mutton broth and deliciously scorched, chewy "jerky bread." Cattle woke up lowing in the stone pens as herdsmen prepared for the day's work. Herdsmen fired up the branding irons and snipped bright yarn for ear-tassels, full of wisecracks because this was the day for playing with bulls. As soon as Fidencio formally handed the herd over to its new herdsmen, senior cowboys turned loose the most villainous old bulls hoping they were still dangerous. They goaded promising yearlings in search of bold challengers for the coming (August) bullfights in town. Men continually leapt out into the corral, prodding bulls into sudden lunges. Those who got knocked down laughed, gasped, and scrambled up onto the rock fence inches ahead of charging horns.

Throughout the day of play-fighting, counting animals, and checking the herd's health, Fidencio alternated between tinya-ing and writing statistics in the Community's notebook (see Figure 4.4). By the fading of afternoon everyone was coated with dust and powdered dung, high on animal power, and a little tipsy. Luis Andrade recorded the action at corral-side. The analysis that follows is based on two recordings taken during the bullfighting, and two from the nocturnal ceremony, as well as subsequent conversations with Fidencio.

Tinyas for cattle in ritual and roundup

It might seem odd that the stirring tinya dedicated to cattle ilas starts with a vocative to two kinds of wild puna grass (*kalwa* and *chilwa*), calling them "unloved" and "not cherished."

> Ay, kalwalaa, kalwalasitalaa
> Ay, chilwalaa, chilwalasitalay
>   Mana kuyaqu(q), kalwalasitalay
>   Mana waylluku(q), chilwalasitalaa
>
> Ay, little *kalwa* plant; oh my little kalwa
> Ay, *chilwa* reed; oh my little chilwa,
>   Oh my little kalwa plant unloved,
>   Oh my little chilwa reed not cherished.

FIGURE 4.4   Fidencio Alejo sings cattle tinyas at the July 2007 roundup. Photo by the author.

But this stanza makes sense in the context of the ritual chamber. Fidencio was addressing uncertainty about gaining the magic animals' favor. Yanabotella, the father-bull, is famously jealous and moody; it is not easy to get him to talk. On this night, for an hour or more, incense embers had failed to sparkle because Yanabotella was hanging back in an unfriendly humor.

The quatrain about wild plants that grow in upper pastures is a highly elliptical passage intended to reassure Yanabotella of Rapaz' devotion. Its unfolded sense is something like this: "[Yanabotella, know this: our love is not diluted by any other love. Seeing the] kalwa plant [of your puna] we do not feel loving. [Seeing the] chilwa reed we do not feel cherishing. [Our love is only for you.]"

In the wee hours after the offering, some of the men, as they intermittently dozed on the floor, said that they felt both happy to have attended and regretful about having "forgotten the old one" and failed to take part in recent "fulfilments" (*cumplimientos*) of ritual debt. It was in this context our friend Néstor murmured the invocation that heads this chapter.

In this context, too, we better understand the sobs and panting breaths that punctuated Fidencio's performance. Emotive sounds expressed the mental state proper to devotional acts. The points of insertion of sobs and gasps within the tinya seems not to obey any prosodic pattern nor do they attach to any meaningful phrase. Rather sobs and panting mimic emotion in tension with the beat of prosody.

Linguists including Jane Hill (1990), William Labov (1997), and Labov and Waletski (1967) observe that performances regularly contain vocal elements that are not words at all, and not "sound symbolism" (onomatopoeia) either, but rather sounds that are supposed to come involuntarily from a total body-mind state. A sob, a laugh, a gasp of pain, a sensuous sigh, a catch in the throat or an off-key note are strong rhetorical acts precisely because they mimic immediate psychosomatic responses—the farthest thing from conscious, manipulative talking. They attach to the speaker-and-his-speech as a package (rather than to speech's referential content). These language devices beyond words embody what Webb Keane would call the characteristic "semiotic ideology" of Rapaz ritual speech (Lambek 2013, 138). The ritualist offers speech in which an appropriate inner state—unguarded sincerity or voluntad—seems to override speech's normal anchorings in reference, deixis, etc.

The first 23 lines of the midnight tinya have the same overall architecture already discussed, that is, a swoop of imagination from the superhuman down to the immediate human here-and-now. In this song animal powers are welcomed into human company. The bull ila and cow ilas are called in as if from their pasture. Where shall they come home to? They are called to come and inhabit their stone effigy bodies, which have been made comfortable in a nest-box full of coca and decorations, right "here," at Jankil.

Ay waya yaya, ay wayay yayay	
Ay waya yaya, ay wayay yayay	
Ay waya yaya, ay wayay yayay	5
Ay waya yaya, ay wayay yayay	
Ay, kalwala, kalwalasitalaa	
Ay, chilwalaa, chilwalasitalay	
Mana kuyaqu(q), kalwalasitalay	
Mana waylluku(q), chilwalasitalaa	10
Pimi, mayshi, torrupadrilay?	
Pimi, mayshi, vakamadrilaa?	
Yanabotéllashi torrupadrilay	
Paryakátala, Ruywasítala	
Kintaléralashi, vacamadrilaa.	15

Maylawtrawshi kantralanran?
Maylawtrawshi rodyulanran?
    Hankill pampa rodyulanray
    Mesay formádulay, mesay postádulaa
Añulapita, watalapita,   20
Yarpanqansiqaa
    Naqami kanan trurarraykan
    Naqami kanan postarraykan.

Transcription: Luis Andrade Ciudad[17]

Ay waya yaya, ay wayay yayay
Ay waya yaya, ay wayay yayay
Ay waya yaya, ay wayay yayay   5
Ay waya yaya, ay wayay yayay
Ay, little *kalwa* plant; oh my little kalwa
Ay, *chilwa* reed; oh my little chilwa,
Oh my little kalwa plant unloved,
Oh my little chilwa reed not cherished.   10
Who and where could he be, my bull father?
Who and where could she be, my cow mother?
    Oh, Yanabotella is my bull father they say,
    Oh, Paryakata, Ruywasita,
    Kintalera are my cow mothers they say.   15
And where could their corral be?
And where could their rodeo be?
    Their corral is right on Jankil flat:
    My ready little mesa, my mesa all set.
From time to time, from year to year   20
As we have remembered,
    Now the mesa is being placed,
    At this moment it's being set.

When the ritualist feels sure his superhuman cattle have come alive in their "corral," i.e., the coca-lined shrine box, he proceeds to "lasso" them, just as the community cattle will be lassoed next morning. He does this by skillfully whirling over their heads a tiny lasso made of red cotton ribbon, no longer than a bootstring. Of course the audience of herdsmen lying on the floor cannot see this, because the ritualist is working with small objects by the glimmer of a single candle. But every mature Rapacino knows the song associated with this rite: the lassoing tinya *Sinta Lasadera*. To understand why lassoing is a sign of devotion, one has to remember that the wild horseplay of roundup day—lassoing cattle, wrestling them to the ground, wrangling them by the horns, teasing and getting tossed—is understood as a joyful party uniting animals and people in fun. (Rapaz bullfighting does not involve killing bulls, though men get hurt often enough.)

Teodora Falcón sang the joyful *sinta lasadera*, which links the little ritual lasso with the real roundup. Its leitmotif is whirling, flying motion like that of the lasso. It is sung at a brisk rhythm suggestive of speed. The whirling ribbon lasso is compared to a flag. At roundups a Peruvian flag is flown to lead the dance, and its windy motion echoes in local sensibility the flight of the lasso.

This whipping flag is called *cáscara bandera* in lines 26–27, a puzzling epithet because it means "potato peel flag." Rapacinos explained the metaphor: an unfurling flag rides the breeze in rippling curves, like a peel separating from a potato in a spiral. (We translate *cáscara bandera* as "flag unfurling.") The verb *qiqa-* in line 31 means "to move uphill, to see from afar" as when cresting a hill. It also denotes the movement of things in the sky, as birds in flight or the sun (Adelaar 1982, 70). *Risqa-* in line 32, unregistered in dictionaries, is another verb applicable to bird flight according to Rapacinos. *Choolo*, "nonwhite man with indigenous ancestors," in lines 3, 5, and other instances just means "[fellow] countryman" and connotes friendly familiarity.

Corre, corre, sintay lasadeera	
Corre, corre, sintay lasadeera	
Mayqantanqa ali choolo	
Huran vákata sarinanpa(q)	
Mayqantaq ali choolo	5
Ali torota sarinanpa(q).	
Tira, tira, sintay lasadera	
Ali choolo kalashqayki	
Mink^{y}ay qayay, mink^{y}ay puriq	
Tira, tira, sintay lasadera.	10
Way, way, way, way, way, way, way	
ay, way, way, way, way	
Achalaw, añalaw, sintay lasadera!	
Achalaw, añalaw, sintay lasadera!	
Mayqantaq ali cholo	15
Torupádreta tunisinanpaq	
Mayqantaq ali cholo	
Ali torota wintinanpa(q)	
Waaay!	
¡Dicen!	20
Achalaw, añalaw, sintay lasadeera!	
Tira, tira, sintay lasadeera	
Minchay puriq, minchay qayaq	
Ma, ari, choolo, tirayk^{y}ulay	
Ma, ari, choolo, tirayk^{y}ulay	25
Achalaw, añalaw, cáscara bandeera!	
Achalaw, añalaw, cáscara bandeera!	
Minkay qayaq, minkay pushaq	
Ma, ari, hombre, tikrarkulay	

Ma, ari, hombre, muyurkulay   30
   Alkun qiqay muyuykulay
   Kundur risqay risqaykulay
   Gavilan muyuy muyuykulay
Tiray, tiray, lasadeera!
Aaaaaaay!   35
¡Dice!

Transcription: Luis Andrade Ciudad

Whirl, whirl my ribbon lasso
Whirl, whirl my ribbon lasso
   Who's the best cholo
To subdue the friskiest cow?
   Who's the best cholo   5
To subdue the best bull?
Throw, throw, my ribbon lasso
   If you're a good cholo
   Who calls the work gang, who goes in the work gang
Throw, throw, my ribbon lasso!   10
Way, way, way, way, way, way, way
ay, way, way, way, way
What a beauty, what a joy, my ribbon lasso!
What a beauty, what a joy, my ribbon lasso!
   Who's the best cholo   15
To wrestle the top bull?
   Who's the best cholo
To wrangle the best bull?
Waay!
So!
What a beauty, what a joy, my ribbon lasso!
Throw, throw, my ribbon lasso!
   If you're the one who calls the work gang, who shows up for the work gang
Come on, cholo, throw it then!
Come on, cholo, throw it then!   25
What a beauty, what a joy, flag unfurling!
What a beauty, what a joy, flag unfurling!
   If you're the one who calls the work gang, who leads the work gang,
Come on, man, whirl round and round!
Come on, man, spin round and round!   30
   Like a falcon in climbing flight, turn round
   Like a condor in soaring flight, soar round
   Like a hawk in circling flight, turn round,
Throw, throw, lasso!   35
Aaaaaay!
So!

Rapaz's tinyas for animals, like those in other parts of the Andes, play on extravagant metaphor (not unlike Evans-Pritchard's famous Nuer cattle-praise songs in East Africa). The following song contrasts what the animal looks like to "you," an outsider, with the owner's visionary perception:

> Viva, vivala, lasaderalaa
> Viva, vivala, lasoychurilán.
>   Kachunchalayta, "kachunmi", ninki   10
> "Iskañay bravalan kachunchalayqa"
>   Nawilantaqa, "nawinmi", ninki
> "Nawinchalayqa luseritalan"
>   Qallunlaytapish, "qallunmi", ninki
> "Qallunchalayqa telayregalan"   15
>   Chupanchalayta, "chupanmi", ninki
> "Chupanchalayqa qayay bergalam"
> Ahiii!

> Hurray, hurray, oh lasso rope
> Hurray, hurray, just start lassoing!
>   You call his horn "a horn";   10
> His horns are just like two wild cane stalks![18]
> You call his eyes "eyes";
> His eyes are just like two brilliant stars!
> And you may call his tongue "a tongue";
> His tongue is just like gift-quality fabric!
> You call his tail "a tail";
> His tail is just like that cock [penis] over there!
> Ahiii!

From the ritual studies point of view, the roundup joins opposite halves as different as night and day. First comes a night of intensification ritual that bonds people tightly with each other. It also bonds them to cattle and molds their personal feelings to the state of mind communal herding demands. Second comes by a day of wild transgressive sport, in which men antagonize cattle and exhibit their individualism in rivalrous play. After *both* they go home happy.

Rapaz is one of many societies in which rituals that celebrate life in close community alternate with rituals that disrupt law and discipline. Where A.F.C. Wallace (Introduction) called the former "rites of intensification," the latter are called "rituals of rebellion." These encourage outrageousness, expressing the intuition that we live *in* society but also *against* it. Rapaz is perhaps unusual in sealing these two extremes of ritual together within 24 hours.

Nonreductionist (or less reductionist) psychological theories of religiosity

In this ethnopoetic excursus, we emphasized links between ritual verbal art and emotion so as to open discussion of rituals as paths to specific shared subjectivities and as engines for shared feeling.

"A religious experience" is a cliché for anything that seems sublime or life-changing. We usually say it ironically. But the cattle ritual at Jankil impressed me with such force that on the way home I pondered the shopworn phrase afresh. During the night, it seemed, I had come closer to the fused feelings of awe, anxiety, hope, and exaltation that believers non-ironically call religious feeling.

Whether such extraordinary feelings are the core of religiosity is an everlasting subject of debate. For over a century, reductionist theories about religiosity (Durkheimian, Marxist, Freudian, sociological, structuralist, and cognitive-evolutionary theories, for example) held center stage among those who take the idea of social science seriously, and these thinkers provided arguments that religious feeling is just a secondary consequence of general social facts.

Within that constraint, however, one vein of functionalist anthropology gave enough importance to emotion to acquire the nickname of emotionalist theory. From the 1920s onward, Bronislaw Malinowski's Melanesian studies famously put ethnographic wheels onto Durkheim's ideas. He attributed the religious tendency to the needs of society-as-such, much as the French master had done (Chapter 2). But unlike the cloistered Durkheim, Malinowski stood close to real-life Melanesian men and women. In magic and sacred ritual, he saw Trobriand Islanders stressfully adjusting their lives to the hazards of luck. Death, accident, and scarcity opened gaps between desire and ability. Every person's anxiety had to be alleviated if he or she was to remain that able, sociable fellow-human needed to incarnate Durkheimian society. Rituals, Malinowski concluded, worked anxieties into routines of reassuring collective actions—actions that overcame, in the minds of actors, the tragic limits of human agency (1948). Considered in a Malinowskian mode, the Jankil overnighter, with its dramatic heightening and resolution of anxiety about cattle, might be seen as one society's way of making rivalrous, anxious Rapacinos into the sort of men who can devote themselves to shared herds.

Although the Malinowskian vein of "emotionalist" theorizing makes cultural channeling of emotion a central endeavor, it still involves reductionism because, intimate and intense though ritual mindsets may be, they are epiphenomena of social functions. No one denies the greatness of Malinowski's ethnographies, but some have bridled at his reduction of ritual experience to "superorganic" Durkheimian causes. The dissenters who will concern us in the next pages hold that regardless of its social framing, subjective experience of the sacred has power over thought and action.

William James' mystical policeman

One of the precursors who made "religious experience" a topic bridging scientific, humanistic, and theological discussions was William James, who died in 1910, just as Malinowski was beginning to study anthropology. Scion of a new-rich New Yorker father with Swedenborgian tendencies and cosmopolitan longings, William was also brother to the novelist Henry James. William became the disciplinary founder of psychology in the USA and an originator of American pragmatic philosophy. In 1902 he published *The Varieties of Religious Experience*, an attempt to characterize universal features of religiosity. Among James' purposes, one was to knock down sectarian religious claims to authority by showing that all specific doctrines were but partial, tendentious expressions of a single human disposition.

For James, religiosity constantly wells up everywhere, spontaneously, in the subjective experience of certain apparently random individuals. The content of this mystic state is a unifying, radiant awareness, felt as experience above and beyond categories of culture or language. For that reason, James' elementary form of religiosity is impossible to put into words ("ineffable"). The fundamental religious vision is non-propositional and indefinable, yet it is felt as a compelling truth. Religious inspiration is not particularly rare. What is rare is the ability to express it, for the mystical experience brings the mind to the end of its tether.

At the book's core is a ravishing display of testimonies from all sorts of people who have known moments of transcendent super-awareness. Prophets and poets have their say, of course, but also:

> an officer on our police force who has told me that many times when off duty and on his way home in the evening, there comes to him . . . a vivid and vital realization of his oneness with this Infinite Power . . . and this spirit of Infinite Peace so takes hold of and so fills him, that it seems as if his feet could scarcely keep to the pavement, so buoyant and so exhilarated does he become by reason of this inflowing tide.
>
> *James 1936 [1902], 385*

James perceives in religiosity "an exciter of the *yes* function" which (like alcohol!) "brings its votary from the chill periphery of things to the radiant core . . . The unlimited absorbs the limit and peacefully closes the account" (James 1936 [1902], 378, 407).

Who would not want to believe it? William James is dear to people who have made their own excursions into the sublime, whether or not they care for churches. To those who have felt intuition or vision that surpasses normal consciousness, James rings supremely true. And many others, who simply consider the whole matter imponderable, nonetheless value *The Varieties* as a noble and reassuring work because of its hopeful implications for religious reconciliation. It also possesses literary beauty in the Edwardian way of an enormous floral centerpiece.

And, gossamer though it is, James' core claim about mysticism may have merit. James intuited a psychological reality, according to neurological researchers who hold that hallucinogens, bodily "spiritual" disciplines, and even temporal lobe epilepsy activate brain loci associated with feelings of bliss. The "biology of belief" has yet to become a consensually respected research field, perhaps because "neurotheologists" have published popular self-help books (Newberg and Waldman 2009). Both bioscientists and interpretivists find shortcomings in such incipient science. Brain-activity arguments tell us that in exaltation, certain brain regions become active. Critics reply, who would have expected them not to? While specifying brain location is a start, neural locations don't tell in what way a particular brain state constitutes a kind of cognition, much less whether that strange cognition amounts to an emergent phenomenon with its own force as James thought. There is a long way to go. But James might have been willing to go that way; he was a scientist (albeit an erratic one), and he might not have seen eventual neurological reduction as hostile to his positive evaluation of religiosity.

A clearer threat to Jamesian views is doubt about James' claim that mystical inclination is the basis of all religious behaviors. Can it really be proven that "The mother sea and fountain-head of all religions lies in the mystical experience of the individual . . . all theologies and all ecclesiasticisms are secondary growths superimposed" (James 1920 [1901], 149)? A hard thing to prove! For if the alleged central cause is something that cannot be seen or spoken, how shall observers know when it is present or absent?

Most important for us is an ethnological fact: the "solemn, serious and tender" attitude of mysticism appears in some but not all religious practices. Even where the mystical state is recognized and valued, it rarely occurs as large-scale collective practice. Nor are the mental powers of religious virtuosi necessarily benign in the way that impressed James. The identification of religious vision with philanthropic transcendence was fashionable in James' time (he wrote the *Varieties* for a Presbyterian-endowed lecture series). And it is true that similar feelings arose variously in other centuries among, for example, early Buddhists. But the association between mystical experience and benevolence never has been universal. Mysticism has often joined forces with combative and judgmental movements.

Nor is mysticism a pan-religious tendency. Religiosity can be, and often is, very dry, very goal-oriented and technical. It specifies and enforces cultural categories and social hierarchies at least as often as it transcends them. An enormous part of the world's religion is seen by its devotees as law, and not primarily as salvation, enlightenment, or any other transcendent personal state. Anthropologists of religion recognize that relatively few of the world's religiously observant people undergo visionary experience.

People nearer the un-mystical pole are sometimes characterized as "orthoprax"; that is, rather than being concerned with vision or belief, they identify religion as behavior founded in revelation that upholds and sanctifies the social order. Orthopraxy values obeying laws, praying for shared goals, memorizing texts, observing taboos, enforcing ethics, etc. Far from embracing the Jamesian idea, orthoprax cultures tend to treat mysticism or ecstatic practice as marginal or suspect. For example, normative Judaism holds Kabbalah at arm's length, and many versions of Islam are unfriendly to ecstatic Sufism. If James were to return today, we would need to challenge him by asking, what is the "mother sea and fountain-head" of the orthoprax tendency? What experiences come to *its* adherents?

Rapaz's mountain-oriented sacred complex shows quite a lot of technical and orthoprax attitude. Yet it also provides several techniques for imparting special states of mind: close physical massing, seclusion in darkness, rhythmic driving, coca- and liquor-induced sensations, cold stress, and sleep deprivation. In staying up late with the herdsmen we sensed great intensity of feeling about sacred things. Among the goals is a collective focusing of intentions toward single-minded *voluntad*. But this is not exactly what popular discourse calls spirituality, and not much like the states James focused on. More tough than tender, more orthoprax than orthodox, Andean ritualism yet generates a kind of mental intensity I have felt nowhere else. There must be more to know about religiosity and experience. Anthropology needs a broader way to account for diversity of "innerworlds" as well as life styles.

Anthropology of experience more generally: a glance at phenomenological approaches

While admitting that James went wrong by privileging one very peculiar sort of experience as the "fount," many cultural anthropologists still sympathize with his desire to understand culture as people inwardly feel it, and not only as bodies of behavioral fact or as symbolic patterns visible to the detached observer. The anthropology that tries to express what life is like to people in different societies is associated with the term *phenomenology*. The phenomenological train of thought originated only about a century ago with Edmund Husserl, a child of multilingual Moravia (in today's Czech Republic). He set out to give us not another objective "natural philosophy" (an older term for science), but a philosophy going in the opposite direction altogether: a philosophy of experience.

A natural scientist in the sense typical of Husserl's age had to live acutely aware that subjective experience includes a mass of fallible impressions. The researcher's duty was to sort his impressions critically as a *via negativa* ("way of negation"). Setting aside known sources of observer error would lead toward images of a real, objective world, called "nature," that exists irrespective of anyone's mental life. "Naturalism" then began by discarding every part of the world picture arising from the observer's position: sense limitations, cultural training, perspectival effects, desires, aesthetic responses, and so forth.

A phenomenologist hoped to do the very opposite. He would set the objective agenda aside as much as he could. He set out to study exactly what the naturalist discarded: "first impressions," and "how consciousness proceeds" in finding and organizing its own impressions (Desjarlais and Throop 2011, 88). What happens if we stop pretending we are alien to ourselves? Is there rhyme and reason in the *mere seeming* of things? In the way things look *to us*? It certainly matters because phenomenal appearances are what people act upon.

Our world-as-lived-in is not like nature. It needs to be studied with different tools—tools that are inherently like ethnography insofar as their object is another's point of view. A wide-branching gamut of humanistic and psychological studies has grown from this program of studying experiential worlds as such. Its grail is not what the world is in itself but what the world is to specific persons or peoples. Beyond this, phenomenology has thrived on the perception that the world of seeming is constructed not only *within* people but *among* them: it is social. Alfred Schutz, a refugee whose phenomenological ideas about the social construction of reality bloomed into a fascinating American sociological movement, stands among anthropology's phenomenologically minded mentors. Even now their legacy stands in provocative contrast to the more "sciency" parts of social science.

What does anthropology bring to the discussion? Anthropologists have a special way to offset "naturalism": they seek immersion in a foreign situation. As a stranger one has a better chance to notice distinctions made about experience than one gets in routine-benumbed life at home. Anthropology's tendency is to insist that these distinctions are inner and yet collective; they are shared constructions among many agents—that is, cultural intersubjectivities. How are they constructed? What are their consequences?

For example, people in many societies (some of them Andean) consider dreams to be realities exterior to the mind of the dreamer, because dreams seem to happen independent of one's will. Consider the sociocultural consequences. For each person, it always matters how others experience her and how her experiences can be exchanged. If the "you" who hurt me or helped me in my dream was an actual agent rather than a figment created inside me, it will make a difference in how I treat you.

"Intersubjectivity" is a phenomenological term for culturally constituted perspectives that organize sharing of experience. Because experience feeds us continual doses of the unforeseen, intersubjectivity never really settles. There is always something more to enter into it. Novelties, misunderstandings, fantasies, and disagreements never cease to disturb the field.

In the hands of a master ethnographer, this kind of theory is like a fine-tuned antenna that registers quivers of experience and intersubjectivity. The ethnography of "lifeworlds" explains the work of culture, especially religion, as "control of experience" in Godfrey Lienhardt's prescient phrase of 1961. Gifted practitioners are many (Csordas 2002; Boddy 1989). One contemporary leader is Tanya M. Luhrmann, known for studying how American Evangelical Protestants experience "gifts of the spirit." She proposes an innovative phenomenological view of differences among religious cultures (2012).

Luhrmann's Evangelical acquaintances are eminently modern people. Theirs is no longer a world in which the authority of religion "goes without saying because it comes without saying." On the contrary, they are acutely aware that Christian belief is an *option* forever challenged by rival models of reality. For many purposes they compromise with secularism, yet they do not want to surrender to it.

Some of their religious experience takes place in what Luhrmann calls an "as-if imagination . . . a deliberatively playful, imaginative, fantasy-filled experience of

God" (2012, 372). They know they can only conditionally disbelieve in disbelief, but doing so is their path to good and useful experience. They cultivate a special habit: they can lightly flip their attention into a mindset that turns away from commonsense categories like coincidence or delusion. Why should they *not* feel free to understand a random mind-picture as an intimation of God? Believers train themselves to an intersubjectivity that receives sudden goosebumps, or a dream, or a coincidence as signs of grace.

Inviting God for coffee (as one preacher proposes) is make-believe. Yet in sacred play "the distinction between belief and make-believe breaks down" (2012, 278, quoting Huizinga). Some phenomenological researchers go as far as recommending that the ethnographer himself take a "ludic" (playful) attitude to cognition. When Kim Knibbe studied devotees of the Dutch "spiritual healer" Jomanda, she played away her academic agnosticism until she became able to take Jomanda's performances at face value—and then, returning to academe, she again became "subservient to her *habitus* as an anthropologist" (Knibbe and Droogers 2011, 285, 295).

For Luhrmann, "ludic" positioning of belief gives religion a new phenomeno-logical perch in modernity. This perception

> has a powerful theoretical payoff. It draws to our analytical attention the observation that the way people understand their minds affects their mental experience. This understanding of the mind is not what we mean by "sub-jectivity." It is a second-order model of the mind: a "theory." . . . Ideas about ideas are also shaped by local culture.
>
> *2012, 372*

The Evangelical theory of mind "straddles" multiple frameworks of truth simul-taneously. It does not try to reconcile visionary criteria for truth with empirical criteria (as modernist revisions of religion tried to do). Instead it entertains the fluttering alternation of miracle and tedium as awareness of what our life really is.

Luhrmann thinks "as-if" forms of religiosity are characteristic of modern "doub-ting societies" in which faith is always a conditional, optional, and challenged intersubjectivity. Does it seem laughable? Think again: "as-if" thinking also under-lies anthropological stances, insofar as the ethnographer strives to flip and re-flip his vision between the "lifeworld" he grew with and that of his foreign interlocutors. The believer who invites God for coffee and the cultural relativist fieldworker are close kin because both believe phenomenological flipping is itself an opening to truth.

Luhrman crucially asserts that other populations' reasons for doubting dogmas differ from such post-Enlightenment reframing. She turns her attention to a dif-ferent set of "doubting" societies. These she calls "never-secular" societies because their members converted to Christianity without forgetting their previous "pagan" ritual life and without ever entering a disenchanted modern condition. They live between religion and religion, rather than between religion and secularism.

Although some Rapacinos think secularly, and although secular rituals abound in the public school and the municipality, Rapaz remains somewhat of a "never-secular" society. It would be awkward if not shameful for a comunero to shun all sacred doings or publicly deny their premises.

Living between one religion and another, as Luhrmann learns from various ethnographers, yields varied phenomenological stances. According to Joel Robbins, Urapmin Melanesian peoples feel "moral torment because their society once had a pre-Christian model" of mind different from the Pentecostal model of transparent inwardness with God. They incessantly make Christian gestures hoping to attain the inner state acceptable in God's sight but never satisfying their qualms. By contrast Birgit Meyers perceives Ewe Ghanaians as differently attuned: "Both the Christian and the pagan supernatural remain real; the pagan supernatural has, as it were, simply changed its charge" by getting reclassified as the Devil's domain (2012, 380–381). And there are other results in other societies. For Luhrmann, what they have in common is that

> In never-secular societies, where the reality of the supernatural as a category has not been profoundly questioned, doubt is focused on *specific* supernatural claims. . . . [C]ongregants do not need help to persuade them to take the entire enterprise seriously in the first place. [italics added]
>
> *2012, 381*

Directions of Andean experience?

In Rapaz the "between religion and religion" issue arises chiefly for the Protestant convert minority. Ardent believers have spread the Ewe-like view that all the powers of the ila animals and mountains are real and that they do exert spiritual powers—namely powers of Satan. Andean sacred things become the infernal opposite of religion, responsible for ills such as drunkenness, black magic, poverty, and sickness. Some Protestants refuse on principle to stay up all night at Jankil or take coca at Kaha Wayi, but most mute their opinions lest they damage the community. Many Protestants do cross the lines between religious groups, meanwhile governing their experience with vigilant "thoughts about thought." They cultivate the ability to repel the blackness of diabolism when it pierces through the white of faith. Pentecostals and Evangelicals share vigilance through a discreet but intense counterculture. For them, musical Sundays at chapel mean taking refuge from the likes of Jankil: a breakthrough from murky plotting with the powers into safety, song, trust, and joy.

Andean ritual tradition, on the other hand, coexists easily with Catholic Christianity. I met people who felt a need to intensify their Catholicism in, for example, religious sodalities or short seminary courses, but not because they had quarreled with Kaha Wayi. Being remote, Rapaz receives visits from its curate only three or four times a year. Although some priests in the 20th century despised Andean rituals and are rumored to have condoned thefts from Kaha Wayi, recent ones admonish more gently against unauthorized rites.

Coexistence is a more fundamental matter than a simple truce between creeds because, from the village viewpoint, there is little need for a truce. A Rapacino knows well enough that Catholic ideas classify as delusions a body of experience (for example, the llama-fat augury) that Kaha Wayi validates. The Rapacino just doesn't see the two as challenging each other. They are true regarding different things and irrelevant to each other. I never heard Andean rituals referred to as religion. (A few people did speak of "faith" toward mountains, etc., but this seemed to mean "good faith" or "loyalty" rather than a bet on metaphysical redemption.)

Instead of being rival creedal commitments, Andean rites and Catholicism are paired bodies of know-how that face in different directions. It is as if Rapacinos' "lifeworld" had a center and a periphery: a central pole of civility and divinity associated with the Church and transcendent authority, and an outer domain to which one is oriented when working with things prior to civility, like peaks, lakes, watercourses, pastures, and fertile mountainside. Life is lived in the field between them. For some purposes, relations with food (Raywana), livestock (Yanabotella) or landscape (Saqsar Wayna Mountain) are experienced as intersubjective, with a strong dimension of mutuality. For other purposes, these are experienced as "natural" things (as resources, etc.) and therefore susceptible to objective technological orientations as well as God's authority. I did not feel at any time that shifting contexts involved "making believe to make it real" or that flipping was a conscious stance. Rather I seemed to feel that the poetic and dramaturgical "control of experience" was an art of consciously awakening within oneself different facets of self, so as to ease into different occasions. That seemed to be the kind of work that the songs, body routines, and ritual scenarios achieved.

Notes

1 Department of Humanities, Pontificia Universidad Católica del Perú.
2 Additional shades of meaning peculiar to Quechua: "your children, your own" as translation for *wawaa, tsurii* misses a poetic effect. *Wawaa* is what a female calls her child (of either sex), while *tsurii* is what a male calls his child (of either sex). Néstor is speaking to the superhuman as a parent whose gender is unknown. He thus gracefully suggests humility in a way that Spanish and English cannot. And Néstor is also using a lexical resource we cannot match in expressing what is called "thought quotation" with the verb *niy. Niy* combines the sense of "think" with that of "say." The invocation says to the higher being: "Think-say us 'my children [female voice], my children [male voice].'" We know that Néstor is emphasizing the thought part of the thought-speech combination because he uses the verb *considerar* in his gloss. We know he is assigning the ambiguously singular/plural first person object marker—*ma*—a plural meaning ("we . . . children") because his gloss uses plurals. Additionally, in a stricter syntax such as one would expect if this were not poetic utterance, one would expect a suffix such as *-ta* (accusative) to mark the receiver of communication, *mana yachaq/mana musyaq* ("the unknowing one/ the unwitting one") (Adelaar 1977, 188). By eliding object-marking, the couplet acquires a somewhat dreamy tone: the speaker reflects on his own ignorance, and then his thought refocuses on the addressee's response. On linguistic resources for naming the sacred in early colonial Quechua, see Adelaar 1994.
3 In Torero's classification. Confusingly, in another classification, Quechua I is called Quechua B, and Quechua II is called Quechua A. But the two classifications roughly agree on the nature and distribution of the differences.

4 Quechua I breaks down into a large subfamily known as Central, and a separate peculiar variety called Pacaraos spoken in a single town not far from Rapaz. Central Quechua in turn trifurcates into varieties called Huáilay, Alto, Pativilca-Alto, Marañón-Alto, Huallaga, and Huáncay. Huáncay is further analyzed into three subdivisions, called Yaru, Jauja-Huanca, and Huangáscar-Topará.

5 "The northern part of Huaura and Oyón Provinces, together with some areas of Cajatambo Province, are home to the northern members of the Yaru subroup. The Quechua of San Francisco de Mangas (Bolognesi Province in Áncash Department) and the Pativilca River form the northernmost edges of this subgroup (Solís Fonseca 2002, 19; 2009, 157). The eastern edge of Yaru's space runs through Pasco Department in the provinces of Daniel Alcides Carrión and Cerro de Pasco. The southern extent of the group includes two varieties in Yauyos Province (Alis and Tomas) . . . as well as varieties in the northerly provinces of Junín and Tarma" (Andrade 2011, 78).

6 Mi papá decía: "Como me hablen la quechua nomás, les voy a cortar la lengua. Así nos decía. Entonces, de ese miedo, nosotros no hablábamos quechua."

7 Mi mamá me decía: "Tu abuelo me ha dicho que en acá hablan dialecto y no tienes que aprender porque no es quechua buena. Pierdes tu tiempo hablando esos dialectos. Esos dialectos no sirven. El verdadero quechua está en el Cuzco." Pero único mi mamá decía: "Bueno, para que llegues a saber que existe quechua en Rapaz," nos hacía contar: huk, ishkay, kima, trusku, pisqa, huqta, qantris, puwa, isqun, trunka. Hasta ahí nomás. Y más no quería mi mamá que habláramos, porque no era verdadero, pero cuando ya vi una vez este . . . televisión, ya en Lima, "Tawa kanal Limamanta pacha", decía ¿no? Entonces, me decía mi mamá: "¿Ya ves? Ya no dice trusku sino dice tawa. Entonces nuestro quechua está equivocado. Y no es quechua. Y no lo vas a practicar." Y es la razón que no nos dejaban.

8 Several good compilations cover the songs/poems of harvesting in other regions, for example Arnold and Yapita 1996, Copana and Apaza 1996. The latter documents Bolivian rites for storing potatoes that resemble rites in Rapaz.

9 The feminine inflection of *Altamirana* (instead of the common surname *Altamirano*) reflects some women's tendency to use surnames as signs of parallel descent: thinking of herself as a female descendant of the Altamiranos she marks her surname in a female way. Salomon also observed this among Ecuadorian Quichua speakers.

10 8 km N-NW of San Pedro de Cajas at 4,420 m altitude. The area lies southeast of Lake Junín.

11 Jankil is called Yanquil on Google Earth. It is at 10° 55' 39" S, 76° 38' 48" W, altitude 13,415 ft. or 4,089 m.

12 Before the recuperation of Lot 29, the ritual and administrative center for cattle was at Karakancha. There the mayordomo and his crew did service to the stone Toro Rumi, to fecundate cows. Ukawayín, the milking station near Karakancha, is still mentioned in invocations. These and other former ritual places are still well remembered as powerful spots.

13 In Santa Leonor Department, Huaura Province, down the Checras valley from Rapaz at 10,500 ft (3,200 m) altitude.

14 Or *illa* in Quechua II.

15 *Ruywa*: reddish-brown, dark "mulatto" color.

16 *Chola* in Peruvian Spanish means a nonwhite woman with indigenous ancestors. Here, it is said in a friendly way to mean "fellow countrywoman."

17 We thank Félix Julca Guerrero who helped us with the subtleties of long vowels, a Central Quechua feature especially productive in Spanish loanwords.

18 Cane stalks grow a good four meters tall.

References

Adelaar, Willem F.H. 1977. *Tarma Quechua Grammar, Texts, Dictionary*. Lisse, Netherlands: The Peter de Ridder Press.

Adelaar, Willem F.H. 1982. *Léxico del quechua de Pacaraos*. Lima: Universidad Nacional Mayor de San Marcos, Centro de Investigación de Lingüística Aplicada. Documento no.45.

Adelaar, Willem F.H. 1986. *Morfología del quechua de Pacaraos*. Lima: Universidad Nacional Mayor de San Marcos, Centro de Investigación de Lingüística Aplicada. Documento no. 53.

Adelaar, Willem F.H. 1994. "A Grammatical Category for Manifestations of the Supernatural in Early Colonial Quechua." In *Language in the Andes*, edited by Peter Cole, Gabriella Hermon, and Mario Daniel Martin. Newark, DE: University of Delaware. 116–125.

Andrade Ciudad, Luis. 2011. "Apuntes dialectales e históricos sobre el quechua de Rapaz." *Revista Andina* 51: 73–108.

Arnold, Denise Y., and Juan de Dios Yapita. 2001. *River of Fleece, River of Song: Singing to the Animals, an Andean Poetics of Creation*. Bonn: Verlag Anton Saurwein. Bonner Amerikanistische Schriften. 35.

Bloch, Maurice. 1989. "Symbols, Song, Dance, and Features of Articulation: Is Religion an Extreme Form of Traditional Authority?" In *Ritual, History, and Power: Selected Papers in Anthropology*, edited by Maurice Bloch. London: Athlone Press. 19–45.

Boddy, Janice. 1989. *Wombs and Alien Spirits: Women, Men, and the Zar Cult in Northern Sudan*. Madison, WI: University of Wisconsin Press.

Cerrón-Palomino, Rodolfo. 1987. *Lingüística quechua*. Cuzco, Peru: Centro de Estudios Rurales Andinos, Bartolomé de Las Casas.

Copana, Norberto G., Cipriana Apaza M. and Emiliana Hilaya M. 1996. "Ofrendas a la papa en la región del lago [i.e. Titicaca]." In *Madre Melliza y sus crías. Ispall Mama wawampi. Antología de la papa*, edited by Denise Y. Arnold and Juan de Dios Yapita. La Paz: ILCA.

Coronel-Molina, Serafín M. 2008. "Inventing Tawantinsuyu and Qhapaq Simi: Language Ideologies of the High Academy of the Quechua Language in Cuzco, Peru." *Latin American and Caribbean Ethnic Studies*, Special issue: *Indigenous Encounters in Peru* 3(3): 319–340.

Coronel-Molina, Serafín M. 2015. *Language Ideology, Policy and Planning in Peru*. Bristol, Buffalo, and Toronto: Multilingual Matters.

Csordas, Thomas J. 2002. *Body/Meaning/Healing*. New York: Palgrave Macmillan.

Desjarlais, Robert, and C. Jason Throop. 2011. "Phenomenological Approaches in Anthropology." *Annual Review of Anthropology* 40: 87–102.

Dransart, Penelope Z. 2002. *Earth, Water, Fleece and Fabric: An Ethnography and Archaeology of Andean Camelid Herding*. London: Routledge.

Duviols, Pierre. 1974. "Une petite chronique retrouvée: errores, ritos, supersticiones y ceremonias de los yndios de la provincia de Chinchaycocha y otras del Piru (1603)." *Journal de la Société des Américanistes* 68: 275–297.

Flores Ochoa, Jorge A. 1977. "Aspectos mágicos del pastoreo: *Enqa, enqaychu, illa* y *khuyarumi*." In *Pastores de puna: Uywamichiq punarunakuna*, edited by Jorge A. Flores Ochoa. Lima: Instituto de Estudios Peruanos. 211–238.

Hill, Jane. 1990. "El llanto como una metaseñal en la narrativa de una mujer mexicana." In *Las culturas nativas latinoamericanas a través de su discurso*, Colección 500 Años, edited by Ellen Basso and Joel Sherzer. Quito: Abya-Yala. 175–205.

James, William. 1920. *The Letters of William James, Vol. II*, edited by Henry James. Boston, MA: Atlantic Monthly Press.

James, William. 1936 [1902]. *The Varieties of Religious Experience: A Study in Human Nature*. New York: Modern Library.

Keane, Webb. 1997. "Religious Language." *Annual Review of Anthropology* 26: 47–71.

Knibbe, Kim, and André Droogers. 2011. "Methodological Ludism and the Academic Study of Religion." *Method and Theory in the Study of Religion* 23: 283–303.

Labov, William. 1997. "Some Further Steps in Narrative Analysis." *Journal of Narrative and Life History* 7(1–4): 395–415.

Labov, William, and Joshua Waletzki. 1967. "Oral Versions of Personal Experiences." In *Essays on the Verbal Arts: Proceedings of the 1966 Annual Spring Meeting of the American Ethnological Society*, edited by June Helm. Seattle: University of Washington Press. 12–44.

Lambek, Michael. 2013. "Varieties of Semiotic Ideology in the Interpretation of Religion." In *A Companion to the Anthropology of Religion*, edited by Janice Boddy and Michael Lambek. Chichester, UK: Wiley Blackwell. 137–153.

Lienhardt, Godfrey. 1961. *Divinity and Experience: The Religion of the Dinka*. Oxford: Oxford University Press.

Luhrmann, Tanya M. 2012. "A Hyperreal God and Modern Belief: Toward an Anthropological Theory of Mind." *Current Anthropology* 53(4): 371–395.

Malinowski, Bronislaw. 1948. *Magic, Science and Religion, and Other Essays*. Boston, MA: Beacon Press.

Mannheim, Bruce. 1998. "'Time, Not the Syllables, Must Be Counted': Quechua Parallelism, Word Meaning, and Cultural Analysis." *Michigan Discussions in Anthropology* 13: 238–281.

Morris, Earl W., Leslie A. Brownrigg, Susan C. Bourque, and Henry F. Dobyns. 1968. *Coming Down the Mountain: The Social Worlds of Mayobamba*. Ithaca, NY: Andean Indian Community Research and Development Program, Department of Anthropology, Cornell University. Socio-Economic Development of Andean Communities, Report No. 10.

Newberg, Andrew, and Mark Robert Waldman. 2009. *How God Changes Your Brain: Breakthrough Findings from a Leading Neuroscientist*. New York: Ballantine Books.

Niño-Murcia, Mercedes. 1995. "Política del purismo lingüístico en el Cuzco." *Lexis* 19(2): 251–288.

Pinto Jiménez, Chris Evelyn, Carmen Martín Espada, and María Dolores Cid Vázquez. 2010. "Camélidos sudamericanos: clasificación, origen y características." *Revista Complutense de Ciencias Veterinarias* 4(1): 2336.

Rivera Andía, Juan Javier. 2003. "Canto ceremonial en las herranzas de los Andes peruanos. Canciones de los ritos en torno a la identificación del ganado en la sierra de Lima." *Gazeta de Antropología* 19(13). http://hdl.handle.net/10481/7328.

Rivera Andía, Juan Javier. 2012. "A partir de los movimientos de un pájaro . . . La 'danza de la perdiz' en los rituales ganaderos de los Andes peruanos." *Revista Española de Antropología Americana* 42(1): 169–185.

Salomon, Frank, Gino de las Casas, and Víctor Falcón Huayta. 2015. "Storehouse of Seasons and Mother of Food: An Andean Ritual-Administrative System." In *Storage in Ancient Complex Societies: Administration, Organization, and Control*, edited by Linda R. Manzanilla and Mitchell S. Rothman. Walnut Creek, CA: Left Coast Press. 189–214.

Solís Fonseca, Gustavo. 2009. "Sobre las lenguas en la provincia de Bolognesi." *Paqariina. Revista de Investigaciones Lingüísticas y Culturales* 2(1): 13–25.

Solís Fonseca, Gustavo. 2002. "Zonas dialectales del quechua en el sur de Áncash." *Arqueología y Sociedad* 14: 151–164.

5

MENDING THEIR SACRED THINGS

(and thinking about religion as symbolism, science, or power)

How to make Kaha Wayi's sacred contents safe, as Rapaz's Community directorate required? I asked the archaeologist Dr. Sonia Guillén in Lima. Archaeologists revere her for founding Fundación Mallqui, a laboratory specialized in conserving prehispanic Peruvian mummies. Sonia scrutinized my photos, which showed many conservation problems: khipu cords speckled with white moth eggs, others frayed and dangling by a thread, some spotted with mold or rotted by animal urine. Soot and mildew stained Kaha Wayi's ceiling and altar. The roof was broken and walls were cracked.

"*Todo vuelve*," she said with a sigh, "Everything returns," meaning everything goes back to dust no matter how much we strive for permanence. "A good conservator could clean the khipus and mend them," she said. "But a good conservator wouldn't accept that as a freestanding job, because everything would just get infested again. The Rapacinos are right about building a protective case. You also need to perform an architectural conservation and clean up Kaha Wayi as a whole. Look how the roof is breaking apart—you can't leave out architectural conservation. You need to study the microclimate. Your project should be a rounded conservation package, not a repair job." She sketched out the staffing and specialties it would need.

"I could probably get those jobs funded," I said. "But there's more to it. Some people are touchy about outsiders even seeing Kaha Wayi, never mind replacing parts. It's sacred. The comuneros aren't going to let anyone do things the way they're done in museums. They'd never let anybody set up lights or use electric tools."

"Well," Dr. Guillén said, "so much the better. That gives you an innovative project in conservation. Usually museum people expect to do conservation work under their control, on their turf. Usually they expect to have things brought to the museum. They're perfectionists. Now the museum will have to go to Rapaz's turf, on Rapaz's conditions. Maybe more will be learned that way. And I do have some ideas about who could do it."

In this way our research crew found ourselves dismantling and manipulating the sacred symbolic heirlooms of Rapaz. During the delicate, painstaking lab work we often wondered what it is that gives sacred objects their compelling hold on people.

By temporarily disturbing the cultural field of play, our work gave glimpses of how these objects embody three powers of religion: symbolism, explanation, and authority. This chapter will move from the actual handling of sacred things toward pondering three branches of theorization.

To foreshadow the question of sacred things a little further: consider their first power, symbolism. The conservation job opened our eyes to the sacred objects as vessels of meaning—a suite of vital emblems whose use constantly regenerates Rapacinos' shared conceptions, attitudes, and motives. This way of seeing religious things is developed in a body of anthropological theory called symbolic or inter-pretative anthropology.

Second, watching people use the symbolic suite meant noticing that it has an explanatory or science-like quality as well as a reverential one. The night with Raywana, the sacrifices and pilgrimages, seemed to the participants investiga-tions—a sort of research, seeking the truth about weather. Rituals had empirical qualities, despite lacking the principle of falsifiability that governs science "proper." This research-like quality is highlighted in a body of theory about religion known as intellectualism.

Third, being supervised by the balterno officers constantly reminded us that Kaha Wayi is a power structure. Its ordering force over agropastoralism is not wholly attributable to members' feelings toward symbols, nor to intellectual assent, nor to voluntary joining-up. Could Kaha Wayi be a tiny Leviathan? A third body of anthropological theory argues that religions are "social facts" of a special kind, namely practices that articulate power. Though recently in the ascendant, this vein of theorizing has no consensual name. Variants that owe a lot to French theo-ries are sometimes called Foucauldian or "genealogical" (because they expose the succession of unspoken power loci). I will simply call them power-centered to emphasize that, unlike Durkheim's sociology, they foreground dominance rather than solidarity.

Convening a crew, and Friday night movies in Rapaz

Sonia Guillén knew Dr. Renata Peters, a Brazilian museologist then working at the University of London's famed Institute of Archaeology. Renata felt a vocation to put fieldwork boots onto the curator's art. I wrote her, and soon she came for an exploratory trip.

Early in 2004, Rapaz's vice-president was showing Renata around Kaha Wayi and the khipus. He warned her that this would be a very special kind of work. Yes, he said, the village expected a thorough conservation. But we would not be allowed to take anything away—people were very nervous about this. He remarked that cultural authorities in Lima seemed to think everything ought to be in huge national museums, but Rapacinos wanted just the opposite—they wanted Andean patrimony to be safe right where it is. "If people in Lima or from other countries want to see our things, why shouldn't they take a bus ride and get to know us?" he asked. "After all, preserving these things is something we did ourselves. Not the Ministry of Culture."

We received our work rules: no electricity in Kaha Wayi, no chemical treatments, no taking of radiocarbon samples without case-by-case approval. Members of the balterno cabinet would supervise at all times. They would have a veto in hiring and scheduling (reflecting their desire for patronage power over wage work, which at the time was scarce). We were even told that mice found in Kaha Wayi shouldn't be killed. We would have to accept ongoing ritual as the top priority. Any time the bendelhombre decided Kaha Wayi was needed for a ritual *mesa*, we would have to suspend work and keep out.

Renata and I conferred. Would we be able to do a proper job under those constraints? Yes, she said. We'd need to build a site laboratory next to Kaha Wayi and get permission for the khipus to live there temporarily. We'd learn ancient techniques and hire local artisans. We'd need to be ultraconservative, cleaning up every thread and every potsherd with pincers and tiny painter's brushes—no chemicals, no power tools.

Fortunately, Sonia Guillén knew who could wield those brushes: the sister team of Rosa and Rosalía Choque Gonzáles. During a conference of textile experts, she'd once noticed that the mends on some bedsheets in her hotel were beautifully sewn and asked who had stitched them. Would the sisters like to cut back on hotel work and get textile restoration training? Soon Rosa and Rosalía went to work in Guillén's mummy-conserving laboratory as virtuoso archaeological seamstresses. Both were already at ease with the life of Andean villages, being daughters of an Aymara-speaking village in the far southern part of the highlands.

At that early stage the project, I also met the young Argentinian-trained archaeologist Víctor Falcón Huayta. Víctor had managed fieldwork for Peru's state archaeological institutions. We talked about how to create a site lab: would any of the buildings around the sacred precinct do? No, he said, old Rapaz houses would be too small, dusty, and dark. Víctor had a better idea: Peru being a mining country par excellence, we should turn to a company that specialize in building high-altitude mining camps.

For our living quarters, we moved into a pair of rough-hewn adobe houses that we rented from the storekeeper-herdsman Néstor Cóndor. Soon the crew from the mining camp company reached Rapaz. From daybreak to past nightfall they laid the cement pad for the lab. After dark the builders found energy for a warming drink and a round of storytelling about their lives at high-altitude mine sites. One had the Quechua nickname Curi ("Golden"), and he lived up to it with superb work. Curi told a tale about a terrible night on the job:

Once we worked building a mining camp in a remote high valley. We made our supper under the stars on a cold night. We told stories, all about zombies (*condenados*), stories to make your hair stand on end. My buddy just couldn't stop thinking about zombies.

We walked onward in the dark. A skunk was there, with its tail curved up forward like a parasol. There was the skunk, digging into the earth to eat those soft white grubs, his food. And as he was digging, he scrabbled with his little hands, making his tail dance and tremble in the air. My friend with the thing about zombies saw him, and he thought it was a zombie. He fell down in a faint.

We gathered round to help him, but he couldn't wake up. He was unconscious and yet his eyes could see and his ears hear. While he was laid out there, a local man came by with a heavy plank on his shoulder, tilted up high. My friend was laid out flat, but his eyes saw that, and he cried, "Oh God, another zombie, bigger!" And he was like dead. We thought he had died.

I loaded him on my shoulders and walked as far as our camp. We prepared a bed. As I was approaching the bed, just letting my friend slide off my shoulders, he woke up and felt himself falling off my back. His eyes opened and filled with terror. In a strangled voice he cried "A zombie has carried me off!" And he died for real.

After the round of stories, instead of being tired Curi was more stoked than ever. But it was late, and freezing, and time to rest. Another worker, his friend Hemer, blew away the altitude blues with a last reminiscence:

Once we went to go and build houses on the hell-and-gone puna, out beyond Cerro de Pasco, just two kilometers from the icecap itself. Even colder than here. We had a new technician, a guy from Lima. He complained that the road was horrible, nothing but potholes, nothing but abysses to fall into. And when the freeze made the rebar crack loose, he complained, "Shit, this is impossible!" We were pouring boiling water into the cement, because if we didn't it would freeze before we could spread it. This guy spat in the concrete. He bitched about ice in the washbasin in the morning and he bitched about wormy potatoes at night. "Boss," he said to the engineer, "this is the absolute shits! Get us out of here!" So the engineer said, "Oh, did somebody tell you the job was in Acapulco?"

Everyone cracked up one last time and we went to bed.

The dry season was well underway by the time the walls were up and our site lab was ready (see Figure 5.1). What a pleasure it was to sit in a sunny white room just a couple of steps from Kaha Wayi! Renata, who had returned to London after the initial site visit, came back to Rapaz. The lab took shape with shelves and tools and a huge work table on sawhorses.

FIGURE 5.1 Temporary site laboratory, later removed from the precinct. Photo by the author.

It was a surprise when Rosalía arrived with her six-year-old son and her twelve-year-old daughter, but after only a few days the kids settled happily into the Rapaz school. Being highland comuneras already, the sisters settled effortlessly into the place. In fact they became celebrities. They were welcomed by women known for being handy with wool. By visiting in each lady's patio and buying samples of all fibers, they learned to imitate local handiwork. Once Rosa's son Wilmer enrolled in the grammar school, Rosa and Rosalía could be found selling fried dough with syrup (*picarones*) at school fund-raisers. Our little camp was finding its place in Rapaz society.

As a part of the planning stage of the project, Gino de las Casas Ríos, a conservation and restoration architect, made preliminary studies of how the structures could be stabilized. While the Instituto Nacional de Cultura, which has jurisdiction over historic buildings, slowly digested his plans, he arrived just in time for the field season. Gino brought along an architectural restoration technician, Edgar Centeno. Edgar was a young contractor from Lima's burgeoning "Northern Cone." For a day job he remodeled kitchens, but his real love was for ancient technology: adobe, stonework, and rough-hewn wood. (He has since become an archaeological curator.)

The return of Carrie Brezine, another early visitor to Rapaz, completed our core crew. Carrie came to prepare the register of Rapaz khipus. At that time she was a graduate student in Harvard's Department of Anthropology under the khipu expert Gary Urton. Carrie provided a precious talent to khipu studies because she was deeply versed in textile studies and at the same time a computer specialist with advanced mathematical training. As she returned from her heroic hikes along the mountainsides, Carrie could be recognized from afar by her handmade dresses of bright cotton print, reminiscent of old Midwestern styles.

A field site is half lab, half commune. As we took turns in the kitchen, we tried to make ourselves at home, each in his or her own way. The Choque sisters, veteran Andean cooks, could whip up tasty meals out of mutton, tubers, and a few limp greens. Víctor, Edgar, and I banked a lot on canned tomato sauce. With Renata's help, we produced Rapaz's first espresso and relished its heat beyond measure. Gino made a show of restaurateur flair on the days when someone brought trout from the high streams. We later hired a young Rapacina, Valicha, to cook and free us up for more working hours. (Since then Valicha has become a successful weaver at the women's textile cooperative.) On Friday evenings after the dishes were washed, the kids jumped on Rosalía's and Rosa's laps. We huddled around a laptop watching *Spider Man* on bootleg DVDs. Outside, the blazing milky way of the heights wheeled through a black sky.

Partnering conservation in the sacred precinct

When it came time to put wheels on Vice-President Gallardo's proposal, we, and the balternos, faced the prospect of trying to meet contradictory needs. First, residents were committed to protecting traditionalistic and inward-looking ritual use of the patrimony. Second, at the same time, many also hoped to make outward-looking, pragmatic use of it, including tourist development. And third, the authorities were concerned for stabilization and protection of the material legacy, despite the stresses that the first two continually inflict on it. Our experience was not that of solving a technical conservation problem, but rather of learning to work out a flexible accommodation among equally legitimate interests.

When archaeologist Víctor Falcón Huayta and I brought our research-conservation plan to the Rapaz New Year's Assembly on January 2, 2005, these interests as well as ours were at risk. Grant proposals had gone in, but would Rapaz give us final permission? Foreign intervention in Kaha Wayi would put the "vice's" political support to an acid test. Víctor wrote in his notes:

> When we were on the way to the Assembly, the outgoing vice-president stopped us on the road. He was walking along with his wooden staff of authority clad in silver and adorned with flowers, and his hat decked with red and white flowers. He walked along with some people and greeted others. He took us to his office and left us there while he attended to other duties. He looked alert and somewhat nervous. He was waiting for his helpers [the balternos] to carry out the change of command. He said he would talk especially to the incoming president to include the question of our project in the agenda. And so it was, he took us before the council and presented us to the new authorities.

Would the project serve the interest of the newly formed Culture and Tourism Committee? Would publications for popularization of research be funded? These and other questions came before the meeting, and others were only asked in undertones: did we foreigners take money from a mining company? Could this job involve scouting for minerals? Or missionary intervention? Or illegal removal of antiquities? Or were we political types operating under wraps? There never was a moment of unrestricted confidence, but once funding became visible the area of confidence grew.

As we started work one thing was clear: the community did have reason to worry about the safety of the patrimony. Since Dr. Ruiz's visits toward 1980, the educator Martín Falcón had led efforts to give Kaha Wayi better physical care, but there also had been periods of neglect. It was Falcón's idea to promote conservation of the patrimony as "Inka" legacy. A steel showcase for the khipus was brought in. It didn't fit. He suggested bringing the khipus out of the shrine so school children and outside visitors could see them. The adepts of Kaha Wayi protested against this as sacrilege. "The comuneros almost lynched me," Falcón remembered. "Because nobody was supposed to see it. It was a sacred thing of the Inkas. Rain would cease, flash floods would break loose, there were going to be epidemics and mass death."

Fortunately for him, that year's weather was good and the harvest large. But nobody revived the idea of linking Kaha Wayi with the school. From the late 1980s to 1992 the Shining Path war, urgent expenses for modernization, and resistance from Protestant factions made work days for Kaha Wayi hard to organize.

Renata and Gino found possibly seismic cracks in the walls of both buildings. Stones and mortar were missing, allowing dust, water, and small animals to get inside. Interior walls were shedding adobe dust on the patrimonial objects. Candles, tobacco, burning embers, and incense in ceremonies had smudged everything with soot. Both roofs were dilapidated. The top floor of Pasa Qulqa had collapsed completely. Rubble from the top floor weighed upon the lower floor, threatening to dump everything into the subterranean ground level. The community had recently rebuilt the precinct's street-side walls, so the outer protection was in handsome condition. But the gate to the precinct was problematic because the Transport Committee had installed a huge steel double door to protect the communal truck and bus inside the courtyard. Also, waste water from surrounding houses was infiltrating Kaha Wayi's patio.

Inside, khipus hung draped over a wooden rod which in turn was suspended from the ceiling of Kaha Wayi. As villagers had often commented, this was not safe for the khipu. The ceiling over them, which was made of wood sticks covered with vegetable fibers and a layer of smoothed earth, had developed gaps and was patchy with mold. Animals had gotten inside the attic and urinated. A large leak just above the khipu had allowed urine to drip onto patrimonial objects. The thatch laid in 1996 had deteriorated so much one could see patches of sky near the ridgeline. The earthen floor had no drainage.

The most obvious khipu problem was fraying of the fibers where the khipu were draped over the rod. The cords were covered with a thick layer of sooty dust that dulled the colors of the fibers and figurines. The central area of the khipu had a dark discoloration and urine stains. Old insect egg cases were stuck to cords made of sheep wool, but the larger amount of camelid wool was almost totally intact. Sheepskin cushions laid on the surrounding stone benches were infested with moth eggs. Some of the figurines attached to the khipu appeared in risk of falling off. A long crack weakened one whole wall of Kaha Wayi.

Fixing the most fragile things

When work got underway in May of 2005, we organized a series of consultations with the comuneros, and especially with the inner cabinet of balternos (see Figure 5.2). They took turns watching over our work. We agreed to absent ourselves from the site during weeks when ritual work was underway inside.

Since we were about to handle sacred objects, we wanted to make sure people could see for themselves that nobody was stealing, desecrating, or altering them. Suspicions could create ugly situations, we were warned. So we decided that during work hours, we would allow visits by any adult who wanted to see what we were up to. After a few weeks knocks on the gate became so frequent that they slowed down work. Nonetheless we were delighted to share people's memories or curiosities. To our surprise, a lot of visitors wanted to donate small sums, so we

FIGURE 5.2 Museologist Renata Peters meets with balternos in the Kaha Wayi precinct, 2005. Photo by the author.

started a ledger for goodwill donations. At year's end the project was able to make a substantial contribution to the Community treasury.

Only the vice-president had the key to the precinct. Every morning we were to sit down in the patio with the maestro of the day's job, waiting for the "vice" to open up. This time was anything but wasted; it was coca time. One speaks of coca-sucking (*boleo, chajchay*) as "finding" the day's solutions, and indeed these pensive, sociable intervals did help us talk through the issues. For example, one of the hardest matters concerned parking. The balternos agreed that leaving the community trucks and its oil drums in the precinct was undesirable, but there was no other place because Rapaz had already built on all its scarce flat land. Little by little a plan emerged: a new terrace would be filled and leveled and the steel gates relocated. Kaha Wayi would get a wooden gate, flagstone footpaths and plantings. By 2007 decorative puna grass and the hardy "flower of the inkas" *cantuta* (Cantua buxifolia) were beautifying the precinct. As of 2016, the new parking terrace is in use.

As has become usual among archaeologists, we observed the Andean proprieties. We sponsored ritual work to "pay" for intruding on the earth. The aged bendelhombre Teodosio Falcón Ugarte came out of retirement to *calzar* (set up and activate) our *mesas* in Kaha Wayi. He taught us to keep coca leaves, *kunuk* incense, llama fat, cigarettes, rum, and special white cornmeal on hand for this end. (I later found out the hard way that putting coca leaf on an expense account makes trouble.) He showed how to carry divinatory embers (*shanla*) on a potsherd. Rosa Choque gracefully contributed a packet of kunuk, coca, and llama fat from her home village in Moquegua. Her llama fat was of superb quality: a shiny globe the size of a baseball, of purest buttery color, humbling the local white goo. As night fell, "Ticocho" initiated us by dabbing white llama fat from Rapaz's own herd on our foreheads and began the series of invocation chants to ask permissions from the mountains, lakes, Kaha Wayi itself, and the khipus. Then we got ready to disassemble Kaha Wayi.

A temple as gallery of symbols

It's characteristic of ritual places and deeds to develop invariant structures. Ritual is sometimes said to be culture at its least flexible. Rustic and dishevelled as Kaha Wayi then looked to outsiders, it looked to its owners like an inviolable assembly of meaningful parts in a meaningful whole. Documenting and safeguarding the assembly was a technical job that would yield (we hoped) some understanding of why it had to be kept just so.

Symbolism has a distinctive anthropological sense. A symbol is any thing or act that stands for a referent in the mind of a beholder. A minimalist system of symbolism such as mathematical signs assigns each symbol to one and only one referent, and it requires the referent to be explicitly identified. The symbolic codes discovered by anthropology tend to represent the opposite extreme of symbolic work, using signs in expansive ways. Cultural symbol systems deploy signs that attach to many meanings simultaneously. Sign-to-referent connections are less explicit, less conscious, and more numerous. The Scottish Africanist Victor Turner called attention to the "multivalent" character of dominant symbols: central symbols' value to society consists precisely in the way they gather *multiple* referents and bind them together in the thoughts and feelings of the beholder.

To take an Andean example of multivalence, coca leaf stands for vital energy, but it also stands for civil order (coca inaugurates meetings), for the superhuman (it is the basic gift to any power), for fertility (wild coca foretells abundance), for motherhood (one says "mama coca"), for wisdom (groups share coca to help them "find" collective decisions), and for respect (coca can never become garbage). Partaking in coca attaches one to all these values at once, in a pleasant mood-making way that shortcuts any need for preaching. That is why the morning coca break put us right for the day. That is why, inside Kaha Wayi, stuffing one's cheek with coca till it bulges is a meritorious sign of commitment. With its deep and wide ramification through Andean cultures, coca is a good example of what the American symbolic anthropologist Sherry Ortner calls "key symbols." A "key symbol" is a multivalent sign that is guarded by special proprieties, appears in many contexts, and evokes strong shared emotions (1973). And what is a temple but a gallery of key symbols?

The meanings of offerings

Thus Kaha Wayi with it sacred clutter seems to the knowing Rapacino an array of things that call out to multiple loyalties all at once. In the physical cleanup and reinforcement work, these things came before us one by one separately—an unnatural way to behold them, but a good focusing experience.

The pile of fresh coca that spills over the edges of the altar table is the active offering of recent encounters, signifying that people here have poured out loyalty and respect for both Kaha Wayi and the powers for whom it speaks. During cleanup, the conservators found several gunnysacks full of used coca leaves leaned against the benches. "What are these?" we asked the bendelhombre. "They're the work," he said. That is, in ritual, every "turn" of coca has to be collected before fresh leaves are handed out, and the sucked-out leaves are saved indefinitely because they are the substance of ritual work. Coca can never be thrown away. After deliberating about whether the "work" would take space needed for the new khipu case, bendelhombre Melecio decided that the bags should be retained as parts of Kaha Wayi by putting them into an archaeological test pit that Victor Falcón had opened along its outer wall, then sealing them when the pit was refilled.

A collection of miscellaneous offerings hangs on strings from Kaha Wayi's cane ceiling (see Figure 5.3). All of them had to be removed in padded boxes and set aside for laboratory cleaning and reinforcement. They included delicate material such as dried flowers, ribbons, cornhusk, bird feathers, a sugar loaf, straw, agave, and desiccated tubers of food. On windless days, the Choque sisters set out their work table beside the laboratory and delicately opened successive boxes, dusting each frail object.

FIGURE 5.3 Some of the offerings restored to their position under Kaha Wayi ceiling after conservation. Photo by Renata Peters.

People stopped to comment, and these comments suggested the objects' roles in anchoring Rapacino knowledge and loyalty. Each object resonates with local ideals and feelings: for example, one of the suspended offerings is a shriveled *pirwa* or *chukrush* (twinned specimen) of the sweet tuber oca. Twinning, as Lévi-Strauss explained in a famous essay, has a very special Andean meaning of abundance combined with danger (1978). It motivates ritual action.

Or another symbol: ritualist Melecio Montes reminded us to be careful with the suspended bottles because, he said, they are used to receive water from the mountaintops. He didn't know their physical origin, but one with the legend BELFAST later proved identifiable as a "ballast bottle," a type made for seltzer water toward 1900 and later brought to many ports as ships' ballast (BLM n.d.). They had been carried up to Rapaz on one of those occasions when sea water had to be brought into Kaha Wayi to prime the cycle of weather—perhaps a long time ago, for ballast bottles are not found in recent material contexts.

The gallery of key symbols has an overall shape: at the edges, participants sit on ground-level benches against walls. The center consists of the altar and its accessories, from which messages in the form of raywanes, liquefied corn, llama fat, smoke, coca, and so forth are dispatched to powers outside Kaha Wayi. Overhead, vectors of communication like birds, sea water, liquor, and food hover suspended from the ceiling. The whole assembly could be imagined in use as a communication center, concentrating ritual work, dispatching it upward and outward, and receiving the replies. This assembly as a whole conforms quite easily with many ethnographic accounts of Andean cosmology, colonial and modern. It is explained as a recirculating system. Water, the stuff of life, flows down mountains to the ocean and up again via the Milky Way to renew the cycle. Life emerging from the moistened surface of earth gives of itself and of its vital tokens to prime the circuit and attract flow toward itself (Urton 1981; Cummins and Mannheim 2011). Kaha Wayi is the pump house for Rapaz's share of this system.

The symbolic or interpretative direction

The vessels of meaning we cleaned and fixed were often literally vessels—baskets, bottles, gourds, pots, bags. Each held substances seen as circulating elements of the cosmos: rainwater, seawater, wind, food, fire, and energy in the forms of coca, tobacco, or liquor. As a suite of vessels, all Kaha Wayi's furnishings seemed to compose a sort of miniature of earth and atmosphere, grouped around a center— the altar—through which human intentions were directed to them and to which superhuman intentions returned in the form of sparking or liquid auguries. A certain kind of anthropologist might think of this chamber of symbols, when filled with its human devotees, as a working model of society in its world.

That kind of anthropologist might be a disciple of Clifford Geertz (1926–2006), who propounded an interpretative anthropology of religion prevailing in the United States circa 1960–1990. He tells us that meaning-intensive settings exemplify models of a special sort. Any cultural model, he held, can be taken in two ways. On the one hand a local set of symbols constitutes a "model for," meaning signs arranged as a program for making things formally resemble the prescribed order. The gourds on the altar are a model for the mountains' desired consumption of human offering. "Models for," Geertz thought, were present in nonhuman nature as well as culture; genes, for example, are "models for" arranging molecules into cells. Simultaneously, however, the same set of symbols can be taken the other way around: they are signs placed into relation with each other as an artificial order for perceiving or receiving (rather than making) exterior realities, and thereby representing them intersubjectively, inside ourselves. Geertz called this use of symbols a "model of." The objects of Kaha Wayi together form a model of the montane environment. Seeing this provides one conceptual component of an overall Andean model we might call animated climatology. Geertz thought model-making in its "model of" function is characteristically human, being a prior condition for both religion and science.

Anthropologists of many schools can agree in characterizing symbolism as the "medium of culture:" signs are what culture moves *through*. Humans create cultural representations out of raw experience by assembling an open-ended variety of symbols, i.e., things that have a "stands for" relationships to parts of experience. Symbols include words, letters, emblems, gestures, images, and the whole open-ended universe of media, whether they are audible, visual, tactile, olfactory, or culinary. To an important degree, culture comes to us as code, in the form of assembled symbols. For this reason, Geertz suggested we think of culture as a sort of text and of ethnographers as decipherers of the many "pages" displayed to us in events from cockfights to shadow plays to ceremonies. Good ethnography should be "thick" and "experience-near": one should interpret unspoken signs like oily perfume of llama fat no less intensively than the arcane words of invocation.

Different symbolic assemblies realize differing human potentials and dispositions. Although Geertz began as a relatively ground-hugging ethnographer of Indonesian wet-rice agriculture, his many-sided ethnographies became more and more symbol-intensive as his theoretical ambition grew, until culture came in his showing to seem almost nothing but the play of symbols and models. In florid prose, he portrayed social activity itself not as socioeconomic cause and effect but as meaningful action in patterns that satisfy needs for certainty and meaning. Whatever else people may be doing, they are always turning raw experience, with its suffering, injustice, and uncertainty, into livable life by continually enacting "models of" and "models for" living.

Geertz perceived separable commonsensical, aesthetic, and religious "cultural systems" that do this work. In commonsensical and aesthetic contexts, a given activity's cultural "text" or scenario is often implicit or partial and hard to "read" ethnographically. What is special about the religious system, he proposes in his most famous essay, is its insistence on explicit "conceptions of a general order of existence" that accept no residue of meaninglessness (1966). In this, he drank deep of the "interpretative" tradition of social theory, especially from American readings of Max Weber's pre-World War I German masterworks. For Weber, social systems are not the invisible, impersonal engines of collective dynamism that Durkheim imagined. For Weber, systems inherently work through systems of meaning present in individual consciousness. These assign value to everything, motivating and organizing action among people. If "collective representations" à la Durkheim make life possible to live, Weberian "values" make it worth living. For Weberians, a shared system of meanings formed one core of society, as much as Marx thought production to be the core, and as Durkheim thought social organization to be the core.

Weber and Geertz were both intensely interested in religious symbolism because they saw it as the guarantor of solidarity in the face of hazards that crack all the other systems. To take part in the guided experience called ritual is, for Geertz, to let the religious symbol system fill in what commonsensical, scientific, and aesthetic mindsets fail to complete. Religious conceptions thus acquire a capacity to saturate experience in general, so that the overall practice of being Balinese or Andean, etc., seems to embody "uniquely factual" truths.

So, for example, a traditional Rapacino as Geertz might imagine him would know in his bones that the principles of life-giving, substance-exchanging reciprocity experienced in a night of mountain cult are the same principles as those of society and of all things. He might find it hard to imagine the world otherwise.

Among those who see culture as a web of symbols, Geertz was extreme. Critics of Geertz feel that, given his prime commitment to "the native's point of view," it seems rather high-handed to imagine culture as a "text" that gives a society all its conscious meanings and yet remains unrecognizable by its authors.

Other anthropologists with loyalties to the "science end" of the discipline are leery of the Geertzian postulate that each culture creates an intersubjective "world" peculiar to itself. "The native's point of view" is all very well, but the Geertzian version of it seems to blur anthropology's other permanent commitment: "the psychic unity of mankind." Geertz's roster of pan-human basics is a rather old-fashioned and arbitrary list of needs he deems primary.

Sometimes against Geertz's own inclination, the relativism that spoke of text-like "cultural worlds" was pushed in the 1990s to a farther extreme where it merged with with literary postmodernist positions. For those attracted to the postmodern idea it could come to seem that other "worlds" of knowledge were created within and through local discourses, so no "world" would be knowable except within its own web of meaning. As "otherness" became a value in itself, cultures came to seem like scattered planets. How then could there ever be ethnographic—or any other—knowledge across cultures? Faced with assertions that cultures are separate universes, the proud old positivist Ernest Gellner asked, "in what inter-stellar or inter-cultural void does our relativist articulate his position?" (1995, 4). The resulting fight has subsided, but successor versions of radical relativism still flourish (Chapter 6).

And yet these side effects of interpretative anthropology would hardly justify abandoning the colorful, commodious, and "experience-near" ethnographic attitude that is Geertz's best legacy.

One other frequent critique of the symbolic school is that in his determination to keep the "native point of view" uppermost (that is, in his resolute phenomeno-logical and antireductionist bent), the later Geertz slighted factors of organization, technology, scale, and economic interest. In countries where anthropology sticks closer to the Durkheimian and British sociological traditions, ethnographers gave symbolic study a different and more sociological emphasis.

For example, Victor Turner proposed that societies (starting with his African hosts the Ndembu) regenerate their systems, in the Durkheimian sense, by peri-odically immersing themselves in intense display of symbols that embody the fundamental bonds. Society undergoes an alternating pulse, between structured normality and ritual states which disrupt our roles, temporarily melting them down into an "antistructural" state of heightened solidarity (1969). Such ritual scenarios put the limelight on symbols that carry multiple connotations about basic social commitments (e.g., for Ndembu, matrilineality, purity, etc.). Multiple commit-ments are thus bundled together as compelling poles of allegiance.

The English Africanist Mary Douglas, pulled the sociological revision of sym-bolism in a partly structuralist direction: people interpret the bodily basics of life (lactation, animal types, dirt and cleanup, etc.) in ways that match the categories of society as they know it. Through symbolic matrices people bring out of their earthly nature natural-seeming doctrines for enforcing social order and even for specu-lating beyond it (1966). For example, everybody experiences having a head and hands. Rapaz attaches to the "naturally" available head/hands contrast the contrast between executive and administrative power: the community's governing board is called the "head," and its enforcers "hands," etc. This "natural"-seeming contrast easily travels upward and outward to all sorts of structures, even to cosmology.

A temple as source of knowledge, and intellectualist theories of religion

One obviously suspect thing about the symbolistic approach is that nobody believes it except us anthropologists. It belongs inherently to the outsider's stance. Nobody ever explained the objects in Kaha Wayi to me as "standing for" anything exterior to themselves. What local traditionalists think is that ritual paraphernalia are substantially the *same* as the entities they manifest, not representations of them. Rapacinos certainly aren't Geertzians.

When we step away from the symbolic or "stands for" analysis, we can recognize that, for its operator, the wind-controlling bag wiya actually, and not metaphorically, contains the wind. Llama-fat sparks actually are the jirkas' utterance. The dust of a footprint, conserved to prevent some "vicuña-like man" from wandering away from the community, actually is part of that man. If one wants to understand "the native's point of view," one may then find the symbolic approach inauthentic: it expands on what "we" think they are doing, not what they think they are doing. Would the mental intensity of the encounter with cattle ilas or mountains occur at all if participants thought they were just manipulating tokens that "stand for" something more real?

To say that Kaha Wayi's belongings add up to a cosmogram or totalizing assembly of symbols leaves out a part of what sacred gear is worth to its operators. These things are equipment for *discovery*—discovery about the climate, hydrography, and the social dispositions of the mountain "owners." They are technology for getting as well as applying knowledge: for making water flow where it is needed, for knowing what people should do and making them work compliantly, and for understanding the lives of crops and herds.

For example: when we were getting close to the day for carrying the khipu collection on its "bed" from Kaha Wayi to its temporary lodging in the conservation lab, Bendelhombre Melecio Montes frowned into Renata's eyes and mine as he insisted that the most crucial matter was to protect his instruments of discovery. Like every Andean mesa, his altar contains objects that are sensitive to and affected by the mountain powers. They are meteorological instruments, except that the force registered through them is mountains' social "will" rather than impersonal forces like barometric pressure. Melecio was most concerned with three gourd vessels. After a ritualist fills them with the three colored varieties of liquefied corn, the gradual lowering of liquid in the vessels is understood as a good response. It shows the powers appreciate the drink and are consuming it—preferably with bubbles, a friendly response.

We too were very concerned with the gourds but for a different reason: the falling liquid level in each gourd is due to corn liquid leaking through its organic fiber structure and onto the altar table. Consequently the altar had

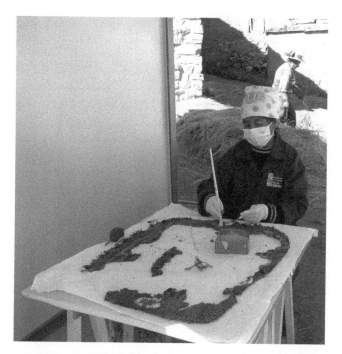

FIGURE 5.4 Rosa Choque cleans Kaha Wayi's altarcloth, later reinforced with a
fungus-proof support. Photo by the author.

become a focus of infestations, from which a bloom of white fungus grew over
the woodwork. Fungus had all but completely eaten away the lower of two
altarcloths.

To alleviate the fungus problem, the ritualist and balternos accepted our suggestion that the three gourd vessels be retained but placed on impermeable saucers.
The small altar table came out of its shelter for a short time to be treated with wood
preservative. On the underside, at the center, it has a grape-sized "navel" made
of hardened llama fat. This little ball is considered the center point of Kaha Wayi,
and it radiates vitality. The navel was the one thing so venerable that we were not
allowed to touch it.

As for the revered altar cloth, only a ring of fringe remained. After drying it
and cleaning it (see Figure 5.4), Rosa began weaving a new synthetic-fiber support
textile and then attached the fringe to it. The support mimicked the old brown
and cream design, so that the restored altar cloth looked whole. Bendelhombre
Melecio, not an easy man to please, smiled to see it on the crated altar.

Another main instrument of discovery is a large broken pot base of brown
ceramic (visible in Figure 6.1). It functions as a brazier for burning the coals of
divination, which contain llama fat and an incense of kunuq twigs. When the
bendelhombre recites invocations to the mountains, he periodically peers into
the brazier to see if the incense is throwing sparks. These sparks, plus various

atmospheric, hydraulic, or animal sounds, are his means for finding out what the mountains say in response: are they listening? Will they join the meeting? Do they feel friendly? Will they send good climate? Melecio was understandably concerned that a careless boot could break the brazier. Fortunately, being free of unburned organic residue, it needed no maintenance.

In anthropology's Victorian beginnings, ethnologists like E.B. Tylor sought alternatives to racial or theological explanations for "primitive" religiosity. They revived a historically deep vein of speculation: arguments that "spiritual" and "magical beliefs" emerge as an apparatus for gaining knowledge. They resemble science by positing invisible but humanly accessible forces in the universe that make things what they are. Early "intellectualists" like Tylor thought notions of spirit force like *mana* of Oceania or *orenda* of the Iroquois had about the same importance as gravity did for us. In their own context, religions were said to serve like sciences: gods, mountains, spirits, and so forth amount to theories. They are "multistranded" theories: in them affirmations of discovery are fused with affirmations of social norms. Nonetheless, said "intellectualists," religiosity and dogma are works of intellect, interpretable only by those willing to give ritual credit for involving reason.

In contrast to Geertzians, who see religion as having latent overall meanings that only a "hermeneutical" (exegetical) procedure can bring to light, several outstanding British Africanist ethnographers proposed that the important religious concern is the overt one: the desire to explain and influence the everyday world by discovering its underlying forces and principles. Science, not theology, is the appropriate translating domain. By this light, rituals, however peculiar-seeming, are not obscure "texts." Rather they serve a purpose "we" already have in common with "them:" study, analysis, and useful action. This vein of theorizing has the nickname of intellectualism.

For example, the great Africanist E.E. Evans-Pritchard was willing to call Azande witchcraft a "natural science." He might have summarized the matter as "science by other premises." Given the local premise that unusual events are caused by unusual human actions, it made sense to attribute what we call random misfortune to human agency (1937). A process of reasoning that was partly divination and partly judicial detective work tried to find out what human deeds were hidden causes of a given misfortune. Andean climate lore also has aspects of investigation and reasoning, embodying as they do not just personalization of nature but detailed study of climate and hydrography. One attraction of intellectualism is that it encourages the ethnographer to explicate local theories as we hear them, and not cook up reductive replacements for them. Even as Evans-Pritchard became a prince of his discipline, he remained reticent about formulating innovative theory because he thought ethnography's true vocation was to elicit local theories from local actions. Evans-Pritchard sometimes foreshadows the idea of cultures' "implicit philosophies," which we will touch on in Chapter 6.

Robin Horton, a British Africanist of the post-WWII generation, revived Evans-Pritchard's theme. He argued against the idea that human thought is somehow fundamentally divided between two kinds of truth, namely, a practical and testable kind, and a non-pragmatic symbolic kind. Against this Horton upholds the unity of thought including "primitive" thought. Ritual man, he said, is not really a distinctive being, but is rather a sub-species of "theory-building man" (1964). Religious modeling is much like scientific modeling. It observes regularities and exceptions and seeks to explain them in terms of underlying forces. Like science, the result reduces complexity and unpredictability toward simplicity and regularity.

The difference between ritual inquiry (auguries, oracles, etc.) and science lies mostly in ways of evaluating models. Traditional African theories differ from post-Enlightenment Western ones "most notably in the absence of any guiding body of explicit acceptance/rejection criteria that would ensure the efficiency with which they pursue their aims" (1964, 97). Horton, like Evans-Pritchard, sees such theories as having strength because they are never put at risk. Models involving sacrifice and divination are never *not* implemented, so for the operators there is no way to tell whether outcomes would be different without them. And at the time of Horton's fieldwork experience, many rural Africans were not acquainted with alternative models of causation. Religions could exist as "closed systems." By contrast, the central premise of Western science as an "open system" is that explanations are always at risk of disproof and abandonment. (We will see this proposition challenged in Chapter 7.)

But if religion is meant to explain, why must it explain in terms of relations with invisible beings? All theories posit invisible entities. "Events and processes which feature in the theoretical model must not be available to the same acts of observation" as the things to be explained, "otherwise they would merely have rejoined the inventory of things to be explained." Science typically finds non-evident parts of reality by downward reduction (Chapter 1), positing underlying entities like atoms (Chapter 1). Religion seeks them by discovering unseen phenomena within the social sphere. "Activities in society present the most markedly ordered and regular area of . . . experience." So they become the wellsprings of hypothesis (Horton 1964, 99–100).

We see traces of this inclination in Western antiquity. Anaximander was one of the first pre-Socratics (6th century BCE) to attempt a physics. Striving to explain interactions among forces such as heat and cold, he said that such forces "pay penalty and retribution to each other for their injustice according to the assessment of Time" (Gottlieb 2016, 9). When social arrangements furnished models, the causes of phenomena in general tended to be imagined as meaningful interactions. Rituals in any age were, so to speak, communications infrastructure for trans-human relationship.

A surprise in the ceiling, and theories about religion as disciplines of power

The Kaha Wayi-Pasa Qulqa system is not considered a "religion," nor is it articulated as a doctrine. It does not encroach on the claims of Christianity by postulating any immaterial or transcendent rival to *Dios*. It housed none of the symbols

FIGURE 5.5 Straw cross found sealed inside the upper floor of Kaha Wayi. Photo by the author.

Christians regard as religious; it simply stands aside from Christianity. So it was a surprise and a mystery to find within Kaha Wayi a hidden symbolic apex that did once belong to Christendom.

The ceiling that divided the ritual chamber from the attic turned out to be hopelessly contaminated with fungus. It had to be replaced. The architectural crew began stripping out rotten canes and exposing bare rafters. As they were breaking the crumbling "cake" of packed and whitewashed earth that formed the attic floor, Gino yelled, "Wait, there's something in here!" He clambered down the ladder and laid a rustic cross on a tarpaulin (see Figure 5.5). Our balterno supervisors crowded round in astonishment. Nobody had expected to find a Christian object in Kaha Wayi.

It looked at first glance like wood, but the balternos quickly saw that there was no wood in it. The material was actually puna straw (*ichu*) bundled into hard cylinders and wrapped around with a different kind of grass called *anqush*.

The balternos recognized bits of inner binding material as the puna grass *shilwa*. A song (in Chapter 4) mentions shilwa as a key symbol of animal welfare because it grows in swampy green spots where livestock love to graze.

A straw cross—what could that mean? In the first place, this cross was not made of wood, the material intimately associated with Christ through innumerable "true cross" reliquary cults. This cross may have been made above the treeline, where there is no wood, or may stand for the treeless heights by metonymy. Puna straw speaks of the purportedly wilder life among herds and predators, high above in-town life. Could it be that, like water brought down from the rain-owning lakes, straw brought an infusion of the mountains' power? But if so, why in the form of a cross? Perhaps it had been made to signify the Christianization of the level most associated with pagan powers.

A hidden cross—what could that mean? Given Kaha Wayi's function as an operative microcosm, full of talismanic "ambassadors" from multiple micro-environments, a token from the puna would be no anomaly. But why a secret one? Andean builders often conceal magically beneficial things such as camelid fetuses inside walls, and similar practices occur in Old World customs about lay-ing cornerstones. A cross might have served to radiate good power. Its invisible but apical position suggested that the cross was inserted during a build or rebuild of Kaha Wayi.

Its meaning became somewhat clearer when we received the radiocarbon results from a bit of straw that fell off the little cross. It yielded two possible date ranges, 1647–1684 (relative area 0.274) and 1729–1803 (relative area 0.726).[1] Both are close to campaigns of extirpation in Rapaz summarized in Chapter 3.

It could then be that a party sympathetic to Christianity emplaced the cross so as to radiate Catholicism over the replica cosmos below. That would have yielded a total assembly something like the one that the pro-Inka "Indian Chronicler" Pachacuti Yamqui drew to represent a prehispanic Andean temple. (Like many Andean Christians and a few clergy, Pachacuti Yamqui suspected the old Inka order had been sanctified by intuitive Christianity.) His drawing contains an altar in a house, surrounded by an array of crop, herd, and astronomical talismans, and surmounted by a starry cross at the roof peak (1993 [1613?], 207–208). The overall order envisioned would have been the Andean "circulating cosmos" with a Christian power installed as its apex, over the altar.

If this is what the straw cross betokened, we would have to guess why it was kept from view while all the other symbols remained visible. Perhaps the Pachacuti-like syncretic solution was controversial in its day because extirpa-tion was above all an attempt to purify rural worship of its pagan components. Andeanizing the cross could have seemed sacrilegious to some clergy. Or, on the other hand, perhaps a faction of the community would have objected to Christianizing Kaha Wayi, had they known about it. It had been usual to ham-mer the cross off coins before offering them to mountains. In some historic transition the governors of Kaha Wayi seem to have forgotten this Christianizing installation.

Imagining this long-forgotten fight for symbolic supremacy brings us to the premise of an anthropological approach different from the vein that emphasizes making a shared symbolic world and also different from the one that emphasizes ritual as intellectual work. This alternative view is the argument of religion as an aspect of power. Was the hidden cross inserted as the keystone of a newly integrated Christian-Andean compulsory order? Should we rather think of it as part and parcel of Christianity's "spiritual conquest of Peru"?

Tiny Leviathan: a temple as a seat of power

Maurice Bloch is a contemporary ethnographer of Malagasy (Madagascar) who exemplifies a power-oriented sociopolitical direction. Rather than seeing religiosity as meaning (like Geertz), or as science (like Horton), he sees it as power. In this he resembles several theorists old and new. Power-oriented theories in their quite divergent poststructuralist and postcolonial flavors dominated graduate-school debates around 2000. Within the landscape that contains Foucauldian "genealogy," subaltern studies, and other kinds of power theories, it is a sign of Bloch's originality that his various critics have never even agreed what he is; he gets pegged contradictorily as a Durkheimian functionalist, a Marxian, or a symbolist.

Here is a Maurice Bloch sentence worth pondering: "The startling quasi-universality of the minimal religious structures . . . derives from the fact that the vast majority of societies represent human life as occurring within a permanent framework which transcends the natural transformative process of birth, growth, reproduction, aging and death" (Bloch 1992, 3). That is, because we exist inevitably as parts of collective arrangements that precede and outlive us, that make or break us, we cannot help but see life as lived under the spell of an overarching, invisible, virtual entity. The transcending construct, such as the church or lineage or state, lives forever while its members die.

Up to this point there is a resemblance to Durkheim. But Bloch's view of the relationship is not so benign as the Parisian master's. The representation of life in rituals

> begins with a complete inversion of everyday understandings. The life invoked in rituals is an "other" life evoked described by such words as "beyond" and "invisible", and located "in the sky". . . or "on a mountain where nobody goes." . . . [I]nstead of birth and growth leading to a successful existence, it is weakening and death which lead to a successful existence . . . [E]ntering into a world beyond process, through the passage of reversal, one can then be part of an entity beyond process, for example, a member of a descent group . . . something permanent, therefore life-transcending.
>
> *Bloch 1992, 4*

The original sociocentric idea now mutates into a sort of black Durkheimianism. Religion does indeed make society visible to itself, as the old French master said.

But the characteristic device by which religion does so is hardly an affirmative gift like the totem feast. Ritual's function is to empower social institutions at the expense of the living man or woman's "ordinary vitality," rather than to "help him live" (in Durkheim's phrase). Indeed for Bloch, religiosity amounts to a tax that the collectivity levies against people's ordinary well-being. It is a tax payable in life or things that stand for life. The transcendent entity's eternal existence is assured by giving some life up: by actual sacrificial killing or a symbolic equivalent, by asceticism and gerontocracy at the cost of youthful values, by practices of submission and constraint, by the exaltation of ancestors above the living, or even by total sacrifice of the self as in suicidal combat, truck-bombing, etc.

"Rites of passage" form a century-old classic theme of anthropology and one of the major categories in ritual studies. Rites of passage are scenarios that relocate a person from one standing in society to another: for example, turning a child into an adult or turning a civilian into a soldier. Bloch sees rites of passage as archetypes of ritual process. The youth or lay person about to be initiated usually is discharged from the "vital here and now" and dispatched to a temporary seclusion or exile. During his period outside normal life he takes part in some strong act of agency on behalf of the overarching entity—typically by performing violence or symbolic violence. For example, he may be made to fight off masked "demons," or attack symbolic enemies, or real human foes. Or, in still other societies, his act of masterly agency may consist of dominating some body of learning.

In his role while away from daily, mortal life, he suspends childish vitality. He is allied instead with an overarching power. He overcomes life: for example, he kills animals, militates against enemies, ritually or really captures women, takes on the voice or message of triumphant ancestors, or challenges spirits. Having now acted as an agent of the transcendent collective, and thus having become imbued with power that mere individuals lack, he comes back "a changed person, a permanently transcendental person who can therefore dominate." He has become a bearer of the collective entity's power.

According to Bloch, similar scenarios of transformation from "prey into hunter" underlie sacrifice, fertility rituals, and many other ceremonial acts. In all of them humans exit normal vitality, assert themselves in the sphere of the transcendental at some expense of ordinary life, and then return charged with force of the transcendental entity so as to act with authority (1992, 10). In this way society produces its own dominators. Societies of many kinds generate roles that enforce institutional commitments and override merely vital motives.

In an essay called "Why Religion Is Nothing Special but Is Central" (2008, 2056) Bloch comments that among his Merina Malagasy ethnographic hosts, a certain frail old man who was viewed as merely burdensome in daily life received in ritual context the deference due a lordly elder, even an ancestor. His lack of ordinary vitality was irrelevant to the ritual frame because the man's elder standing formed part of an imagined (genealogical) double of the social order. This overarching shared construct is what Bloch calls the "transcendental social."

As I handled the coca bags and offering bottles the bendelhombre of Rapaz must carry in his dealings with mountains, I was reminded of that article. Not because of senility, but because a certain bendelhombre was in daily life poorly regarded for his selfish behavior. He was crabby and brusque and he drank alone, which is considered a sign of bad character. And yet, when in his role at Kaha Wayi this man received deference from the most respected balternos. Just as the relevant fact about the old Merina man was his seniority as an incipient ancestor, the relevant fact about the bendelhombre was his titular standing as a specialist empowered by his "rebounding violence"—his brave confrontations with "ornery" mountains.

Before a ritual ascent a bendelhombre and his assistant must separate themselves from ordinary vitality by sexual abstinence, fasting, and solitude. When they sacrifice small animals and vitality-giving intoxicants to lakes, they acquire the clout of the "transcendental social." When he picks a fight with mountains he is not only defending Rapaz but replenishing himself and Kaha Wayi with authority. He comes home newly filled with transcendent authority that overrides his individual persona. Bloch thinks that "the transcendental social . . . and religion are part and parcel of a single unity."

Other theorists of power/ritual stand closer to the Marxian or Foucauldian veins of social theory than Bloch does. They see ritual as a site in which institutions—and not just religious ones—enact arrangements of domination. Talal Asad turned the tables on earlier anthropology of religion by taking Christian religious authority as a prime object of research and using the results to challenge Geertzian interpretivism (1983).

Asad argues that Geertz errs in thinking that the individual religious actor ("man," in lofty Geertzian lingo) creates, chooses, and shares symbolic constellations. For Asad everyone is already at the start a product of particular power arrangements, and that is the template for his activity. At no point does man face the field of symbolic action as a language-like field from which he freely chooses signs to express something, or from which he may stand apart. Rather, known signs have unequal weight. Social consequence is derived from the "social discipline" that ritual enacts; that is how one becomes a person. The person must usually display such signs, for reasons of establishing himself as a credible agent, regardless of whether he believes. (Believing is a side effect.) The ritual posture deploys particular symbols not because they are cosmic—how often do people seek the cosmic anyway?—but because they derive from and point to the enforced existing order. Geertz, he says, has ignored the issue we should be addressing, which is how symbols get their authoritative, natural-seeming power in the first place. The answer is that some people and not others, some institutions and not others, are in a position to impart them as authoritative.

The Oxford English Dictionary mentions an etymological doubt about the word *religion* that evokes the difference between the Geertzian view positing text-like symbols and the Asadian power perspective. In Roman times, Cicero thought *religio* came from a Latin word meaning "to re-read," whereas later scholars derived it from a verb meaning "to restrain or bind." In departing from the Geertzian theme of text-like, quasi-readable meaning, Asad discards the former for the latter. Ritual constrains us to being what we are supposed to be. By changing the subject from transcendence to discipline, Asad proposes a more even playing field for comparing sacred practices. "Faith-based" presuppositions no longer have any privilege. Orthopraxy, the definition of religiosity as behavior rather than belief, is foregrounded. Unlike Bloch, Asad lets us do without a supposedly general inclination to perceive "transcendence." Indeed, as we will see in Chapter 7, he goes as far as challenging the category of religion itself.

The work of power in Kaha Wayi: khipus, for example

Asad has reminded us that to think about Kaha Wayi as a constellation of symbols, or as an engine of knowledge, still leaves out perhaps the most obvious of its attributes: power. For local decision-making in the traditional system (never forgetting that today it is part of a more complex system), the little temple is the proverbial smoke-filled room of politics. Balternos gather there as in their clubhouse, confidentially discussing people's access to resources and influencing the choice of future officers. Hierarchies and authorities are continually regenerated there.

Temples as centers of power form one of the oldest themes in scholarship about religion, a discussion within which anthropology (including archaeology) has intermittently contributed distinctive views. Asad's viewpoint rarely matches the entrenched positivism of Ernest Gellner, yet the two might agree on Gellner's judgment that utterances made in sacred precincts like Kaha Wayi are accredited in a special way. They are "true (that is, referentially valid, correctly linked to nature)" and at the same time "true (that is, true/loyal, conforming to normative conceptual expectations)." The balterno pensively sucking on coca leaves does not hear the officiant's voice as fusing two strands of thought that we think we should distinguish, namely objective cognition of the climate and social attachments. "Loyalty to concepts [such as the idea of weather as interaction] makes possible loyalty to the community" (1988, 54–55).

For Rapacinos and visitors alike, Kaha Wayi owes part of its solemnity to what are thought of as its immemorial inscriptions. While radiocarbon gives us relatively recent dates, the perception of inscription as central to the old legacy of the commons makes some sense. Archaeologists have often noted that the power structures of agrarian cult and administration seems to have been important in the genesis of writing and the culture of recordkeeping. Speaking of the Mideast in the 4th millennium BCE, but also generalizing about ancient China, Mesoamerica, and Egypt, the archaeologist Jerrold S. Cooper holds that "The particular aspect of [political] complexity that led to the invention of writing was administrative, tracking incomes, disbursements, and transfers within large organizations, be they what we might call palace, temple, or community" (2004, 72). Indeed, political thinkers since Rousseau in the 18th century have argued that records, perhaps more than weapons, are the fulcrum of both priests' and governors' power over people—very much so in Rapaz, where the temple and community functions were fused.

FIGURE 5.6 The khipu collection suspended in Kaha Wayi before conservation.
Photo by the author.

In the prehispanic Andes, recordkeeping (not necessarily writing in the strict sense, but data registry) took place through a system of notation different from that of any other continent: assemblies of colored, twisted, and knotted cords that convey formatted information. They are called khipu in Quechua (see Figure 5.6), and they continued to serve administration of church and state during the first century of Spanish rule (Curatola and de la Puente Luna 2013, 9–32; Salomon 2004, 109–135). The origin of khipu notation and its relation to political/cult administration is only now coming to light. Rapaz is one of several places where the nexus of khipus and ritual-framed administration endured into modern times, although nobody today claims ability to decipher the khipu collection in Kaha Wayi. Rather, these cords are understood as the opaque but compelling proof of Rapaz's "Inka" political legitimacy. The khipus are among the objects that receive invocations in nighttime ceremonies.

How could this matted skein (see Figure 5.7) have been the matrix of ritually enforced power? We will glance at this subject just enough to suggest how the work of power in ritual is executed through inscription. Slung over its suspending rod, the collection looks at first like one immense Inka-style khipu, and indeed it has often been misreported as such.

It quickly turned out that Rapaz cords (see Figures 5.8 and 5.9) resemble Inka khipus hardly at all.[2] Compared to slim Inka cordage, these are oversize, having 2–5 times the usual Inka diameter, and together making a mass of about ten kilograms. They also lack the usual Inka format, which consists of a sustaining

FIGURE 5.7   Khipu case installed in 2005, with Community Vice-President
(*kamachikuq*) Víctor Gallardo and the author. Photo by Renata Peters.

main cord from which data-bearing pendants and subsidiaries hang. Rather than
being a single giant khipu in Inka-like format, the Rapaz legacy consists of 267
discrete cord objects, draped over the suspension stick and loosely grouped in 14
bundles, belted with lengths of khipu cord. (We call each discrete length a KR
object because many do not seem to be whole khipus.) Because cords were looped
through each other and intermingled over the suspension rod, the cords' respective
central portions were obscured in a tangled mass.

We hoped that our simultaneous enterprise of conserving the khipu collection
and describing them would make it possible to elicit or detect their role in society
with the same clarity yielded by the Tupicocha khipus and others recently discovered in Huarochirí (Hyland 2016) or in archaeological contexts (Urton 2017).
Perhaps we might even learn parts of their original code. Although we did complete both conservation and description, the code is still far from clear (Salomon
and Peters 2009).

Nearly all the specimens are single long cords made of alpaca or llama wool (see
Figures 5.8 and 5.9). One cluster of cords (group 2) is sheep wool. Each bears pre-
sumably meaningful small objects attached in varied sequence along their length.
Rapaz khipus can be incredibly long compared to other cord media, even exceed-
ing 15 meters. Present length is not, however, a reliable datum because many cords
show mends made in the 20th century, such that some single cord objects now

FIGURE 5.8 A representative long, mended khipu, KR 040. It is folded many times over the hanging stick, a part of which is visible at lower right. Photo by the author.

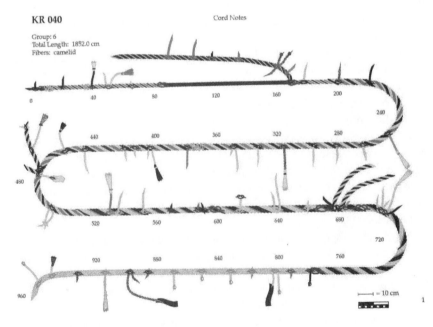

FIGURE 5.9 KR 040 as drawn by Carrie Brezine.

combine lengths of originally separate cordage. Some of the cords have dyed plies of blue or yellow. Radiocarbon dating, which works poorly for recent centuries, did not yield clear dates of origin but did narrow dating to the point where we can say the khipus were all finished within the same period and that the period in question is most likely posterior to 1809.[3]

What are the signs fixed onto cords? The Quechua word *khipu* means "knot," but knots scarcely if ever appear in Rapaz in ways that promise significance. In the whole collection there is not a single Inka-type "long knot" (long knots having multiple turns to signify numbers under ten). Neither did we find figure-eight knots, which are common in Inka style. Overhand knots appear only as ways to attach things, rather than signs in their own right. The meaningful objects are probably the small things attached. These attachments are small objects tied or looped on: tags of rawhide or animal skin with wool, tufts of unspun wool, pompoms made of yarn, and in ten cases, little figurines made of textiles. They are not attached with the Inka half-hitch.[4]

Some Rapaz khipus at first glance seem to have pendants in the Inka fashion (see Figure 5.10), but this is an illusion. Rapaz khipu makers, like modern Rapacinos, tend to ply wool tighter than industrial spinners do. Tightly plied yarn has a tendency to double back on itself forming a double helix. Many main cords are made this way. Their seeming pendants are lengths which have redoubled in the direction opposite to their final plying. This tendency may have been a useful feature because KR objects can be extremely long and therefore unhandy. Redoubling

FIGURE 5.10   Rapaz khipu KR 025 appears to have pendants, but they are actually redoubled stretches of main cord. Photo by the author.

may have been used intentionally to condense very long cords: with a redoubled specimen in hand, a user might have been able to quickly find a particular reference point instead of running long stretches through the hands.

Each freestanding cord, then, forms a highly individual line or path, along which a wide variety of smaller objects are attached by short subsidiaries.[5] It seems sustaining cords were designed for individual recognizability, and not just a standard support for signs. Main cords are much less standardized than Inka cords, which vary within limited parameters. A few Rapaz cords have peculiarities that are hard to explain except as identifiers.[6] For example, Rapaz cords, unlike Inka ones, are often composed of odd numbers of plies—in one case, three plies made of three threads each.[7] Allowing odd-numbered combinations of plies doubles the number of acceptable structures, as compared to Inka work, and therefore the number of identifiable designs. Moreover, Rapaz cords allow more color combinations than Inka cords do, again suggesting design individuation.[8] And finally, Rapaz cords vary much more in diameter than Inka ones do.[9]

Is such an object—a single, highly individuated line with attached signs— believable as a medium? A few Oceanian, Mexican, and North American cultures invented formally similar devices for helping to remember episodic items.[10] None of these show the complexity or diversity that Rapaz cords exhibit, nor do they occur in such a large accumulation. But it is not unreasonable that a group might make a central deposit of artifacts referring to individual sequences if they were of collective relevance. One such function could be a register of individual members' or households' services.[11]

The khipus' "little people"

Carrie Brezine, like many visitors, was fascinated with ten strange little dolls that hang from KR cords. Perhaps, she speculated, they are images of the major categories that their respective main cords represent—that is, the owner or person to whom the cord referred? That would be a most interesting finding because archaeological khipus are rarely if ever associated with images. Carrie dedicated a whole chapter of her doctoral dissertation to describing the figurines (2011, 75–122).

Who then are the "little people" (see Figures 5.11–5.13)? For example, they are herdsmen carrying tiny coca bags, a soldier in 18th-century dress uniform, and a lady in a long white skirt. Some dress in peasant homespun decorated with bits of bright factory fabric. The miniature coca bags that two figurines carry under their ponchos tell us they are ready for a ritual function. The soldier and the lady wear elite costumes of military and gentry style. On the whole the assembly evokes the 19th century and the hacienda economy, times when the "Indians" of Rapaz interacted with soldiers of the new Peruvian nation-state and its landholding elites (Salomon, Brezine, and Chapa 2011). This was the era when the old khipu art had long been marginalized by the "lettered city" in script and print. Yet in Rapaz, some version of cord-based "technology of intellect" apparently carried enough authority to be the institutional memory of Kaha Wayi.

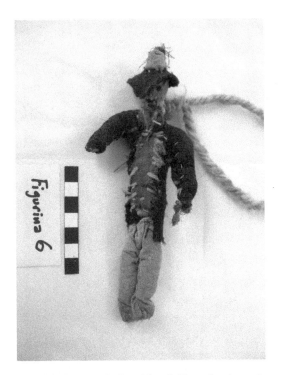

FIGURE 5.11 Figurine KR 06, the "little soldier." Photo by the author.

FIGURE 5.12 Figurine 8 carries a small mollusk shell resembling a conch trumpet. Photo by the author.

FIGURE 5.13 Figurine KR 09, "the lady." Photo by the author.

But what could khipus mean?

The vast majority of objects fixed onto cords are tufts, tags, and pompoms. When I asked what these could be, one repeated answer was *unancha*. *Unancha* was a word meaning "sign," "symbol," or "standard" well known to early colonial scholars of Quechua II (Szeminski 2006, 584–585). Adelaar recorded *unancha* as an "old-fashioned" word meaning "flag, sign" in the Quechua I of Tarma (1977, 486). Today in Rapaz, the Hispano-Quechua verb *unanzar* means to attach a mark of ownership to something (as a colored tuft on a herding rope or colored tassels in an animal's ear), to brand, or to paint initials on a dish, etc. A saint's insignia are also called *unancha*. One important fact about unancha is that it is authoritative. A fake unancha would be a serious infraction.

Main cords with their attachments look to Rapacinos like chains of unan-chas. Summing up: first, the main cords are linear paths. Second, they are unique records made for recognizability, not standardization. Third, in contrast with the uniqueness of main cords and their little branches or subsidiary "carrier cords," the attachments on them belong to a few standard types such as white wool tuft, bicolor tassel, hide tag, and figurine. That is, each khipu probably constitutes a unique freestanding record, which attributes to individual cases a relatively small set of standardized attributes in varying numbers and sequences.

I made an elicitation guide containing color photos of the unanchas and figu-rines. I went house to house interviewing older people and those with Kaha Wayi experience. I found three repeated interpretations but no consensus.

The first was that of people close to bendelhombre work: they think the khipus record how particular people served the mountains with ritual duties. For Melecio Montes, the current bendelhombre, the "little people" constituted the *cabildo de los cerros* or "council of the mountains." Each figurine seemed to him the human-like avatar of a specific mountain. (Mountains sometimes appear as humans in dreams and visions.) The khipus then are to him concretions of their will as revealed in auguries, etc.

People whose careers centered on herding with no particular claim to ritual authority thought otherwise. For them, cords were the accounting of communal animal herds, made before the Comunidad started writing paper records. They saw the almost entirely animal-derived character of khipu materials as supporting this view. Attachments' default values were simple indices: raw wool for shearing, raw-hide for killing and skinning, pompoms of yarn for wool processing. In favor of that hypothesis one might note that the wool is in khipus is of low quality. It resembles the less-valuable wool found on animals' legs and rump. The Choque sisters suggested that unsaleable residues left behind on a shearing floor would serve to make low-cost unancha. According to this hypothesis, "little people" might be individuals who held power over animals or herd work: the "lady" perhaps an hacienda owner, the "little soldier" perhaps an officer in charge of confiscated or military livestock, the coca-carrying herdsmen community herd officers such as mayordomos. I found no agreement about whether each cord represented a season or a person or a herd.

Some men who had held high balterno posts and constitutionally elected offices pointed out a third alternative: political administration. Because nobody wants to serve the numerous community work days unless they are sure everyone else is doing his part, comuneros demand extremely detailed records of service—today in ledgers, but once on cords. Villagers conduct an exhaustive public audit at the New Year's Assembly (Salomon 2004, 75–76). Since 1935, Rapaz has archived the resulting record books. Perhaps some of them carry on what were formerly khipu functions (Hyland 2016).

Mario Alejo suggested that the most important of all records is the "book of cargos," which has one page to register the "curriculum vitae" of each comunero. Only after serving in a fixed number of accountable offices (cargos) does a comunero become eligible for semiretired (pasivo) benefits.[12] When it is time to assign jobs, the book of cargos becomes the very measure of justice. In Mario's opinion, each highly individual cord must represent the course of an individual career: the main cord corresponds to the person's identity, and the successive attachments to successive duties such as holding a balterno office or attending a work day. Mario asks, how could Rapaz ever have lived without this kind of knowledge? How else could power have been applied acceptably?

At a triple intersection of theories: diverging ideas about how religion works on and in people

So in Rapaz ten kilos of matted wool seem to embody all three components of the triad symbolism/knowledge/power. The khipu collection shows how any one of these may seem primary, depending on the angle from which one looks. As symbols, khipus possess that "multivalent" quality Victor Turner emphasized: they simultaneously bring to mind the remote grandeur of Inka sovereignty and the familiar fellowship of *campesinos* visible as "little people." As instruments of knowledge, they seem to Rapacinos annals of archaic information, not legible now but still valid as prototypes for the self-recording bureaucracy through which comuneros validate each other's participation. They are said to "know" almost everything. As tools of power, they incarnate the "transcendent collective." The taboo on touching khipus and the still faintly lingering reluctance to let women view them express the coercive power of the overarching whole. The content encoded by the makers is now in dispute among the heirs. But it seems certain to the heirs that they manifest the disciplines Rapacinos must follow, whether in relations with the superhuman or in their duties to the commons.

Notes

1 University of Arizona Neutron Activation samples AA68916 and AA68918 from the body of the straw cross yielded T test 95% probability of statistical equivalence. Aggregated date: 232+25 Bp, calibrated to H-Sur, 1648–1803 CE.
2 The collection looks so unlike Inka khipus that I wondered whether the application of the term might be the result of modern re-labeling posterior to Ruiz Estrada's visits. But Dr. Ruiz is a native speaker of Quechua I, and he told me that he never heard them called anything but khipu. So we still think that the objects were in their day a device classed with khipus. We heard no opinion from any Rapacino contrary to the local view that this device was a data registry of some sort. We did not observe objects similar to Rapaz khipus in any context outside Kaha Wayi (although a few elders did know how to make numerical records on cord in Inka decimal style).
3 23 radiocarbon samples from the khipus, the straw cross, and Kaha Wayi were C14 tested at the University of Arizona Neutron Activation lab in 2007. The summary of findings by Raymundo Chapa says that "Although radiocarbon dating has failed to determine an accurate chronology for the khipu collection, 2σ calibration has revealed that construction of the khipu did not occur before 1700, or between 1722 and 1809. This suggests that they are likely not Inka or early Colonial in origin."
4 A first kind of attached objects consists of tied-on tufts of unspun wool. These may be knotted onto a subsidiary cord or tucked within the redoubling loop at one end of a subsidiary. A second kind consists of tufts bent double and bound so as to form tassels. It is common for tassels to be bicolored. They too are held in place by subsidiaries connected to KR cords. A third kind of attachment consists of thin rawhide tags. Some of them bear wool and others do not. A fourth kind of attachment consists of figurines dressed in textiles. This unusual feature, apparently unique among objects classified as khipu, is considered in detail below.
5 We called all cords that branch off main cords subsidiaries. This class falls into four subtypes, none matching the Inka type (which is attached by a half-hitch). A first sort consists simply of cords overhand-knotted onto a KR. A second sort is made by passing the subsidiary between the plies of the KR before tying it. A third sort of subsidiaries consists of a cord equal in diameter to the respective KR tied onto it with unequal ends hanging. A fourth sort of subsidiaries is attached by blanket stitches. The third and especially the fourth kind may be repairs.
6 For example, KR 215 and 250 are bicolors made entirely of mane hairs, from horse or cow, an extremely difficult fiber to work with because of its stiffness.

7 About 33% are made with 1, 3, 5, or 7 plies. In one case two levels of structure were both odd: about this tendency Carrie Brezine reported, "The notable thing is that the Inka system proceeds by a series of doublings, while here we apparently find an additive system. There seems to be a basic difference in the structuring system. Uneven structures provide different possibilities for polychromy." Allowing odd composition also doubles the number of admissible unique designs. So much diversity does this yield that Brezine concluded "there are no duplicates in the khipu. Each cord has its own configuration of cord patterning, subsidiaries, knots, and attachments" (Brezine 2011, 84).

8 Almost everything in the Rapaz collection is polychrome. The overwhelming majority of cords are of two colors plied together in spiral or "barber pole" fashion (also common in Inka work). Three-color cords are common, and there are cords with four or even five colors. One-color design is rare overall but more common in sheep wool than in llama/alpaca cords.

9 Diameter may reflect a hierarchy of data or emphasis, as has been found in ethnographic khipus where thick cords record broad classes and thinner ones subclasses. Rapaz presents cords up to 10 mm thick, and subsidiaries as thin as .8 mm. Diameter does not seem to vary continuously. Rather, as in ethnographic herding khipus, it goes in brackets. A range of thin cords goes from 1 to 3.5 mm, and another range covers 5 to 7 mm. A few giants approach 10 mm. After scrutinizing hundreds of cord segments, Carrie judged that "the hierarchy and contrast of diameters is always very clear. There is no doubt about which is to be understood as the lesser. Main cords (if we want to use the term) generally measure 5 to 7 mm." These reflections make it likely that cordage as such carried hierarchized meanings together with identities.

10 Jürg Wassman reported in detail on a New Guinean people's one-cord device to aid in the correct singing of long ritual sequences (1991 [1982]). A comparable New Guinean cord registers ancestral itinerary (Silverman 1998, 429). J.D. Leechman and M.R. Harrington reported on "string records" among the Yakima Native Americans of Washington State, including a forty-foot example made by a woman in British Columbia before 1911 (1921). Like the Rapaz cords, it contains many small objects tied in as signs: human hair, bits of colored cloth, sinew, roots, deerskin, beads. A Yakima cord keeper, Sally Jackson, explained that her 35-foot string concerned deaths and funerals. The same authors mention a Kiowa unilinear record on a surface (not string) concerning Sabbaths of the Peyote religion. Huichol Mexicans used the single-cord format to make memoranda of sexual sins which had to be confessed in their temple prior to the peyote hunt (Lumholtz 1902, 127–128).

11 Cords combining eight or more simple threads are found exclusively or almost exclusively in the secondary or "subsidiary" cords that are attached to a main cord. If more distinctive cords occupy positions away from the central cord, it suggests these outer parts bear more specified, complex messages. About 20% of the subsidiaries have more than one level of structure. It appears that the main cord signified an identifiable owner(s) or sequence, while its subsidiaries and attachments register successive facts about the subject matter of the main cord.

12 Namely, twelve leadership/administrative offices during at least thirty years of membership, plus attendance at all required functions such as meetings, work days (faenas), and festival-organizing tasks. As well as dozens of duty cargos per year, some comuneros assume voluntary ones.

References

Adelaar, Willem F.H. 1977. *Tarma Quechua Grammar, Texts, Dictionary*. Lisse, Netherlands: The Peter de Ridder Press.

Asad, Talal. 1983. "Anthropological Conceptions of Religion: Reflections on Geertz." *Man* 18: 237–259.

Bloch, Maurice. 1992. *Prey into Hunter: The Politics of Religious Experience*. Cambridge: Cambridge University Press.

Bloch, Maurice. 2008. "Why Religion Is Nothing Special but Is Central." *Philosophical Transactions of the Royal Society* Series B (363): 2055–2061.

Brezine, Carrie Jane. 2011. *Dress, Technology, and Identity in Colonial Peru*. PhD dissertation. Department of Anthropology, Harvard University, Cambridge, MA.

BLM [United States Bureau of Land Management of US government]. N.d. Historic soda bottles. www.blm.gov/historic_bottles/soda.htm#Early%20Soda/Mineral%20Water%20Styles.

Cooper, Jerrold S. 2004. "Babylonian Beginnings: The Origin of the Cuneiform Writing System in Comparative Perspective." In *The First Writing: Script Invention as History and Process*, edited by Stephen D. Houston. New York: Cambridge University Press. 71–99.

Cummins, Tom, and Bruce Mannheim. 2011. "The River Around Us, the Stream Within Us: The Traces of the Sun and Inka Kinetics." *RES: Anthropology and Aesthetics* 59/60: 5–21.

Curatola Petrocchi, Marco, and José Carlos de la Puente Luna. 2013. "Estudios y materiales sobre el uso de los quipus en el mundo andino colonial." In *El quipu colonial: Estudios y materiales*, edited by Marco Curatola Petrocchi and José Carlos de la Puente Luna. Lima: Fondo Editorial de la Pontificia Universidad Católica del Perú. 33–64.

Douglas, Mary. 1966. *Purity and Danger: An Analysis of Concepts of Pollution and Taboo*. New York: Praeger Publishing.

Evans-Pritchard, Edward Evan. 1937. *Witchcraft, Oracles and Magic among the Azande*. Oxford: The Clarendon Press.

Geertz, Clifford. 1966. "Religion as a Cultural System." In *Anthropological Approaches to the Study of Religion*, edited by Michael Banton. London: Tavistock Publications. ASA Monographs, 3. 1–46.

Gellner, Ernest. 1988. *Plough, Sword and Book: The Structure of Human History*. Chicago, IL: University of Chicago Press.

Gellner, Ernest. 1995. "The Uniqueness of Truth." In *Anthropology and Politics: Revolutions in the Sacred Grove*, edited by Ernest Gellner. Oxford and Cambridge, MA: Wiley. 1–10.

Gottlieb, Anthony. 2016. *The Dream of Reason: A History of Western Philosophy from the Greeks to the Renaissance*. New York: W.W. Norton.

Horton, Robin. 1964. "Ritual Man in Africa." *Africa* 34(2): 85–104.

Hyland, Sabine. 2016. "How Khipus Indicated Labour Contributions in an Andean Village: An Explanation of Colour Banding, Seriation and Ethnocategories." *Journal of Material Culture* 21(4): 10–20.

Leechman, John Douglas, and Mark Raymond Harrington. 1921. *String Records of the Northwest*. New York: Museum of the American Indian, Heye Foundation. Ser. Indian Notes and Monographs.

Lévi-Strauss, Claude. 1978. "Harelips and Twins: The Splitting of a Myth." In *Myth and Meaning*, edited by Claude Lévi-Strauss. New York: Schocken. 25–33.

Lumholtz, Carl. 1902. *El México desconocido: Cinco años de exploración entre las tribus de la Sierra Madre occidental, en la tierra caliente de Tepic y Jalisco, y entre los Tarascos de Michoacán*. Balbino Dávalos, trad. Vol. 2. New York: Charles Scribner's Sons.

Ortner, Sherry B. 1973. "On Key Symbols." *American Anthropologist* 75(5): 1338–1346.

Pachacuti Yamqui Salcamaygua, Joan de Santa Cruz. 1993 [1613?]. *Relación de antigüedades deste reyno del Piru*. Estudio etnohistórico y lingüístico de Pierre Duviols y César Itier. Cusco; Instituto Francés de Estudios Andinos and Centro de Estudios Regionales Andinos, Bartolomé de las Casas.

Salomon, Frank. 2004. *The Cord Keepers: Khipus and Cultural Life in a Peruvian Village*. Durham, NC: Duke University Press.

Salomon, Frank, Carrie Brezine, and Reymundo Chapa. 2011. "Khipu from Colony to Republic." In *Their Way of Writing: Scripts, Signs, and Pictographies in Pre-Columbian America*, edited by Elizabeth Boone and Gary Urton. Washington, DC: Dumbarton Oaks. 353–378.

Salomon, Frank, and Renata Peters. 2009. "Governance and Conservation of the Rapaz Khipu Patrimony." In *Intangible Heritage and Tourism*, edited by Helaine Silverman and D. Fairchild Ruggles. Frankfurt and New York: Springer Verlag. 101–125.

Silverman, Eric K. 1998. "Traditional cartography in Papua New Guinea." In *The History of Cartography: Cartography in Traditional African, American, Arctic, Australian, and Pacific Societies, Vol. 2, Book 3*, edited by David Woodward and G. Malcolm Lewis. Chicago, IL: University of Chicago Press. 423–442.

Szemiński, Jan. 2006 [1560]. *Léxico quechua de Fray Domingo de Santo Thomas*. Cusco, Peru: Convento de Santo Domingo-Qorikancha, Sociedad Polaca de Estudios Latinoamericanos, and Universidad Hebrea de Jerusalén.

Turner, Victor. 1969. *The Ritual Process: Structure and Anti-Structure*. Chicago, IL: Aldine.

Urton, Gary. 1981. *At the Crossroads of Earth and Sky: An Andean Cosmology*. Austin, TX: University of Texas Press.

Urton, Gary. 2017. *Inka History in Knots: Reading Khipus as Primary Sources*. Austin, TX: University of Texas Press.

Wassman, Jürg. 1991 [1982]. *The Song to the Flying Fox: The Public and Esoteric Knowledge of the Important Men of Kandingei about Totemic Songs, Names, and Knotted Cords (Middle Sepik, Papua New Guinea)*, translated by Dennis Q. Stephenson. Boroko, PNG: Cultural Studies Division, National Research Institute. Apwitihire: Studies in Papua New Guinea Musics.

6

A TEMPLE BY NIGHT

(and religions as other ontologies)

On icy evenings in my Rapaz sleeping bag, I strapped on a headlamp and warmed up reading Richard Dawkins' homage to the scientific worldview, *Unweaving the Rainbow*. One night, I chanced on Dawkins' discussion of rainmaking as the very exemplar of deficient reasoning in pre-scientific culture (2000, 161, 182). Dawkins thought that the same purportedly non-empirical views of nature (reverential, moralistic, or personalistic views) that hobbled primitive people still handicap rationality in modern societies because people hold to religious and romantic thinking.

Since I'd been dedicating every day to studying a rainmaking temple, this rankled. As much as I appreciated Dawkins' polemic against antiscientific thinking, it bothered me that he anachronistically lumped a vast swath of cultural inventions in with 19th-century romanticism. Cultures, we anthropologist believe, have their reasons—widely differing ones, which we want to understand both in their own terms and *also* in terms of cosmopolitan knowledge (Chapter 5). I pondered in my sleeping bag about ways to do that without falling into the recently deepening chasm between naturalists and culture theorists. A new cognitive-evolutionary reconciliation with ethnology? A cultural analysis of the sciences?

On the way back from Rapaz I found that I'd missed a chapter in this kind of discussion. The basic notions of "culture" and "nature" themselves had come into question, for reasons different from the postcolonial and epistemological objections that had already been boiling when I left. In these pages, I'll comment lightly on how Kaha Wayi might look in the light of debates I'd missed.

Doubling down on relativism

After about 1980 the ethnological conversation bifurcated. Discussion of alterity as such was conducted on almost purely culturological bases. Meanwhile anthropologists inclined toward sociology and economics downplayed the theme of alterity in favor of globalization, an argument trending toward uniformity. The culturological branch of anthropology sought ever-deeper definitions of difference while postponing anthropology's other prime commitment, "the psychic unity of mankind." Cognitivists, evolutionists, and now "new materialists" picked up that turf, as Chapters 1 and 7 note.

By the 1990s most North American cultural anthropologists had long since put Dawkins on their blacklist. By relativist logic he just doesn't get it: every natural fact is a fact only as reckoned within a given cultural frame, a "lifeworld." Irony quotes had hardened around the word *nature*. Cultural variability, we were taught, undercuts the very possibility of cosmopolitan science or a unique nature. This proposition was all but consensual in cultural anthropology graduate programs circa 2000; citations of positivistic works tailed off as citations of "science studies" (the study of sciences as cultural phenomena) zoomed. The trend put relativists on an adversarial course in relation to majorities in natural sciences and "harder" social scientists.

Around the millennium the main battlefield was epistemology, the inquiry into what knowing is and what counts as knowledge. Relativism of that era pegged scientific cognition as the local "knowledge system" or "episteme" proper to certain relations of power. A 2010 draft of the American Anthropological Association's mission statement went so far as to remove science from the Association's list of goals (Medin and Bang 2014, 91). That draft was not approved. But the resulting uproar exposed advanced damage to the scientific-humanistic coalition that had long been American anthropology's social contract. Many anthropologists with commitments to natural-scientific method (archaeologists, human biologists, and paleontologists) stopped attending the Association's meeting or quit altogether. At some universities the cultural and natural-science ends of anthropology broke apart. The cultural subdiscipline set about to uphold its stature within the increasingly science-oriented spectrum of academe by positioning itself as the champion of critical science studies, of "engaged scholarship" with humanitarian or political commitments, and of diversity in the face of globalization.

Far from moderating earlier claims of strong relativism, a younger cultural-anthropological generation doubled down on the relativist bet. They did so by relocating the debate on philosophically different ground. As first proposed by the Amazonianist Eduardo Viveiros de Castro, the new arena of diversity was to be ontology: the part of philosophy concerned with being rather than with knowing (1998 [1996]). What counts as an entity? What entities may we ask about? Viveiros proposed as the ethic and premise of future anthropology no less than the "ontological self-determination of peoples." The opening question was to be, what do "they" assume there is in the world? Human jaguars? Jealous mountains? God the omnipotent and benevolent? Very well; we are to find out just what sort of a world has such entities in it and acclimate our rationality to it.

So Walt Whitman's proclamation was reversed. From now on, "what you assume I shall assume." We are no longer to take unfamiliar assertions as "cultural beliefs," or multiple "representations" about an underlyingly single world called "nature" (as we saw Horton doing in Ch. 5). By whose authority is it called single? Nor is the goal to square "beliefs" or "representations" with any larger intellectual project or theory of which "we" are the owners, such as natural science or interpretative humanities.

Rather we ought to take "a world" to mean the conjoint sum of all that is given to a portion of humanity by circumstance (formerly, "nature," "history"), plus all that it takes as given (ex- "worldview"), and all that its members build out of these ("culture," as was). What humans do is not to represent but to create a world—or many of them? Here is a philosophically explicit statement of the position by an outstanding ethnographer of Mongolia, Morten Axel Pedersen:

> If . . . one takes as the theoretical premise . . . many worlds that all exist *as* construction (or becoming, or transition) . . . then cultural exegesis no longer depends on a representational theory of symbols, meaning, or context. If things are not distinct from their meanings, but are rather meanings in a certain form, and if immaterial things are not less (or more) real than material things, but simply real in another (and possibly more virtual) ontological register, then their interpretation does not require a conventional social or political-economic context, for as postplural entities, they contain the potential to act as their own scales . . . and thus potentially to serve as particular kinds of concepts in their own right.
>
> *2011, 180*

During the decade when I was researching this book, South Americanist ethnographers played the leading part in the "ontological" tendency. Two scholars who became prominent participants had been graduate school advisees of mine. Their ontological innovations have nothing to with that fact—except that, *ex post*, personal sympathy heightens my interest. In the next pages I look back on Rapaz experience in the light of ontological programs. My reservations about the ontological moment will become obvious. But I don't doubt that it is a movement worth discussing because it is today's expression of loyalty to the "gold standard" of ethnography: resolute, respectful study of "the native's point of view" (Candea in Venkatesan 2010, 175).

The "ontological turn" is the latest in a series of similar controversies that occur every decade or so in American anthropology. They occur whenever popular culture and ideology have reduced the previous terms for studying alterity to conceptual dust bunnies. This happened to epistemological relativism by the 2010s ("It's true for *me*"). Anthropology's paradigm breaks occur when demand builds up for a more challenging and bracing approach to human differences. Ethnography is the study of alterity, a venture inherently vulnerable to routinization. Ethnographic commitment includes a demand for surprise and therefore a relatively rapid cycle of self-imposed shock therapy, as compared to many other disciplines. One component of these intentional jolts is the impulse to invent language free of habitual assumptions, and thus, to generate jargon. Once when I showed irritation about this, Marisol de la Cadena, who was then developing ontological ideas, shrugged and said, "Jargon is just what happens when people are getting excited." Good point. I decided to tolerate some of it.

Ontology's traditional issues nag at cross-cultural thinking more than ever. How will I know when the statements I hear from "you," the native, need to be taken as ontologically unfamiliar? Should we think of cultures as rules for accrediting "things"? For example, are we to allow that an abstraction (say, discord) can simultaneously be a person (Eris or Discordia in Greek myths) and thus posit a kind of entity never welcomed in scientific ontology? Ontological anthropologists remind us that when people tell us mountains are persons, we aren't obliged at the start to pigeonhole the idea as "myth" or "metaphor" and thereby ready it for dissection under the terms of an academic subdiscipline. "Ontographic" ethnographers (Holbraad, Pedersen, and Viveiros' word) think we should instead find out the consequences of "their" having built a world that contains mountain-persons—and what intellectual opportunities open up through dialogue with a world where unfamiliar ontology prevails (2014, 4).

Friends of the "ontological turn" often emphasize that the distinctive ontology of natural science and of much western political philosophy errs at the start by splitting natural from cultural phenomena. For the old school, nature is that which exists irrespective of "us," whereas culture is what exists by virtue of "our" (human) thought and work. Since under this doctrine the two domains have different ontological status, different disciplines must study them.

By 2010, ontological critics were loading these premises for the landfill. "Western" ontology, they held, is only one way of accrediting "things," albeit a pragmatically powerful one. It is not a universal; to assume its universality is both impoverishing to "us" and dismissive to our interlocutor "the Other."

Freed from the obligation to find equations between things implicit in cultures and "natural" things, ontological-minded ethnographers became especially good at capturing cultural notions that seem vague, elusive, or illogical to the outsider. That same Pedersen who wrote the puzzling passage on the philosophical basis of "ontography" quoted above, also wrote this enlightening passage about the entities known as spirit beings in post-Soviet northern Mongolia:

> Instead of thinking of *ongod* [shamanic spirits] as single and stable entities, it is therefore more accurate if we conceive of them as inherently labile and capricious assemblages of heterogeneous elements. Indeed . . . spirits simply *are* movements, more than they are discrete entities imbued with the property to move . . . As swarmlike assemblages of human and nonhuman affects, *ongod* move through time and space, land and sky/skies, words and things, along transversal lines drawn by their incessant jumping from one body to the next, as manifested in their unpredictable "strokes" of misfortune and good luck.
>
> *Pedersen 2011, 175–176*

If we judge "ontography" by its fruit, we should admire it for producing such a fresh, convincing rendering of cultural phenomena that seems important to natives but merely confusing to "us." This, surely, meets the "gold standard."

The ontological turn is thus a circling-back to earlier commitments of cultural anthropology, namely the effort to recognize "Other" human constructions of life as importantly, deeply different. Like many previous versions of ethnography (dialogical anthropology, reflexive narrative, humanistic anthropology, postcolonial anthropology) it swears off "sameing" our objects of study. Instead, ontological writers tell us to confess at the start that we simply don't know what they're talking about. So we must set aside the question of truth. Instead of representing a local reality for the sake of merging it in a project outside itself (as a "case" within some wider inquiry, such as cognitive evolutionism), they aim to put the foreign world into our path as a reality which we must simply enter, helplessly at first. Checking up on its, or our, epistemological basis is now off the agenda.

Some such arguments fall within what Webb Keane calls "weak" ontological pluralism (2013, 186). That is, they see cultures constructing subjectively self-sufficient working versions of an ultimately unitary world, whose unity we nonetheless cannot directly approach. Since we can't inhabit a one-and-only world, we are constrained to a penultimate pluralism. For "weak" ontology, the way forward involves identifying the specific parts and practices of culture which "entify"—that is, which confer thing-like status. Bruce Mannheim, an Andeanist and theoretically minded linguistic anthropologist whose ideas we will revisit soon, argues that the "entifying" work of culture is not free mental play, but rather is constrained by the same faculties and biases we summarized in Chapter 1's discussion of cognition. He argues that ontological differences among cultures, far from being amorphous and imponderable, arise from specific interplays among the programs that neurology, language, and social habit provide (Mannheim and Salas Carreño 2015). "Weakly ontological" ethnography seems to me the most promising path forward, both because it points toward a renewed symbiosis between the "science end" and the "culture end" of anthropology, and because it rescues us from making cultural difference into a conundrum that defeats rationality.

But today's cultural-anthropological limelight is rather on "strong" ontological pluralism. My Peruvian friends who share the world with such beings as person-mountains, it's suggested, are not just paying attention to different aspects of this world, or just applying their mental faculties in unfamiliar ways. They are living in an incommensurably different and separate world. We are not to explain their mountains as symbols or representations of geological or social facts. We are not even to distinguish between theoretical models present in their culture and objects named by it. In other words, "strong ontographers" require of fieldworkers that we refrain from imposing "meta-ontological" models (like theory versus essence or epistemology versus ontology) that allegedly drag our findings willy-nilly back to Western common sense.

It's hardly a surprise that this demand for the bewildering as a minimum criterion for veracity has resulted in reams of difficult debate. The maximalist notion of diversity obviously presents big problems for ethnographic method. It incurs Gellner's paradox (in Chapter 5) all over again: from what "interstellar" viewpoint is the deep-pluralist notion spoken?

> The problem with . . . adopting ontological pluralization as an anthropological methodology is that this move ends up being so ironically, tragically, and embarrassingly modern. Stripped to its core, our modernist ontology is inseparable from what we might call the exceptional position of non-position . . . Whatever the world is, there must always be some position of nonposition outside it for the Western liberal subject to occupy . . . [T]here is nothing more profoundly modern than the effort to step outside modernity.
>
> Severin Fowles in Alberti et al. 2011, 907[1]

And supposing for the moment that there is some answer to this, we are still up against another difficulty. As many critics of "ontography" have noted, the more difference we attribute to "worlds," the more we incur Wittgenstein's famous "lion paradox": "If lions could speak we would not understand them." Certain of "ontography's" critics puts it thus: "How the proponents of the ontological turn are able to . . . translate [incommensurable worlds] into understandable anthropological text remains a mystery" (Vigh and Sausdal 2014, 57; Dressler 2015, 20). This mystery of how to export ontological difference need not be unanswerable; it is now the object of concerted assault by linguistic anthropologists interested in "translation theory," as we will see at the end of this chapter.

The "speech of lions" problem is not how I wanted to lionize my Rapaz neighbors. Yes, they say things that might make a visitor think their lifeworld strange. But in any case, a visitor is at a disadvantage in guessing what place these verbal or ritual constructs have in their lives. When we assess what place to give ontology among the multiple ways of describing difference, we should hope to have some criterion beyond just assuming that ontological difference is crucial. It won't do to simply make ontological difference the default explanation for everything. I think it's interesting that Rapacinos have differences among themselves, and not only with us, that look like they might be ontological. I wonder if it's possible to tell whether they are.

Do Rapacinos disagree among themselves at the ontological level?

When lifelong companions who share most of their experience disagree with each other about what exists, their disagreements (assuming we understand them) are more interesting than the puzzlement of a newcomer, who can never be sure why he is so unsure. Even after due diligence of fieldwork, ontologism is a hard conclusion to draw. The following three sections will characterize three positions voiced about Kaha Wayi-Pasa Qulqa and seek their emergence amid "communicative situations." The disagreement occurred within a triangular cluster of issues much like the cluster Guillermo Salas Carreño observed in certain Cuzco communities in the same period: Catholic versus Protestant affiliation, effects of a mining boom, and tourism. Each of these destabilized practices and world views in ways he subtly parses (2010). After characterizing Rapaz disagreements, I'll end asking us to ponder how well ontological views explain the dissensus about Kaha Wayi–Pasa Qulqa.

The old allegiance and the weather

Our conservationist commitment to Kaha Wayi and Pasa Qulqa unintentionally brought local philosophical and practical differences to the fore. These local disagreements apparently incurred ontology: not rival interpretations of what mountains do, or how we know them, but rival suppositions about what mountains are. I'll summarize three local understandings concerning how "men and mountains meet," calling them respectively the old allegiance, doublethinking, and dissent.

By the old allegiance, I mean the "habitus" of Kaha Wayi's loyalists (who are at the same time Catholics). People of the old allegiance proved at that time to be the strictest of "conservators" because their idea of conservation meant (in principle) not changing anything at all. They might rather let Kaha Wayi fall to pieces than disturb its venerable soot. In sponsoring conservationist interventions I unwittingly defied an old-allegiance majority, but a majority which for a long time I could not hear because their case was not one likely to come forward as a proposition.

By 2005, the childless elder Teodosio Falcón had been retired for many years from his service as bendelhombre. Sometimes he reminisced at his hearth as his wife Teodora prepared supper. Beribboned trophy skulls of favorite animals smiled toothily down on us amid a cloying vapor of mutton fat, coal smoke, steam, leather, and entrails. His mind returned to the old ritual order. Teodora, having recently become Protestant, grumbled under her breath about my encouraging him to reminisce about "those satanic things." But the next day she'd urge me to return because remembering heroic nights in Kaha Wayi or up on the heights alleviated her old man's sadness about passing into obscurity.

In July of 2005, the moment for removing the khipu collection from Kaha Wayi to the site laboratory was approaching. Teodosio, who sometimes stopped by to watch our work, took it on himself to ask about performing a *mesa calzada* for permission to move them (see Figure 6.1). He loved the inside of Kaha Wayi in all its murk and moldiness; it evoked a high point of his career and recalled fellowship among men of his generation. He took pride in his cohort's long labor of bargaining with the mountain powers. The soot and mildew the chamber had accumulated seemed to him venerable and comforting. He found the whole idea of conservation disturbing because it smacked of irreverence and profanation: too much daylight, too many strangers. Yet like the current bendelhombre Melecio Montes, Teodosio reluctantly accepted that the spell would temporarily have to be broken, and he set about allowing that by conducting a night of invocations.

In the next three months the hills turned from green to tawny. Cows began to slump home looking haggard. Milk became scarce. Conventionally, rain is supposed to begin in late October, but none fell. As much as we were hurrying to gather straw for Kaha Wayi's new roof, it wasn't filling out fast enough. Protestant or not, Teodora let her former allegiance get the better of her. One morning

FIGURE 6.1   The retired bendelhombre Teodosio Falcón Ugarte performs a mesa in
Kaha Wayi, observing ember augury. Photo by Víctor Falcón Huayta.

she spoke to me in an urgent whisper, nodding toward Kaha Wayi's bare rafters:
"Please, when is it going to be finished? Because the potato planting is almost finished. And as for rain—nothing. The sprouts are starting to die. What can be done
if there's no place for carrying out a mesa? Haven't they done a mesa yet?"

At the morning coca sit-down before work, Mario Alejo, a balterno, warned
me that people were saying the rains were hanging back because Kaha Wayi wasn't
in normal condition. Melecio, too, worried aloud as he reprimanded me:

> They're talking about me all over. Can't you just finish up quickly so it
> can rain? There are rumors. People ask, "Did they knock over the altar?"
> People say you're breaking a law because [the mountains] won't give rain if
> anybody's cutting high grass before the wet season. We used to serve Kaha
> Wayi. We paid our obligations to Kaha Wayi. Now that you've damaged
> Kaha Wayi by taking off the old roof, Kaha Wayi is telling you to give what's
> due. Rain is given for fulfillment.

Vice-President Gallardo, head of the balterno corps, said, "They're pressing me hard, too hard. Especially the ladies. Every day I hear people say, 'Can't you do more to bring rain?' Just a little more and—" His gesture mimed a knife across the throat. I was horrified to feel the public chill.

In early December Rapaz's need for reconciliation with the rain powers and our need for reassurance became acute. Melecio intervened and required us to back off from the site while he worked ritually though the night. After a few days of indecisive drizzle, a five-hour soaker arrived. Water cascaded in arcs off tin roofs. Sitting on the ground in his sopping pants, Mario said, "But this is excellent! People will say it's because Kaha Wayi's roof is almost finished. If we get more they'll say it's because Pasa Qulqa is getting better."

And so it was. On December mornings, individual clouds the size of dogs or people drifted along the streets. At midday, mist filled up the Checras Canyon like water rising in a tub. When it rose higher than town level, a clammy flood of fog flowed over Rapaz. Instead of seeing heroic vistas one could only see a few feet of mud underfoot, and an occasional sparrow darting through murk. Villagers plodded around in drenched ponchos and galoshes. Women acquired a coneheaded look as they wrapped their carefully plaster-whitened hats in sheet plastic. The men looked like wet mutts. Life was good again.

So the crisis about weather and profanation that I'd feared never came to a head. But as I breathed an inward sigh of relief, I realized that from the start I had been greatly mistaken about the old allegiance. While negotiating scientific access with the community's elected officers, Víctor and I had unwittingly been hearing a biased sample of local discourse. What we hadn't known then was that male villagers versed in metropolitan law, language, and rhetoric were the ones routinely elected to the directorate because they appeared best able to engage outsiders like us. But those men didn't speak for the majority where internal matters were concerned. As spokesmen for the village, these men screen outsiders off from the opinions of less cosmopolitan people. Appalled by the near-crisis about rain, I asked some balternos what percentage of Rapacinos thought conservation endangered relations with the "old ones." I was told eighty to ninety percent.

Tourism, "doublethink," and the day/night solution

The old allegiance commands no clear consensus. A large and influential minority of comuneros are of two minds about it; they have no trouble accepting talk of mountain lords in some contexts, but they also accept and practice technologically informed modernism. Peaks that are lords in one conversation are resources in another. Schooled people are well acquainted with the positivist notion of nature. With equable doublethink, they want the old temple to be at once an heirloom the community "holds" within an overall modernist mindset, and yet also a hallowed power that the community "is held by" (Geertz 1971, 17, 61). They find this a rewarding posture, for it gains in livability what it surrenders in consistency. This

FIGURE 6.2 Mario Alejo, a balterno in 2005, is both a Kaha Wayi traditionalist and a modernizer; he helped organize and supervise conservation work. Photo by the author.

of course is nothing unusual. It is the typical posture of post-enlightenment people who nonetheless feel some appetite for ritual, including its "strange" ontology (discussed in the last part of Chapter 7). Just because this apparently ontology-doubling mindset is so close to modern common sense it's worth looking into anthropologically.

Many stalwarts of the old allegiance have finished their required turns of leadership and enjoy semiretired (pasivo) status. For their school-bred successors now in middle age, Pasa Qulqa's sacrifices, Kaha Wayi's deliberations, and the mayordomos' nocturnal honors to animal ilas have become more self-consciously set apart from the utilitarian sphere. Some public contexts for the old allegiance, such as sowing and harvesting parties on lands of the communal endowment, have ceased. Schooled people and returning migrants from cities absorbed "disenchanted" viewpoints decades ago. At least some of the time, they contemplate weather and mountains as part of a natural realm called the environment, or ecology, or the resource base. Such people initiated and defended the Kaha Wayi-Pasa Qulqa conservation project (see Figure 6.2) on secular grounds, while at the same time taking part in the precinct's sacred work.

Kaha Wayi's modernist friends are no less sincere than their traditionalist peers, and, as far as I can tell, they feel no cognitive dissonance. They seem to credit the rain temple as a trustworthy approach to climate. Experience does not falsify it because effective rainfall agropastoralism still does, to a good degree, depend on conformity with Kaha Wayi's rules of circulation, especially the ones that concern collective supervision of crops, herds, and land tenure. This double posture allows *balternos* to confidently discuss with outsiders the details of sacred geography and to present "beliefs" (*creencias, fe*) as a part of "our culture." They address anthropology in its own language, using terms popularized in the period of the Columbian quincentennial (1992) and recently echoed in the public discourse of multiculturalism.

Rapaz houses a few scientifically minded people such as the locally born health extension agent (*promotor*) and also some extreme modernists such as sympathizers of leftist or technocratic movements. If cognitive consistency were crucial we might expect such people to disconnect from Kaha Way, or belittle it as "folklore." But they don't. Most native-born people with technological training (e.g., for vaccination or cattle breeding) value the old complex and favored its conservation during our project.

Such Rapacinos want at the same time to connect the village's peculiar internal life with a "national" landscape of antiquities and tourism, such as one finds promoted by the Ministry of Tourism and commercial media. Why, they ask, shouldn't this "Inka" treasure be Rapaz's own monument of Peruvian authenticity and local legitimacy?

No longer is Rapaz obscure and marginal. Cosmopolitan-minded comuneros have sought and found many interlocutors with urban audiences. The agrarian historian Pablo Macera (1995) and Ruiz Estrada (1983) made the Rapaz church's rustic-baroque murals famous in Lima as much as three decades ago. In 1996 the Association of Rapacinos resident in Lima began sending letters to UNESCO asking for Rapaz's designation as a Patrimony of Humanity (Encarnación Rojas and Robles Atachagua 2011, 147–151). Journalists oriented to culture tourism publicized "cultural treasures" (Capurro 1995; Raffo 2000; Alva Salinas 2006). A team of restoration architects with support from the Getty Foundation have successfully worked on protecting Rapaz's seismically damaged church (Beas, Grau, and Maguiña 2000; Estabridis 2004; Navarro, Vargas, and Beas 2006; Patrimonio Peru 2000). A modest tourist traffic began as a few weekenders on the lower Checras river hot springs circuit began taking the rugged detour up to Rapaz. Backpacking adventure tourists from Lima, dirt-road bicyclists, rural technicians, and mine personnel sometimes stop by. By 2007, Rapaz had a simple hostel for visitors.

For Rapacinos who are at the same time actors in the old practices of life-circulation, and activists of development, tourism posed new questions. The contexts of tourism and of sacrifice seem to be in conflict. How can a place be arcane and at the same time public?

Rapaz simply divides day from night. Rapacinos who intend to hold "custom," and at the same time be held by it, assign the ritual work of Kaha Wayi and Pasa Qulqa exclusively to darkness. Such duties are markedly set apart from secular routines; balternos are bidden to arrive and depart by darkness so as not to be seen. They are to enter and leave by the precinct's small side door rather than make noise opening its gates.

In the daytime, outsiders are allowed through the main gate to visit, if closely supervised. First, visitors must find the "vice" or kamachikuq. He alone may unlock the precinct and show them around. This keeps down the amount of visiting because Rapacinos, including the officers, spend much of their time in remote fields and pastures. The "vice" guards control of Kaha Wayi's visitor traffic as a jealously held privilege and hardly ever delegates it. As guides, the successive "vices" have learned a more or less standard narrative that exalts the "khipu house" as a living pre-Columbian relic, but reveals nothing about its current function as the seat of the nighttime *rimanakuy* or conclave of governance. They meet visitors' expectations by emphasizing "Inka" antecedents and ancient chieftaincies.

Kaha Wayi does good service to Peru's multicultural ethos. Visitors who gain admission are usually glad to leave a few coca leaves on the altar with their friendly wishes. Many visitors told us it was their first actual contact with indigenous ritualism and that they experienced it as a cordial moment. Often, visitors erroneously perceived the shrine as expressing the *pachamamismo*, or Mother Earth worship, bruited globally as indigenous piety, but nobody among their hosts objected. In 2005 tourism gradually became formalized with a guestbook. Small donations became frequent.

By daylight Kaha Wayi's balterno guardians give every sign of modernism. When they speak of mountain-feeding as an Inka homage "to nature," they seem to speak of nature the way positivists do: a nonhuman exteriority which cultural constructs represent. They are able to objectify culture for tourists and even asked me to write a sort of guide's script that would help them do so. More and more visitors to Kaha Wayi are also guided to the new cooperative weavers' and knitters' store, a women's organization subsidized by the mining company. But tourism has not become anywhere near as profitable or dynamic as it has in the hinterland of Cuzco Department.

It seemed to me almost as if some Rapacinos had heeded Gellner's 1992 valedictory essay "The Uniqueness of Truth" (1995). Gellner's final reflection on the cognitive diversity of our age—an approach to anthropological wisdom rather than theory—is to commend a degree of doublethink, sacrificing some philosophical consistency for the sake of a satisfactory lifeworld. Those who inhabit the "well-lit" but arid mental space of the "enlightenment puritan" are Gellner's heroes. Yet he admits his epistemological foes do provide some values that one would hardly want to do without. The gifts of relativism are generous tolerance and colorful pluralism, a value enacted in the touring context. The gifts of fundamentalism are centeredness and moral seriousness, a value enacted in the *qaray* or sacrificial context. If these different values are pursued in consciously differentiated contexts, their discrepant epistomological underpinnings can serve their respective "worlds" without pushing each other out of shared real life. In this respect Rapaz and the globalized liberal ethos are not after all poles apart.

Protestant dissidence and "cosmopolitics"

One branch of the ontological discussion takes Viveiros de Castro's "ontological self-determination" proposal in a frankly political way. By this view, the crucial question is what happens when incommensurable ontologies belong to groups with rival interests? When a political sector faces a rival group that espouses its interests in terms of strange "things," may the political sector demand that its rival drop ontologically nonconsensual arguments? If ontologies disagree, can there be a common forum at all? If somebody says political agency belongs to "strange" things like jealous mountains or the Trinity, does that change him from a legitimate adversary to a person incompetent for political encounter? Would a constitution that combines respect for diversity with egalitarian sentiment require a parliament of worlds? And what might that look like?

In this matter the Andes are at the forefront of debate. Marisol de la Cadena prominently discussed as a case of "cosmopolitics" some Andean activists' claims for political recognition of "earth beings" as entities having rights (2010, 2015). The rights concerned are typically control over water or minerals. Community spokespeople who express inherited rights as the rights of mountains face corporations and state ministries as adversaries. Their claims have been derided as political "pachamamismo" by Ecuadorian and Peruvian heads of state. In Bolivia the rights of "earth beings" have been elevated to a constitutional issue.

De la Cadena valuably teaches that these fights are not an encounter between alien cultural worlds, nor a matter of ethnic polarization. She brilliantly summarizes the differentness of historically Quechua or Aymara people in the Andes as an "articulation of more than one, but less than two, socionatural worlds" that escapes the familiar rubrics of ethnicity and class. Media continue to represent the mestizo-Andean spectrum as a separate "indigenous" cultural sector, but this misleads insofar as Quechua- and Spanish-speaking existence are completely interpenetrated, even within the individual person.

As one might expect from people who are unrealistically conceived by their "others," Andean claimants sometimes express their interests in ways that others see as unreal. For de la Cadena, the monolingual Spanish political class' unwillingness to let nonhuman entities be parties to political process reflects the ancient bipolarity between nature and culture, with politics assigned to the whiter pole of "culture" and "native custom" to the pole of "nature." De la Cadena's ideal "cosmopolitics" on the other hand would take place among "partially connected heterogeneous socionatural worlds negotiating their ontological disagreements politically . . . without making the diverse worlds commensurable" (2010, 360–361).

FIGURE 6.3 Tomás Alejo Falcón, a Protestant Rapacino and balterno officer, helps conserve Kaha Wayi's patio. Photo by the author.

Is de la Cadena's "utopia" already happening (2010, 346, 361)? In the two local views sketched above, namely the old allegiance and doublethinking modernism, is Rapaz "interconnect[ing] such plurality without making the diverse worlds commensurable"? Is it conducting cosmopolitics in the here-and-now? The question becomes much more pointed when we regard the third of Rapaz people's postures toward the Andean sacred legacy.

The third party, an influential minority in the village, consists of Protestant converts. This group includes many of the most active, best-earning comuneros and some of the ablest holders of local office. Protestant numbers are varyingly estimated around 20 or 30 percent of the comunidad. On the whole Protestant households today enjoy peaceful relations with Catholic ones. A younger generation, born into Evangelical or Pentecostal religions rather than converted to them, has grown up with a relaxed attitude to diversity. Most Protestant "brothers" and "sisters" have Catholic relatives, so cross-cutting loyalties put a brake on conflict (though mixed marriages can cause rifts). The Community provides candy and soda as alternatives to ritual coca leaf and liquor, which Protestants consider objectionable. Some Protestants assume balterno roles with only nominal deference to Kaha Wayi and some helped in its conservation work (see Figure 6.3). The political order depends on this modus vivendi because if Protestants refused to accept civic offices the Community might become ungovernable.

But at the time our fieldwork began, now over a decade in the past, a significant number of Protestant Rapacinos wanted to have done with Kaha Wayi and Pasa Qulqa once and for all—either by neglecting them to death or by reducing them to heirlooms. The Pentecostal Assembly of God especially preached angrily against both Catholic "idolatry" (meaning saint veneration) and against "pagan" or "satanic" Andean customs.

Both people of the old allegiance and modernist doublethinkers spoke just as harshly about what they call "the sects." Referring to garbage tossed over the Kaha Wayi precinct wall, one woman said, "Why has that been allowed? It's because of the new sect [i.e., Protestantism]. Since that started, there's been no respect. They damage the town." Some felt stung by ridicule of their tradition. Some resented the condescension of converts, who considered themselves more educated because they pray from books (Salas Carreño 2010, 665). One lady of the old allegiance snapped, "All they ever talk about is God. They don't have any religion."

The more vehement Protestant comuneros opposed the old allegiance with quiet intransigence. They were able to nonviolently obstruct anything pro-Kaha Wayi in the Assembly by quorum-denying tactics or contentious amendments. They refused to schedule *faenas* (days of mandatory collective work) to maintain Kaha Wayi. That is how the structures had gotten into such shabby condition by 2004. After some Protestant "brothers" gained election to the 2008 board of officers, the board could not reach consensus to contract the *awkin* or ritualist. The 2008 "search for weather" was never carried out. Villagers loyal to the old system said that 2009's January freeze and the resulting midget crop of potatoes resulted from this dereliction. But the "brothers" blew them off. "What do we need all that diabolical magic for? Why spend on things that belong to Satan? In the end everything depends on God alone."

Rather than calling Andean ritual objects by their common Quechua names, the most ardent converts spoke of the animal essence talismans (ilas or lifestones) as "devils' eggs." They called Pasa Qulqa "Satan's storehouse." The lexical curtain that prevented converts from talking with loyalists on the village's usual terms suggested at least a posture of ontological dissent, i.e., separation of life-worlds. Opposite to the ontological commuting of modernist doublethinkers, Protestants proclaimed a sort of ontological boycott by refusing to help create ritual-verbal contexts in which lifestones' animal essences emerge as things in their own right.

But are "devil's egg" and "ila" parts of discrepant ontological outlooks? Perhaps not. Between converts and traditionalists the problem of "not knowing what they are talking about" hardly seemed prominent. Kaha Wayi loyalists had no trouble imagining the characteristics of a devil's egg, nor converts those of an animal lifestone. They just disagreed on which thing ilas are. It appeared that as Protestant discourse became Andean, it developed a lexicon that was dissident in relation to older ritual habit but still aligned with it. Moral valences were reversed, but the paradigm of entities a believer faced was conserved.

How did that happen? Separate practices produce different discursive frames. Each entails ways of ratifying experiences and classifying know-how. As with modernity and the old allegiance, practical Protestant know-how discerns and names emergent objects. "Devil's egg" is not an entity foreseen in dogma but a newly labeled quasi-entity generated metaphorically while practicing convert normality. Convert normality includes the daily practice of defamiliarizing the bad old world and taking critical distance from the things known in pre-conversion life by speaking inventively about them. It is in this process, and not in a "top-down," ex-post, totalizing image of Protestant life as an intellectual system with its own criteria for entity, that we can imagine the referent of "devils' eggs."

Questions and options in the "ontological turn"

Anthropologists continue to swing around "the turn" at undiminished speed. As of 2015 the databases *Anthropological Index, Anthropological Literature,* and *Anthrosource* showed steadily high production of English articles with "ontology" titles. Part of this production is self-criticism within the ontological current—which was, in a sense, its original mission.

G.E.R. Lloyd is an anthropologically minded, philosophically attuned British historian of ancient sciences. In 2012 he published a slim book with the Olympian title *Being, Humanity, and Understanding.* It brought his researches on Greek and Chinese antiquity together with mostly Amazonian ethnographic arguments. His purpose was to find a way of acknowledging deep cultural differences without condemning them to incommensurability. An eight-author "book symposium" about it in the journal *HAU* (2013) became a milestone in assessing the ontological turn's value and its costs.

Lloyd is receptive to the claim that ethnographic ontology amounts to more than "a posh and trendy synonym for 'culture'" (Holbraad in Venkatesan 2010, 179). He tries it out by describing some non-modern postulates (such as *logos* or *yin/yang*) as ontological entities irreducible to culture-neutral phrasing. But he joins the "weak ontologists" in insisting that within cultures several overlapping processes of cultural construction, and not only latent philosophical premises, generate perceived entities. Some of these processes result from the genetic template, others from "universals of experience" such as enculturation (Brown 1991, 47–49). Some arise from the imperatives of mutual accommodation (Sangren 2013, 182). Some seem to be dictated by our language-generating apparatus for information-sharing. These are good reasons for not *presupposing* incommensurable ontologies are the essence of difference.

Although it is a gentle book, Lloyd's work goes after weaknesses of "strong" ontologism. Others have joined him in criticizing them. Lloyd's anthropological ally Paolo Heywood argues that beyond duly recognizing the *possibility* of ontological-level differences, which is a good idea, "ontographers" elevate the *premise* that differences are ontological into "a kind of meta-ontology" of its own, with peculiar results. They "have moved too far from the call to 'take seriously' other worlds, and started positing worlds of their own" (Heywood 2012, 144). They do this, he suggests, because they do not follow the strict route of tracing "ontological commitments" as the philosopher W.V.O. Quine prescribed. Quine's route would narrow the range of entities that ordinary statements must imply. Instead, "strong" ontologists assume that "in order to have meaning a named object must exist" even if only as an unrealized potentiality. For example: if a Rapacino says "there are no such things as devils' eggs" the "ontographer" holds he is nonetheless giving us devil's eggs as for him an ontological fact. What a strange country that leads us into! The object of study becomes hard to hold in mind. Distinction between meaningfulness and realness collapse. ("Things are not distinct from their meanings," as Pedersen told us above.) And since we don't understand the resulting scene well, "ontographers" tell us, we had best practice "ontological generosity" by acting as if we were visiting a fully different world.

Pedersen, the ethnographer of Mongolia, scolded Heywood for applying a commonsensical "meta-ontological" filter without critical awareness (2012). The surprising thing about Pedersen's rebuttal, however, is that he actually seems persuaded by Heywood's objection. In several passages Pedersen backs away from "strong" ontological claims. Renouncing claims is not a big deal, he says, given the movement's "relative lack of commitment to the heuristic concepts that it creates." He concedes that "The ontological turn . . . does indeed involve a concept of a 'bloated universe'" such as Quine warned against. He suggests ways "of deflating the ontological bubble." And he does not deny that when ethnographing an unfamiliar scene one inevitably represents it in some extraneously constrained way. He guesses "the time may well have come to put the ontological turn to rest."

Another critique derives from the observation that treating vernacular "implicit cosmologies" such as the mountain cult as if they were exotic philosophies leads to inappropriate readings. The old allegiance is, as Laidlaw and Heywood put it, mostly a matter of "taken-for-granted assumptions and unarticulated notions . . . conceptions and commitments that might be thought to be implicit in a way of life" (2013, 197–198; see also Alberti 2011). This sort of "implicit cosmology" is non-propositional and non-critical in the first place, and therefore inherently unlikely to be put forth as a theory or a creed. "Implicit cosmology" is a very different matter from the propositions people state when they take distance from their cultural milieu for critical purposes. Critics of cultural anthropology have long called it a mistake to discuss "implicitly cosmological" postulates like sentient mountains as if they were the iceberg-tips of systematic philosophies waiting for translation.

They are not systematic philosophies because they arise in social conversations directed to quite other ends than analyzing what there is. That is, they differ from philosophy on a variable that the ontological turn is slow to discuss, namely the embeddedness of thinking in practice. Of what "communicative situation" are utterances about animated mountains products? Surely nothing like the classical Greek fora where competition for pedagogical influence spurred mutual critique (so G.E.R. Lloyd finds, 2012, 57). Rather they are parts of practical conversation in which statements about the nonhuman are inseparably loaded with messages about solidarity, practicality, and authority within the human group.

Viveiros interestingly rebutted such doubts about whether "implicit philosophies" teased from non-self-critical local discourse should be put on the same agenda with formal ontology (2013 [2002], 486–487; see also Severi 2013, 195). He holds they should, because the product of ethnography "reflect[s] . . . a certain relation of intelligibility *between* two cultures." A local idea such as, he says, the Melanesian partible individual is "a concept . . . as imaginative as Locke's possessive individualism" and has comparable standing "as . . . a form of *understanding* in its own right" even if it has not been locally worked up as explicit philosophy.[2] Native worlds are full of potential, still "imaginary" philosophies. We needn't wait for their full formalization to begin from learning them.

Perhaps Viveiros is right that the iceberg-tip usage is an inspiring idea for philosophical purposes, even if it oversteps the evidence. Remarkable things have been done with this position, as in Eduardo Kohn's *How Forests Think* (2013). Kohn has taken an implicit cognitive inclination, the Amazonian hunter mentality, and analyzed it as "animist" exchange of meaning (Chapter 2) among jaguars, dogs, and people that amounts to an implicit natural philosophy. Perhaps an environmental scientist willing to consider the sentience of mountains as a scientifically suggestive model for how Andean biosphere-culture relations work could also go far toward what Kohn calls "an anthropology beyond the human." But it's important to notice that Kohn's approach is not "strong ontography" because it does not require incommensurability *a priori*. It employs concepts from bioscience (especially Jesper Hoffmeyer's idea of the "semiosphere" [1993]) as interpretative tools.

Keane brackets some ontological theories as "weak" versions (2013). Kohn distinguishes "broad" from "narrow" versions, to partly similar purposes (2015). I would speak instead of "constrained" versions because, as I see it, the nub of the debate is not whether to dilute the ontological concept but rather to define conditions when one should apply it or abstain. A "constrained" approach would concentrate on the explaining the genesis of ontological differences within or among cultures, rather than simply equating cultural difference with ontology wholesale.

Bruce Mannheim, a linguistic anthropologist greatly interested in the mountain cult as practiced around Cuzco, has offered a program for doing so. He takes note that "research by cognitive psychologists has moved many of the questions traditionally raised by philosophers onto an empirical plane." Every speaker's "core cognition" or sense of "things" is constrained by the inborn faculties discussed in Chapter 1: "intuitive physics," disposition to posit "other minds," and "intuitive biology," etc. Implicit theories attach to domains like "animate things:" living things move autonomously, possess agency, etc., and these entailed theories guide the formation of ontology in the mind without fully determining it. "Core cognition constrains but does not specify a denotational set of ontological categories" (Mannheim and Salas Carreño 2015, 203). The remaining determinants of whether something appears "thingish" (Pooh Bear's word) in the mind of beholders arise in structures of their language(s) and in the local rules of social interaction. These layers of mental process do not always fit together in unique solutions about what perceptions are things. "There is crosslinguistic and crosscultural variability in the recruitment of concepts to domains (in Quechua, both mountains and rock are frequently treated as living kinds, whereas in English neither is)" (Mannheim and Salas Carreño 2015, 204).

And this is a sociocultural-linguistic matter. Our ways of "projecting" under-lying domains and theories onto perceived items vary because "projection" takes place as part and parcel of varied practices. For example, whether a mountain can be "recruited" to the animate class is not an imponderable "weirdness" of Andean culture. It depends on whether one's relation to the mountain is part of one's biologically organized activity.

Mannheim and Salas Carreño, have given a helpful account (2015). For them, the reason interaction with mountains contains a social and moral strand is nei-ther an archaic cognitive limitation nor an unfamiliar *a priori* philosophy. Rather, it arises from the way Andean agropastoralists manage a single inclusive domain of practices, namely the circulation of the substances of life. "Ultimately, human bodies are produced through the incorporation of the materiality of places, medi-ated through the consumption of food, which is cultivated and cooked by human relatives." Food in turn goes back to higher, nonhuman relatives in the form of sacrifices, sown seed, and burials.

One kind of circulation (agropastoral) is not a metaphor for the other (culinary). It isn't possible to say which is the basis and which the comparison. Rather both belong to a single common domain of feeding and being fed, receiving and paying, producing and consuming, all of which share lexicon and many other features. (A Rapaz example from Chapter 2 is *qaray*, a verb meaning both "to feed" and "to sacrifice.") "Animacy and sentience, as social constructs in Quechua culture, are based not upon a set of abstract beliefs that attribute them randomly to some beings and not others, but rather on practice of co-residence and the provisioning of food that are grounded in the quiddities of face-to-face interaction" (2015, 63–64).

Within this context, the "animate" ontological domain readily "recruits" the cordillera. Mannheim's bottom-up account of how groups generate putative "things" has the merit of giving local ontology a cognitive logic that goes only as far as it needs to. It does not oblige us to take named, ritualized constructs like *awkin* mountains as the shibboleths of alien "cosmovisions."[3] In explaining how particular detailed practices of grammar and lexicon commit the Quechua speaker to a world that contains "strange" things, the psychological-linguistic-pragmatic approach gives one an exciting sensation of approaching the particle-wave minima of cultural construction. When we enter into a society's prosaic talk and deeds, we learn how its bits of experience are forever gaining (or losing) "thingishness." It's no wonder that a visitor sometimes doesn't know what they're talking about. But it's one thing to perceive the continual emergence of unfamiliar entities and another to interpret ontological variation as if it made "other" cultural scenes imponderably alien. We want to render culture as it is, partly foreign but also partly our shared condition, incomplete and imperfect, always welling up from ordinary life.

Notes

1 A related argument occurs in Keane 2013, 187.
2 The "partible individual" is Marilyn Strathern's characterization of a Melanesian way to conceive of the person: not as an indivisible unitary subject, but as the site of the various social relationships that made him.

3 The term *cosmovisión*, from German *weltanschauung* "world view," was used by Mexican indigenist scholars before World War II. In current popular usage it tends to denote "implicit cosmologies" considered as philosophies of particular cultures.

References

Alberti, Benjamin, Severin Fowles, Martin Holbraad, Yvonne Marshall, and Christopher Witmore. 2011. "Worlds Otherwise: Archaeology, Anthropology, and Ontological Difference." *Current Anthropology* 52(6): 896–912. http://doi.org/10.1086/662027.

Alva Salinas, José. 2006. "Universo Rapaz, un desconocido tesoro colonial en la sierra de Lima." *El Comercio* (Supplement): 8–9.

Beas, María Isabel, Patrició Navarro Grau, and César Maguiña. 2000. "La arquitectura religiosa del Valle de Oyón, Perú." In *Terra 2000, 8th International Conference on the Study and Conservation of Earthen Architecture, Torquay, Devon, UK, May 2000.* London: James and James. 4–8.

Brown, Donald. 1991. *Human Universals.* Philadelphia, PA: Temple University Press.

Capurro, Hugo Ramón. 1995. "El quipu gigante de Rapaz." *Restaurantes y Turismo* 1(1): 17–21.

Dawkins, Richard. 2000. *Unweaving the Rainbow: Science, Delusion and the Appetite for Wonder.* New York: Harper Collins.

De la Cadena, Marisol. 2010. "Indigenous Cosmopolitics in the Andes: Conceptual Reflections beyond 'Politics.'" *Cultural Anthropology* 25(2): 334–370.

De la Cadena, Marisol. 2015. *Earth Beings: Ecologies of Practice across Andean Worlds.* Durham, NC: Duke University Press.

Dressler, William W. 2015. "'Culture'. . . Again." *Anthropology News* May–June 2015: 20.

Encarnación Rojas, Eulalia, and Narciso Robles Atachagua. 2011. *Breve Historia de San Cristóbal de Rapaz.* Lima: Gráfica Quinteros E.I.R.L.

Estabridis Cárdenas, Ricardo. 2004. *Iglesia de San Cristóbal de Rapaz: Análisis iconográfico de la pintura mural.* Report to Getty Grant Program Patrimonio Perú. n.p.

Geertz, Clifford. 1971. *Islam Observed: Religious Development in Morocco and Indonesia.* Chicago, IL: University of Chicago Press.

Gellner, Ernest. 1995. "The Uniqueness of Truth." In *Anthropology and Politics: Revolutions in the Sacred Grove,* edited by Ernest Gellner. Oxford and Cambridge, MA: Wiley. 1–10.

Heywood, Paolo. 2012. "Anthropology and What There Is: Reflections on 'Ontology.'" *Cambridge Anthropology* 30(1): 143–151.

Hoffmeyer, Jesper. 1993. *Signs of Meaning in the Universe,* translated by Barbara J. Haveland. Bloomington, IN: Indiana University Press.

Holbraad, Martin, Morten Pedersen, and Eduardo Viveiros de Castro. 2014. "The Politics of Ontology: Anthropological Positions." *Fieldsights: Theorizing the Contemporary, Cultural Anthropology Online.* http://culanth.org/fieldsights/462-the-politics-of-ontology-anthropological-positions

Keane, Webb. 2013. "Ontologies, Anthropologists, and Ethical Life." *HAU: Journal of Ethnographic Theory* 3(1): 186–191.

Kohn, Eduardo. 2013. *How Forests Think: Toward an Anthropology Beyond the Human.* Berkeley, CA: University of California Press.

Kohn, Eduardo. 2015. "Anthropology of Ontologies." *Annual Review of Anthropology* 44: 311–327.

Laidlaw, James, and Paolo Heywood. 2013. "One More Turn and You're There." *Anthropology of This Century* 7. http://aotcpress.com/articles/turn/.

Lloyd, G.E.R. 2012. *Being, Humanity, and Understanding: Studies in Ancient and Modern Societies.* Oxford: Oxford University Press.

Macera, Pablo, Arturo Ruiz Estrada, Luisa Castro, and Rocío Menéndez. 1995. *Murales de Rapaz.* Lima: Universidad del Pacífico and Banco Central de Reserva del Perú, Fondo Editorial.

Mannheim, Bruce, and Guillermo Salas Carreño. 2015. "Wak'as: Entifications of the Andean Sacred." In *The Archaeology of Wak'as: Explorations of the Sacred in the Pre-Columbian Andes,* edited by Tamara L. Bray. Boulder, CO: University of Colorado Press. 47–72.

Medin, Douglas L., and Megan Bang. 2014. *Who's Asking? Native Science, Western Science, and Science Education.* Cambridge, MA: MIT Press.

Navarro Grau, Patricia, Julio Vargas Neumann, and Maribel Beas. 2006. "Seismic Retrofitting Guidelines for the Conservation of Doctrinal Chapels on the Oyón Highlands in Peru." *Proceedings of the Getty Seismic Adobe Project, 2006 Colloquium, Getty Center, Los Angeles, April 11–13, 2006.* Los Angeles: The Getty Conservation Institute. 135–146.

Patrimonio Peru/Getty Grant Program. 2000. *Inventario, catalogación, y estado de conservación de bienes culturales. Iglesia de San Cristóbal de Rapaz. Cuenca de Oyón, Lima. Obispado de Huacho, Perú.* Lima: n.p.

Pedersen, Morten Axel. 2011. *Not Quite Shamans: Spirit Worlds and Political Lives in Northern Mongolia.* Ithaca, NY and London: Cornell University Press.

Pedersen, Morten Axel. 2012. "Common Nonsense: A Review of Certain Recent Reviews of the 'Ontological Turn.'" *Anthropology of this Century.* http://aotcpress.com/articles/common_nonsense/.

Raffo, Cecilia. 2000. "Norte de Lima de Churín a Huancahuasi." *Bienvenida* 12(52) 6–93.

Ruiz Estrada, Arturo. 1983. "El arte andino colonial de Rapaz." *Boletín de Lima* 28(5): 43–52.

Salas Carreño, Guillermo. 2010. "Conversiones religiosas y conflictos comunales: Las iglesias evangélicas y la creciente importancia del turismo en comunidades campesinas del Cusco." In *Perú: El problema agrario en debate. SEPIA XIII,* edited by Patricia Ames and Víctor Caballero. Lima: SEPIA. 644–680.

Sangren, P. Steven. 2013. "Ontologies, Ideologies, Desire." *HAU: Journal of Ethnographic Theory* 3(1): 179–185.

Severi, Carlos. 2013. "Philosophies without Ontology." *HAU: Journal of Ethnographic Theory* 3(1): 192–196.

Venkatesan, Soumha, ed. 2010. "Ontology Is Just Another Word for Culture: Motion Tabled at the 2008 Meeting of the Group for Debates in Anthropological Theory, University of Manchester." *Critique of Anthropology* 30(2): 152–200.

Vigh, Henrik Erdman, and David Brehm Sausdal. 2014. "From Essence Back to Existence: Anthropology Beyond the Ontological Turn." *Anthropological Theory* 15(1): 49–73.

Viveiros de Castro, Eduardo. 1998 [1996]. "Cosmological Deixis and Amerindian Perspectivism." *Journal of the Royal Anthropological Institite* (N.S.) 4(3): 469–488.

Viveiros de Castro, Eduardo. 2013 [2002]. "The Relative Native." *HAU: Journal of Ethnographic Theory* 3(3): 473–502.

7

THE GROUND TREMBLES

(closing thoughts on secularity and the "material turn")

"Religion" as a term has never fit well into anthropology because one can hardly use it without pulling in premises alien to some cultures we study as well as alien to our methodology. To many it seems a creepy, bullying word because in its usual usage it surreptitiously asserts as definitive something ("spirituality") that can never be consensual.

In 1995 in *Ordered Universes* Morton Klass carefully surveyed a century of efforts to redefine the term "religion" in a way that would make it anthropologically useful. To be anthropologically useful, it had to be, first, a secular term, independent of and equidistant from the tenets of particular sacred cultures. And second, it had to entail enough empirical referents to prevent its application being arbitrary. Klass found that all attempts at an anthropologized concept of religion finally belonged to only two sorts: first, arguments defining religion as the part of culture that refers to a certain kind of object, namely "the supernatural"; and second, arguments defining religion as the part of culture that does a certain kind of work, as for example, generating solidarity, providing overall meanings to live by, or deflecting overall conflict (1995, 18). Klass' analysis is still respected for its subtlety and fairness.

But when the University of Toronto anthropologist Simon Coleman set out to characterize "recent developments in the anthropology of religion" only fifteen years after Klass, he reported a third judgment on the venture of making "religion" anthropologically useful: it was a mistake in the first place (2010). If not totally mistaken, at least in need of drastic criticism.

Secularity/religion on trial

Coleman was writing in the wake of Talal Asad's "genealogical" or Foucauldian critique of secular approaches to religion. Since 1983, Asad's argument has gradually become the most influential critique affecting the anthropology of religion. It begins by noting that ethnographers of religion, religious studies professors, the American Academy of Religion, and so forth claim to expound a domain called religion, as marked off from the neutral secular forum. But wait: the idea of "the secular" as the default framework for knowledge, separable from "religion," is not to be taken for granted. It is not recognized everywhere, much less taken as a privileged arena of cognition. And it is not all that old. When were we licensed to think of "the secular" as the level field of normality on which religiosity sits as if within a special redoubt?

Asad taught that "the secular" is a rather local cultural framework, just as much in need of anthropological explanation as any cult. The secular cultural domain arose from a struggle in one part of the world: from Western countries affected by Reformation and Counter-Reformation struggles over state-sanctioned religious power in (especially) the 17th century. At that time certain sectors sought to define some political, commercial, and scientific institutions as *not* Church-governed. In a few places they eventually redefined state power as altogether separate from clerical authority. It was in this context of fragmenting Christian authority that attempts to contrast "religion" as a class of behaviors in contrast with secularism flourished. But from within many other societies, this contrast is not so visible. In many places ritual and the sacred domain are (at least ideally) best seen as a facet or aspect of social existence in general.

A corollary is that "religion" as an object of study may itself be ethnocentrically misconceived. Even if observers distanced from religious authority perceive far-flung commonalities of ritual language, mental intensity, intellectuality, and so forth, by what title are these commonalities elevated to the status of a defining essence? Perhaps it is only because "we" academics are estranged from ritual that this group of traits always catches our eyes.

The more committed an observer is to the secular academic platform, the more anomalous ritual and the sacred ethos look to him. Could it be that we have come full circle from the Jacobin "cult of reason" in the 1790s to a "cult of religion"? Have we been mistakenly reifying the ritual aspect of action into a virtual entity called Religion, somewhat as the "cult of reason" transformed the rational aspect of action into the virtual entity called the Goddess Reason? That would not leave standing much of Catherine Bell's optimistic homology between ritual and scholarship.

Asad's followers are just being good anthropologists when they show themselves leery of Eurocentric conceptions that might mis-orient their teaching. They have derived from his core argument (one to which Klass in 1995 gave a friendly nod, 149) the position that secularist definitions of religion remain inseparable from Western states' recent dominance.

For Asad the crucial function of the sacred ethos is social discipline; it is a specific form of power. Its material signs (e.g., the kneeling or prone posture) are not just a handy means by which people share optional ideas, but rather compulsions that shape human life into preexisting orders and set people's possibilities for living. A kneeling or prone person, for example, is denied full bodily agency. Taking that limitation into oneself is the very thing that validates one as a communicant person, a member. Communicant status governs the body, inculcates habits, and preconditions cognition. It attunes a person's range of agency to relations of power existing among those who kneel, and forecloses others. But the person so constrained is also empowered insofar as he partakes of that social order's impersonal power. And this is a very great social fact.

Power as conceptual common denominator has proven an easy sell to cultural anthropologists because we are subject to a gnawing suspicion that we have drifted too far from tough-mindedness.

If the present book had been written by a PhD of a later generation than mine, it might well have come out as a portrait of a composite social discipline: one authority in Kaha Wayi, another in the Church, a third in Protestant congregations, all framed as religions by the mostly secularist Peruvian state. That could have been a cogent study. But I see some room for doubt about whether it would be enough to consider Kaha Wayi's authority as the kind of "religion" that is contained within and defined by secularist statehood—a church of the mountains, as it were, or in other words an "Andean religion" to be filed in the same paradigmatic list as Catholicism, Islam, and so forth.

Fenella Cannell, an anthropologist who, like Asad, is adept at defamiliarizing Christianity, voices a caution: "Asad's close focus on the history of the secular in the West, logical for his own project, means that he does not engage at length with polytheistic (or nontheistic) formations of religion or with the unexpected forms of secularity which might emerge in such contexts" (2010, 95). For this reason, even if we class Peru as a society of the secularized West, we may find that Andean ritual life does not sit within it the same the way Christian churches do. Although we have seen many reasons to think of it as religious, it may not be quite the same thing as "a religion."

As of 2016, Kaha Wayi still had its old peculiarity as an institution that had never been forced to define itself on the secular/religious divide or to fit the disciplines of modernity in the usual ways. Although it strongly possesses sacredness in the simple Durkheimian sense, when balternos discuss Kaha Wayi among themselves, they don't categorize it as a religion. Nor does the walled precinct carry any of the insignia rural Peruvians recognize as religious or civil. Kaha Wayi states no creed and has no scripture. For those who hold what I called the "old allegiance," the "implicit cosmology" enshrined in Kaha Wayi counts as knowledge or know-how, not belief or spirituality. "Voluntad" within unwritten law rather than "faith" is the state to which members discipline themselves.

Not that Kaha Wayi is isolated from ecclesiastical religion. In contexts external to its own functions, those who demur from some of Kaha Wayi's disciplining demands say *"no tengo esa fe"* ("I don't have that faith") or *"no tengo esa creencia"* ("I don't have that belief"), using churchy language. Balternos who demonstrate Kaha Wayi to visiting outsiders use such expressions as *"la fe en la naturaleza que tenían los incas,"* "the faith in nature that the Inkas had." They seem then to be speaking the language of post-Enlightenment religious pluralism in denominational contexts. Those who distance themselves from Kaha Wayi can speak of its obligations as if they were faith orientations.

"New materialism": toward an anthropology of all things

Having taken to heart the Asadian critique, sociocultural anthropologists early in the 21st century have begun over. They search for common denominators for describing ritual life without qualifying it on criteria originally internal to Western theology (creed, transcendence, spirituality, faith, ultimacy, and so forth).

Many of the contenders cued by Asad's insistence on religion as a "material discipline" have returned to the theme of materiality. The central perception is culture's physical presence. Obviously we make culture out of environmental features, artifacts, and visible, audible media but, less obviously, we make it out of our bodies and what happens inside them. Whatever else religion (and culture) are, they are approachable as swarms of *stuff* and *flesh* in culture-making motion. It is hoped this will prove a more impartial and refreshingly humble premise.

In seminar lingo the rubric for this turn is "new materialism." The word "new" signals a rupture from once-dominant Marxian materialism. One can get an idea of what is curiously coalescing in the name of "material culture studies" from the publisher's keywords listed for *The Oxford Handbook of Material Culture Studies*: "archaeology, anthropology, geography, science, technology, material practices, landscape, built environment, Coca-Cola, chimpanzees, artworks, ceramics, museums, cities, human bodies, magical objects" (Hicks and Beaudry 2010). When applied to our subfield, the material culture approach is sometimes called "material religion." Rapacinos' lifestones, khipus, wind-sacks, empty fasting bellies, and flowery staffs are not insignia attached to a preexisting thing called a religion. What brings persons and groups into being as religious actors is a constellation of specialized objects together with bodily activities that activate them.

A flock of other partially overlapping names call us toward other angles of vision on the human-thingish horizon. The variant called the "media turn" puts emphasis on the fact that a religion's content is inseparable from the palpable streams of signs through which people co-construct culture and shape selves: gestures, words, icons, and scriptures as much as digital technology. Media cease to be viewed as neutral transporters of religious propositions. They emerge as the structures that organize every ritual collectivity. Once religious collectivities are imagined as media webs, anthropology of religion meshes with semiotics (Mayer 2013) and linguistics (Keane 1997).

Another tendency, nicknamed "embodiment," focuses on the human body as the material of religion. By turning to the body, its adepts strive to make up for the abysmal misunderstandings we accumulated when long ago "we" embraced as religion par excellence those sacred cultures which reject, devalue, and "transcend" carnal life (in both East and West). Instead, the embodiment approach puts the accent on religions as systems of practice that bond and organize people in the flesh, through the flesh: the "fulcrum of culture is embodiment," (Morgan 2005, 3). All five senses and proprioception (the self-body sense), as well as all bodily functions like birth, feeding, and dying are disciplined as actions constituting the religious bond.

Perhaps, we learn, "embodied" religion matters even more than the conscious, discursive parts of ritual. It is less vulnerable to argumentative attack. Bodily practice can expand to govern the whole rhythm and manner of life, as well as to manifest and enforce everyone's place in society. Surely the herdsmen's all nighter we recalled in Chapter 4 is nothing if not a way of creating joint human-livestock society by joining the stink of burning animal fat, icy night, and the heat of close bodies, blackness, silence, song, the bellow of bulls, the pounding of their hoofs.

Embodiment theory also helps explain unselfconscious, habitual piety. That might be the world's most common form of religiosity—and a consequential one, before which more cerebral theorists stand fidgeting in helpless consternation.

A host of philosophically linked projects in "new materialism" with names such as "vital materialism" and "agential realism" point in the same general direction: the line between people as anthropology's "subjects" or "agents," and the non-human world of "nature" or "objects" needs to be erased (Hazard 2013, 64). This is a broader way of proposing what in Chapter 6 we called "anthropology beyond the human." The theoretical scene is swirling with such innovations.

Post-humanism?

Theorizing in the new-materialist vein is sometimes called "post-humanist." On first hearing this phrase, the gentle reader may well murmur, "I don't want to hear about it." It seems to suggest tech fetishism or punkish attitudes. But the "new materialism" is not (at least intentionally) hostile to the ethical concerns of humanism. Rather it suggests that research can be fully cultural, and even humanitarian, without clinging to the anthropocentric bias of traditional humanities. What happens if we suspend such slogans as "Man is the measure of all things" (an Aristotelian phrase ancestral to cultural relativism) or "the proper study of mankind is man" (a 1733 admonition against theological bias)?

The ecological revolution has already left its mark on us. Having re-measured mankind, and having judged ourselves an unreliable component of the delicate blue-green mist that covers our lonely planet, we feel with a chill that our half-millennium-long exploration of the world in human-centric terms may have run its course. In Chapter 6 we already glanced at ecologically influenced proposals for "anthropology beyond the human."

Self-designated post-humanists think today's marginalization of liberal arts results from the false supposition of a chasm between humans and the rest of the world. Looking back on it, our distinctive human form of awareness ("consciousness") ought not to have inhibited reasoning about the fact that most of our attributes are shared with "animals," and most of our agency is mixed with "things." Some successful areas of theory, such as systems theory, have already become quite indifferent to the supposed gulf between people and things. So why should our ethnological science balk at crossing the line between humans and all other phenomena?

Humanities disciplines will continue to matter, the "new materialists" suggest, and anthropology can keep on partnering with them. But first the former have to be "provincialized" (to use a fashionable word borrowed from subaltern studies) as parts of something more inclusive. Humanistic ventures such as Max Weber's foundational sociology used to be called *Geisteswissenschaften*, "sciences of the spirit," pre-eminently including the anthropology of religion. That term brings to the surface the assumption we are now asked to renounce: the notion that beings who possess a type of self-regard we recognize as soul, spirit, or mind must by that token be set apart and studied separately from all else.

In 1991 (translation 1993), Bruno Latour, already a renowned ethnographer of life among scientists, proposed an immensely influential alternative. For the sake of a more unified way of knowing, we are to unseat the founding dichotomy of modernity: nature versus culture (meanings versus facts, persons versus things, subjects versus objects). This monumental reorientation would amount to a U-turn reversing the "linguistic" and "symbolic turn" of the late 20th century and leaving behind old symbolist friends like Geertz. Instead of dissolving everything solid into "cultural construction," Latour meant to reconceive cultural construction in seamless relation with materiality.

Although Latour's name is often associated with "the new materialism," his vision of the material world makes room for many things that earlier materialisms tried to argue out of existence, including cultural constructs (which are "embodied" as they exist in neural formations and sensations).

Latour asks us to imagine that an interactive "democracy of entities" forms the common ground containing people and everything else. "The beings of this new, nonmodern world, are neither purely natural nor purely social, but rather 'networks' that hybridize nature and power, language, language and the ozone hole" (Proctor 1995, 384). The entities we should envision are "assemblies" of human and nonhuman that all have effects on the world. Even that purported charter member of reality, the individual human, turns out not to be an irreducible entity, but a many-million-fold assembly of microorganisms, organs, substances, and artifices, all of which form an "actor network." All these actors make "her" or "his" vital processes and deeds occur.

And if the human person is an actor network, so too are other entities. Thus many nonhuman things, such as climate, medicines, cars, animals, foods, radiation, computers, and viruses are to be thought of no longer as "objects" but as active parties to human affairs, without any of them receiving a priori privilege as "the subject." Whatever we find, in or beyond society, is the swarming of a material myriad. In a superb pro-Latour article titled "The Material Turn in the Study of Religion," Sonia Hazard writes that "religions are buzzing imbroglios populated by things, human and and nonhuman, like Bibles, golden plates, transatlantic telegraph cables, radio waves, pheromones, and strands of DNA . . . To trace religion through all this, of course, we must pass through and around the human" (2013, 69).

In the works of Bruno Latour the range of phenomena previously characterized as agency, namely the ability to make changes in the world, is decoupled from subjectivity, namely "inner life." It is also separated from particular chains of causation like human agency as compared to genetic linkage or energy-flow linkage. When seen as parts of "actor network" fields, cars, symbols, viruses, and computers are assemblies that make things happen in ways unforeseen by subjective intention. Indeed, say "new materialists," it is futile to describe our condition without recognizing the universal distribution of material agency.

The "new materialist" train of thought does still allow the individual subjective "lifeworld" the standing of a material (neural) phenomenon within all this. The new style is anything but dismissive of human culture. But it pushes back against the notion that through "cultural construction" mental activities are the grounding of all reality.

"Actor-network theory" and its relatives obviously fit Kaha Wayi like a glove. It wouldn't be news to any Rapacino that the world consists of an interactive web among beings who are both social and natural. The archaeologist Luis Jaime Castillo Butters comments that our current "internet of things" just reinvents an ancient supposition of Andean and Mayan peoples: that things in general form a sort of society, partake of reciprocity, and have agency of their own. Long ago, Andean and Mesoamerican myths say, nonhuman beings rebelled against humans for using them badly: "Mortars and grinding stones began to eat people. Buck llamas started to drive men" (Neuman and Castillo 2017; Salomon and Urioste 1991, 52). In reading Latour's *We Have Never Been Modern* I sometimes felt that he was rendering explicit a way of thinking whose iceberg-tip I had already experienced when hearing about Andean mountains.

For Latour hybrid "monsters," as both he and his critics call them, are neither a peculiarity of the hypermodern, nor a mythical archaism. On the contrary, human-nonhuman composites are what all sorts of societies and ages posit, just as Rapaz does. By accepting this commonality, actor-network theory promises to put the observer equidistant from any and all cultural orders. And for this reason Latour's paradigm is catnip to ethnographers.

What then makes "our" consciousness, namely "modernity," so different from all others that we find Rapaz utterances about hungry mountains hard to believe? The peculiarity of the modern, Latour thinks, is not what we have been given to believe, namely, a chasm between an old, primitive kind of thought and a new, enlightened kind. Replacing this "Great Divide" is one of Latour's central commitments. ("Great Divide" refers to the shared premise of all theories founded on a dichotomy between the "West and the Rest," "open" versus "closed" cultures, "oral" versus "literate," "savage" versus "domesticated" mind, and so forth.)

Let's get real, says Latour: when we are not being overtly theoretical we casually attribute person-like agency to all kinds of things. For us, just as for Rapaz people and everyone else, no part of our world is any more natural than it is cultural. Cars partake of humanness and we humans are car-symbiotes. Every driver gives her car a nickname, scolds or strokes it, and counts on it to act as her agent in showing others what sort of person she is. A professor's spotless 30-year-old pearl-gray Volvo *causes* an adjustment in relations; it might make me think of her in a certain way and perhaps vote for her as Department Chair.

The sculpted battle shield of a Marquesan "big man" works the same way. Alfred Gell, a specialist in Pacific island art whose ideas prefigured Latourian notions, characterized both Marquesan art and British "vehicular animism" as typical second-tier forms of human agency. It sounds as if he picked up on the word *agent*'s double suggestion in naming a *doer* who is also a *delegate* (1998, 18–19). Latour and Gell don't need a special theory-of-Western-selves. Theory should explain "their" monsters and "ours" together. Anthropology should become "symmetrical."

In the course of western society's expansion, the art of multiplying hybrids has become perceived as knowledge par excellence: science. A somewhat elusive argument (1993, 13–48, 108–112) claims that the technological surge since about 1650 is itself what generated our taboo on recognizing the part-culture, part-nature character of everything (Latour 1993, 13–48, 108–112). By inventing scientific instruments, early-modern natural philosophers brought into view un-socialized, non-cultural properties of the material world. They allowed us to imagine nature supposedly as it is in itself, uncontaminated by "us." An inverse taboo defined the social as the area of sovereign subjectivity, different from nature.

This great new divide created an epochally successful research path and a platform for disenchanted philosophizing too. But natural philosophy also demanded a strange amnesia. In the service of science, the West imposed on itself a taboo on remembering how science happened: namely, the fact that measuring (etc.) was a sociocultural activity in the first place. Instead we learned to suppose that science and its objects must be different from everything else about ourselves. And our selfhood must be different from all "factish" things. Having tabooed the perception that scientific findings are hybrids, Great Dividers, such as the "naturalist" whom we heard Husserl scolding back in Chapter 5, perceived all knowledge as "discovery" of an ever-greater and ever more alien "nature."

So what really is peculiar about "us?" For Latour, it is our ironclad unwillingness to *know* that we live among assemblies and hybrids. When asked to account for ourselves intellectually, we posit a primal, fundamental difference of substance separating the things we study as "objects" from those we think we know through cultural intersubjectivity. We put their respective studies at opposite ends of the campus. We talk about them in mutually incomprehensible jargons.

Yet all the time we go on behaving as if we accept and really want a universal distribution of agency. We avidly create ever-more domineering hybrids by fusing intersubjective with scientific knowledge (for example, in automated management systems, "consumer science," Facebook, and so forth). These devices stand to us somewhat as mountains stand to Rapacinos, as agentive, part-human things. What's up with that? Why should our self-image depend on pretending all things are either cultural or natural?

In the brilliant (or perhaps just flashy?) sixth chapter of *We Have Never Been Modern*, Latour proposes a way to make anthropology "symmetrical." Let's picture a western ethnographer. She thinks people like Rapacinos make up fantastic cosmologies because they mix "signs with things," and "nature" with "politics and social interests." Symmetrically, the Rapacinos may be judging her a mixed-up person. They might say she superstitiously pencils in the nature-culture polarity over her actually much more tangled world view. "All natures-cultures are similar in that they simultaneously construct humans, divinities, and nonhumans" (1993, 106).

A population in its "natureculture" involvements is what Latour then calls a "collective." The difference between "premodern" and "modern" collectives is not qualitative, as we'd been thinking for centuries—it's not a divide at all. It is quantitative: "Collectives are all similar, except for their size, like the successive helixes of a single spiral. The fact that one of the collectives needs ancestors and fixed stars [like Rapaz circa 1614 in Chapter 2] while another one, more eccentric, needs genes and quasars, is explained by the dimensions of the collective to be held together." A society that needs ancestors is a smallish one, in which kinship and descent carry the load of organizing life as such. Rapaz circa 1614 was like that, and so was the society envisioned in the early strata of the Bible.

A society that needs genes is a big society, one that must organize colossal numbers of people not known to each other as relatives. Nonetheless, capacities for working with genes and quasars are achieved in the same old way: by multiplying part-human tools for recognizing "actants" in new assemblies. Modernity and growth of scale are inseparable. As networks among humans and "resources" become globalizing aggregates of billions, with a physical horizon measured in billions of light years, "they add many more hybrids in order to recompose the social link and extend its scale" (1993, 109).

Latour calls his position "a-modern" (rather than anti-modern). In its practical implications, his teaching is not particularly heterodox. Like any progressive citizen he fears our sorcerer's-apprentice technophilia, yet at the same time prizes the Enlightenment legacy that underpins it.

At the same time, his teaching's interpretative implications are quite heterodox. Among many other novelties, they include a variant of relativism eminently hospitable to the non-reductionist study of religion. It is not relativism about societies but relativism about the facets of living within any society. Unlike Great Divide theorists (but like Talal Asad?) he is in a good position to deal with religion's ascendancy at times and places where it was least expected. The reason is that he regards religiosity as an inherent aspect or posture of the human being *in* "natureculture," rather than a proposition or doctrine *about* it.

Envoi: researchers and religionists

At this point anybody wanting to do anthropology of religion might well feel both excited and perplexed. Latourian ideas make the "strange" things envisioned in religion less weird than most theories do. But once we are on the ethnographic ground, how will the rather phantom-like Latourian entity mesh with the earth-bound study of people in action? "Assemblies" seem to lack edges, and "agency" seems to include activity in general. If you go this route, you are likely to hear a member of your doctoral advisory committee charge that your proposal counts inanimate things as "social" only in a "recondite way, so as to avoid the crucial issues" about what sociality actually consists of (Collins 1994, 674). Andrew Kipnis, though friendly to Latour, similarly charges that "posthumanists . . . wish to flatten the differences between human and nonhuman agency." Latour might be agreeing with Rapacinos in saying "a mountain makes its way in order to maintain itself in existence," but in saying so he buys ethnographic "symmetry" at the expense of clarity about agency. Kipnis suggests moderating the Latourian omni-agentive vision by "granting agency to nonhuman entities but emphasizing the difference between human and nonhuman agency" (2015, 44, 49).

Still, you might want to go the Latourian way because he engages more substantively with the religiously conceived world than any major theorist for a long time. That may be because he is among the few who perceive religiosity from the inside as well as the outside. A decade after formulating "A-NT," Latour published a surprising book called *Rejoicing, or the Torments of Religious Speech* about this posture.[1]

It empathizes tenderly with a nameless, Latour-like protagonist. This sophisticated fellow has long since accepted the Enlightenment demolition of the supernatural, yet he drinks deep of the Catholic tradition and loves it. As a member of the secularist European intelligentsia he suffers from the knowledge that his secularist peers see his religious attachment as eccentric if not ridiculous.

On the way to celebrate Pentecost Mass, Latour's alter ego "grinds his teeth" about "the menacing choice that vulgar common sense demands of anyone who sets out to talk about religion: 'But are you a believer or a non-believer?'" In the face of such bullying he "wants to disinter religious utterance . . . a form of expression that used to be so free and inventive." It has been disoriented and devalued by its misclassification as bad cognitive information. For Latour's stand-in, religion "isn't information, and it leads nowhere [cognitively]—but it can perform plenty of other miracles." Latour considers religion a special type of practice that delves into the phenomenal world in a way complementing the theoretical view. Instead of stepping back for coolness and distance, religious action comes forward as close as possible, feeling "natureculture" within and without. During his moment as an intense worshiper, Latour's proxy disappears into the here-and-now, "creating closeness" as "a surfer . . . might say that she struggles to become 'one with the water'" (Kipnis 2015: 47).

Hmmm. "Miracles?" Can we swallow that?

Latour's idea that it makes a difference whether the ethnographer embraces religion experientially has arisen many times before. The incomparable Africanist E.E. Evans-Pritchard argued (mostly by example) that theories of religion had to be evoked from, rather than imposed on, ritual life. Late in life Evans-Pritchard felt it followed that "the believer" enjoys an advantage in this task because he is free of the need to condescendingly render religiosity in terms of "translation domains" unrecognizable by his hosts (1965, 121). Evans-Pritchard's younger contemporary

Victor Turner (Chapter 5), like the old master a Catholic by choice, startlingly concluded that a certain Ndembu crisis cult expressed the same ineffable "ground of being" perception that led Thomas Aquinas toward a doctrine of the divine (1962). Turner was moved to entertain in the teeth of relativism the idea of pan-religious ultimate concerns. (Robin Horton, whom we also met in Chapter 5, bitingly demurred.)

Don't these examples seem to border on missionary ethnology, which is often considered one of anthropology's disreputable ancestors? The likeness is no illusion. Evans-Pritchard quoted credulously from Father Wilhelm Schmidt, a later-discredited Viennese proponent of "primitive monotheism." Turner's ver-sion of primitive Thomism too was discredited, on grounds related to analytic philosophy as well as for interpretative excess. We may not want to go very far in these thinkers' direction lest someday we find a "No atheists allowed" sign posted on our classroom doors. Yet when Fiona Bowie reviewed the matter of "believer" ethnographers in 2008, she concluded that "It is the gap between this [ritual] experience and the intellectual culture of the academy that paradoxically both provides intellectual rigour to the study of religion" and "also all too often emasculates its subject matter" (2008, 872). That rings true.

In choosing Asad and Latour for this book's *envoi*, I chose two ritually expe-rienced anthropologists. They, unlike the converts Evans-Pritchard and Turner, prefer not to shorten the "gap" between academe and religious participation. They think, as I do, that the religious/academic distinction should remain sharp. But they also think that we should be able to think about how that sharpness is achieved and know how it feels to be cut by it. Different as they are, Latour and Asad are alike in that they reject the usual ethnographic project of describing religiosity "as if" from within while actually repudiating it. The "gap" symbolized by Latour's path to his village church is a good place to stop and think. Latour and Asad seem to theorize from within a field of tension between un-ironic ritual experience and experience in critical secularism.

Asad is the son of an Austrian Jew who converted to Islam and spent his life pro-posing modernizing versions of Muslim statehood. He is also the son of a mother completely at home in "embodied," orthoprax Muslim piety, so he knows the ritual mindset empathetically:[2]

> It was not meaning that was taught first but just a way of life and a way of inhabiting one's body, of relating to other people, and of learning certain kinds of rituals. Even when one is taught in words it's not really the symbol-ism of rituals that matters. I remember as a child being taught by my father: "You stand like this when you're doing your prayer; bow down like this and make rukū' and then prostrate yourself and make a sajdā."
>
> *Asad 2015, 261*

As for Latour, he characterized his young self as a "militant Catholic" (Skirbekk 2015, 46). His 1975 PhD thesis was in theology and had the title *Exegesis and*

Ontology, with Reference to the Resurrection (Schmidgen and Custance 2014, 13).[3] He had not forgotten this when he wrote *Rejoicing* 40 years later.

These are anthropologists of religion who know what they are talking about when they discuss sacred culture, even as they talk in fora that are and should be foreign to it. Scholars who experience the anthropology of religion in this way, knowing first-hand both sides of Bell's homology between theorizing and ritualizing, sometimes gain an unusual ability to speak with undivided conviction.

Notes

1 Overlapping the third part of *On the Modern Cult of the Factish Gods* (2010), which in turn reproduces Latour's chapter in the 2005 edited *Science, Religion and the Human Experience* (James. D. Proctor, editor).
2 As a doctoral student of Evans-Pritchard, Asad produced a Sudan-based Oxford dissertation: *The Kababish Arabs: Power, Authority and Consent in a Nomadic Tribe* (1970).
3 *Exegèse et ontologie à propos de a resurrection*, Université de Dijon, 1975. Latour began ethnographizing while embarked on this exegetical train of thought, during his colonial National Service (1973–1975) in Abidjan, Côte d'Ivoire.

References

Asad, Talal. 1970. *The Kababish Arabs: Power, Authority, and Consent in a Nomadic Tribe.* New York: Praeger.

Asad, Talal. 2015. "Talal Asad Interviewed by Irfan Ahmad." *Public Culture* 27(2): 259–279.

Bowie, Fiona. 2008. "Anthropology of Religion." *Religion Compass* 2(5): 862–874.

Cannell, Fenella. 2010. "The Anthropology of Secularism." *Annual Review of Anthropology* 39: 85–100.

Coleman, Simon. 2010. "Recent Developments in the Anthropology of Religion." In *The New Blackwell Companion to the Sociology of Religion*, edited by Bryan S. Turner. Oxford: Blackwell. 103–121.

Collins, H.M. 1994. "[Review of] *We Have Never Been Modern* by Bruno Latour." *Isis* 85(4): 672–674.

Evans-Pritchard, Edward Evan. 1965. *Theories of Primitive Religion.* Oxford: Clarendon Press.

Gell, Alfred. 1998. *Art and Agency: An Anthropological Theory.* Oxford: Oxford University Press.

Hazard, Sonia. 2013. "The Material Turn in the Study of Religion." *Religion and Society: Advances in Research* 4: 58–78.

Hicks, Dan, and Mary C. Beaudry, eds. 2010. *The Oxford Handbook of Material Culture Studies.* Oxford: Oxford University Press.

Keane, Webb. 1997. "Religious Language." *Annual Review of Anthropology* 26: 47.

Kipnis, Andrew. 2015. "Agency between Humanism and Posthumanism: Latour and His Opponents." *HAU: Journal of Ethnographic Theory* 5(2): 43–58.

Klass, Morton. 1995. *Ordered Universes: Approaches to the Anthropology of Religion.* Boulder, CO: Westview.

Latour, Bruno. 1993 [1991]. *We Have Never Been Modern*, translated by Catherine Porter. Cambridge, MA: Harvard University Press.

Latour, Bruno. 2013 [2002]. *Rejoicing, or the Torments of Religious Speech*, translated by Julie Rose. Cambridge: Polity.

Latour, Bruno. 2005. "Thou Shalt Not Freeze-Frame, or How to Not Misunderstand the Science-Religion Debate." In *Science, Religion and the Human Experience*, edited by James. D. Proctor. Oxford: Oxford University Press. 27–47.

Latour, Bruno. 2010. *On the Modern Cult of the Factish Gods*. Durham, NC: Duke University Press.

Mayer, Birgit. 2013. "Mediation and Immediacy: Sensational Forms, Semiotic Ideologies, and the Question of the Medium." In *A Companion to the Anthropology of Religion*, edited by Janice Boddy and Michael Lambek. Chichester, UK: Wiley Blackwell. 309–326.

Morgan, David. 2005. "Religion and Embodiment in the Study of Material Culture." *Oxford Research Encyclopedias: Religion*. http://religion.oxfordre.com/view/10.1093/acrefore/9780199340378.001.0001/acrefore-9780199340378-e-32.

Neuman, William, and Luis Jaime Castillo Butters. 2017. "The Internet of Things Is Coming for Us." *New York Times*, Jan. 22, 2017. https://www.nytimes.com/2017/01/21/sunday-review/the-internet-of-things-is-coming-for-us.html?smid=nytcore-ipad-share&smprod=nytcore-ipad&_r=0.

Proctor, Robert N. 1995. "[Review of] *We Have Never Been Modern* by Bruno Latour." *American Scientist* 83(4): 384.

Salas Carreño, Guillermo. 2010. "Conversiones religiosas y conflictos comunales: Las iglesias evangélicas y la creciente importancia del turismo en comunidades campesinas del Cusco." In *Perú: El problema agrario en debate. SEPIA XIII*, edited by Patricia Ames and Víctor Caballero. Lima: SEPIA. 644–680.

Salomon, Frank, and George Urioste, eds. and trans. 1991. *The Huarochirí Manuscript: A Testament of Ancient and Colonial Andean Religion*. Austin, TX: University of Texas Press.

Schmidgen, Henning, and Gloria Custance. 2014. *Bruno Latour in Pieces: An Intellectual Biography*. New York: Fordham University Press.

Skirbekk, Gunnar. 2015. "Bruno Latour's Anthropology of the Moderns: A Reply to Maniglier." *Radical Philosophy* 189: 45–47.

Turner, Victor. 1962. *Chihamba, the White Spirit: A Ritual Drama of the Ndembu*. Manchester, UK. Published on behalf of the Rhodes-Livingstone Institute by the Manchester University Press.

GLOSSARY OF NON-ENGLISH AND FIELD-SPECIFIC TERMS

Bolded terms refer to theoretical concepts. *Italicized* terms are non-English words, signaled as follows:

(Q)   Quechua I or central Peruvian Quechua

(Q II)   Southern Peruvian (Quechua II) terms possibly introduced via Inka influence, ecclesiastical Quechua, or neo-Inka indigenist lexicon

(HQ)   Hispano-Quechu word, meaning a Quechua word of Spanish etymology

(SQ)   Spanish word of Quechua etymology

(S)   Spanish usages within or near the Peruvian "educated norm"

Normative Quechua spelling is applied to words transcribed exclusively from Quechua oral context. Spanish words of Quechua etymology and Quechua words of Spanish etymology are spelled in the Spanish orthography used by local writers. Words encountered in colonial documents are spelled in the Spanish orthography of the sources.

agency   ability to make changes in the world

allawka, allauca (Q, SQ)   upper moiety in Rapaz hydraulic organization and ceremony

alqasaku (Q, SQ)   bag-lifter, the person who executes the count of incoming crops

analogism   in P. Descola's model, that mode of cultural cognition that organizes a maximally diverse array of entities according to paradigms of shared traits at multiple levels, similar antitheses at multiple levels, etc.

ancestor veneration   ritual communication with or propitiation of deceased kin

animism   in older usage, attribution of a vital or magical force to entities; in P. Descola's model, a mode of cultural cognition that organizes beings as differently embodied but possessing inwardly similar subjectivity

anqi (Q)   an agricultural sector defined for purposes of rotation *anqush* (Q)   a type of puna grass

apu (Q II?, SQ)   lord, often meaning a major mountain

armar (HQ)   to set up, especial a ritual array

auto da fe (Portuguese, used in Spanish and English)   ceremony demonstrating orthodoxy by punishment of religiously irregular persons or things

away walqi (Q)   coca bag for ritual use

awkin (Q, SQ)   old man, ritualist, venerable or authoritative male

ayllu (Q)   descent group, ancestor-oriented kindred often with patrilineal bias

balterno (HQ)   member of the corps of traditional civil authorities

bendelhombre (HQ, SQ)   contracted ritualist or priest; authoritative benefactor

benio (HQ)   'biennium' period of office

boleo (S), *chajchay* (SQ)   act of sucking coca leaves in the cheek

cabildo (S)   civic council

caja (S)   chest, treasury, cash repository

calzar (S)   to set up and activate an array of ritual objects; to effect a ritual with it

campesino (S)   peasant or small-scale farmer and/or herder; countryman

campora (S)   female consort and co-officer of a *campo* or balterno in charge of rural operations

cayan (Q)   village plaza or civic/ritual ground

cerro (HQ, S)   mountain

chacleado (SQ?)   ceiling made of plant stalks

chaco (SQ)   surround hunt to shear vicuña

chaguay (Q)   cellar or semi-subterranean part of a building

chajchay see *boleo*

chakwas (Q, SQ)   old woman, authoritative female

chilwa (Q)   a type of puna grass

chúcaro (S)   ornery, untamable

chukrush (Q)   a twinned or otherwise auspicious plant specimen suspended to dry (*chukruy*) in storage

cognitive-evolutionary   theories of religion combine cognitive arguments about perceptions of sacred beings as side effects of evolved cognitive dispositions, with evolutionary arguments about the adaptive or prosocial value of certain cognitive biases

compañera (S)   female companion, female friend by virtue of a shared activity

comunero (S)   formally inducted member of the corporation of the commons, representing a member household

comunidad campesina (S)   state-recognized, non-commercial corporation owning inalienable shared resources in the name of a population

condenado (S, HQ)   zombie, heinous sinner wandering in the form of living dead

cordellate (S?)   a coarse woollen fabric

costumbre (S, HQ)   unwritten law

cumbi (Q II)   luxury-grade fabric

cumplimiento (HQ)   fulfillment; goods or services owed as an obligation

curacazgo (SQ)   colonial hereditary chieftaincy with tribute exemption *derecho* (S, HQ)   goods or services owed in recognition of a superior's rights

doctrina (S)   group instruction for neophyte Christians

emergence   interaction of small, simple elements in ways that produce new levels of complexity or types of patterning not visible at the underlying elementary level

emotionalist theories   of religion consider sacred dispositions as cultural means to alleviate mental stresses by processing them ritually, or to create solidarity around extraordinary states of feeling

espanto (S)   a serious psychosomatic illness brought on by disrespect of a mountain or many other transgressions

ethnography   systematic, fieldwork-based description of a particular human group's way of life

ethnology   comparative, critical, and synthetic study of ethnographies as a corpus

extirpation of idolatries   a series of ecclesiastical persecutions against rural, vernacular "Indian" religion during the 17th and early 18th centuries

faena (S, HQ)   a day of required collective work levied by a community authority

fiscalejo (S)   town crier

functionalism   theories that explain cultural traits by demonstrating their contribution to the ongoing viability of a society, or a part or subsystem of it

hanka (Q)   ice, extreme altitude

huama (SQ, Q II?)   diadem

huamanripa (SQ, Q)   a *Senecio* plant species esteemed as medicine

huari (SQ)   population primordially associated with valleys, agriculture, and stable polity; antithesis to *llacuaz*

huaylapa (SQ, Q)   a puna grass

Ichku (Q)   lime

ichu (Q, SQ)   puna grass or straw

ideology   cultural discourse through which a social group explains and justifies itself to itself

Ila (Q, SQ)   stone talismans embodying the life force of specific species

Inka Tinkuy (Q II, SQ)

intellectualism   theories of religion that envision rituals and ideas about spirits as efforts to understand the causes and hidden nature of things, positing analogies with scientific inquiry

interpretative anthropology   tendency construing culture as the sum of symbolic exchanges, and therefore regarding ethnography as the representation of foreign cultures in a manner comparable to translation and interpretation of text

ispinsira, espensera (HQ)   female official in charge of Pasa Qulqa, consort of vice-president or *kamachikuq*

jirka (Q)   mountain, herding location on mountainside

jurka (Q)   solution of cornmeal in water for ritual use

kalwa (Q)   a puna grass

kamachikuq, kamasichuq (Q II, Q, SQ)   highest officer of *balterno* corps, in charge of community's traditional internal governance, and also vice-president of the community in constitutional law context *kasha* (Q, SQ) stickpin; thorn

key symbol in S. Ortner's formulation, a central or dominant symbol with attributes of multivalence, ritual privilege, and emotional potency

khipu (Q, SQ) cord artifact made as register for information

khuyaq rumi (Q II) "loving stone" or herd talisman hidden in corral

kunuk (Q, SQ) woody resinous herb used as incense

kushuru (Q) an edible alga

Lamash (Q) lower moiety in Rapaz hydraulic organization and ceremony

llacuaz (SQ, Q) population primordially associated with high altitude, herding, and aggression; antithesis to *huari*

llactayoc (Q) original inhabitant of a settlement

llahta (Q II?) community, village

llama wira (Q, SQ) llama fat

llanques (SQ) moccasins

llipta (Q) alkaline ash added in small amount to coca leaf for *chajchay*

machay (Q II, SQ) mortuary cave

mactación (SQ?) rite of adolescent passage, including sexual initiation

malki (Q) mummy

maltón (SQ?) young llama of reproductive age

manta (S) shawl, cloak

marcación (S) roundup of herd; branding or other signaling of ownership

materialist theories of religion tendencies partaking of the premise that only materiality constitutes existence, and therefore characterizing religiosity as a domain of humans' physical activity, including technologies, economic relations, and the life of the flesh

mesa, mesa calzada (HQ) ritual composed of a sequence of invocations, auguries, and offerings at an altar or before an array of sacred objects

milqa (Q) amount that a woman can lift in her skirt

mita, mita plasa (SQ) colonial-era obligatory labor service by turns

mortuary cult ritual activity in relation to the dead, including burial, mummification, etc.

naturalism theoretical tendency attributing final reality to the world as given independently of consciousness, unconditioned by perception or conceptualization

nature/culture antithesis theoretical tendency attributing to human consciousness and its cultural expressions a different ontological status from nature, and requiring different disciplines for study

"new materialism" theoretical tendency postdating Marxian and positivist materialisms, tending to repudiate the antithesis between materiality and culture in favor of "natureculture" concepts such as the hybrid human-nonhuman actor

ontological approaches regard cultural variation as variation in cultural recognition of being or existence itself, rather than in cultural interpretations of one underlying existence ("nature"). Because ontological differences violate the "naturalist" premise they tend to be seen as "supernatural," i.e., religious

obraje (S) colonial-era factory or workshop employing coerced native labor

ontological domains in cognitive scientific terminology, areas of perception predefined by inherited "module" characteristics of the brain, such as living creatures, inanimate objects, and persons

orthodox/orthoprax antithesis contrast between religions that assign priority to internalizing teachings or beliefs (*doxa*, dogmas), as against those that assign priority to behaving in conformity with religious law (*praxis*, practices)

pachaca (Q II, SQ) Inka administrative unit of (ideally) a hundred households

pachamanca (Q II?, SQ) feast of earth-baked mixed meat and vegetables

pago (HQ) fulfillment; goods or services owed as an obligation

palla (Q II) Inka princess, today a role in the pageant Inka Tinkuy

Papa ilan (Q) talismanic stone fostering the vitality of potatoes

paqtsa (Q) waterfall

partikur (HQ?) ritual gesture of folding an altar cloth corner to restrain rainfall

pasa (Q) time, season, world

pasa cerro (HQ) a round of coca-taking asking permission to tread on mountains

pasivo (S) semi-retired *comunero* with reduced entitlements and duties

pastor (S) herder

patrón, patrona (S) boss, patron

pecho a pecho (S, HQ) round of drinks in which outgoing and incoming officers toast each other "chest to chest"

phenomenological theories explain religion in terms of ritually or discursively shared frames for subjective experience that accommodate "strange" or extreme perceptions as meaningful

physicality/interiority in Descola's model, two variables on which any given culture classifies beings as alike or different: the former regarding what substance they are considered to be made of, and the latter regarding what subjectivity they are considered to have

pirwa (Q) storehouse; auspicious plant specimen considered talismanic to a storehouse

pollera (S) wide skirt

porongo, poronguito, purungu (HQ? S?) gourd container

positivism philosophical premise that only empirical information about natural objects and their relations, irrespective of subjectivity, can count as knowledge

post-humanism philosophical tendency that rejects separation between studies of culture ("humanities") and studies of nature, instead perceiving a world of inextricable "natureculture hybrids"

pozo (S, HQ) well, deep container

principal (S, HQ) civil executive officer

prorrata (S) tax assessment

prosocial tending to increase the coherence of a group

puna (Q, SQ) grasslands over tree line

pupu (Q, SQ) umbilicus

qaray, qarakuna (Q) to feed, to offer sustenance as a social gesture

qhapaq simi (Q II) noble language, a modern regionalist term for the Cuzco variety of Quechua II

Qhapaq Hucha (Q II)   Inka term for a cycle of imperially coordinated ritual, centralizing and redistributing sacrifices including human youths from all quarters of the Inka state

qucha (Q, SQ)   lake or other body of water; vessel functioning as symbolic lake

Quechua I/Quechua II   contrast between central-Peruvian group of Quechua varieties, and the more widespread, later Quechua dialect group extending northward into Ecuador and Colombia as well as southward into Bolivia and Argentina

quenual (Q, SQ)   Polylepis spp., a group of tree species more resistant to altitude than any others

qulqa, colca (Q, SQ)   storehouse

qunupada (HQ, SQ)   warming-up ritual of llama-fat anointment

rasapa (Q)   an edible alga

ratay (Q)   rotation of land to fallow

raymi, laymi (Q II?)   turn or period of agricultural rotation

raywan (Q)   ritual term for food; Raywana, a female superhuman considered owner of food

raywan entrego (HQ)   New Year sequence bestowing ritual care on growing crops and transferring their care to new *balterno* officers

recio (S)   harsh, rigid

reducción (S)   colonial-era forced resettlement of Andean populations

reductionism   explanation of a class of phenomena in terms of simpler and more general phenomena

relativism   theoretical tendency holding that there is no knowledge independent of particular frames imposed by culture, language, etc., and that truth is therefore governed by context

religion   culturally prescribed complex of actions that seeks public or private ends through actions that are both ritualistic and sacred

reparto (S)   the portion of harvest immediately distributed to participating household

reserva (S)   the portion of harvest put aside for storage and later distribution in the communal interest

rimanakuy (Q II?)   conversation, especially political discussion

ritual   cultural program for acts (of speech, gesture, display, and so forth) in formalized sequence, manifesting invariant features of role structure, symbolism, and performance style, and contrasted with less programmed and more pragmatic activity

sacred   set apart by requirements of special conduct that express respect or reverence

sarsillus (HQ)   earrings

sectorial rotation or *raymi* fallowing   rule of land use requiring that arable sectors be rotated through planting and fallow in fixed multi-year sequence. The sequence is: potatoes, then other tubers, then barley, then fallow

semilla (S)   portion of the harvest retained as seed for the following year's planting

shanla (Q)   glowing embers

shilwa (Q)   a type of puna grass

shuqush (Q)   special flute used in irrigation ritual

sinta lasadera (HQ)   miniature ribbon lasso used in ritual for vitality of cattle

social discipline   body of mandatory practices shaping, binding, and coordinating persons into a given social order

social fact   in Durkheimian views, cultural norms and social structures which a given society imposes on its members by virtue of its organic nature rather than as a result of members' purposeful choices

sociological theories of religion   Durkheimian views that conceptualize religiosity as a universal social fact, consisting of intensified sociability around symbols that make the social whole visible to the individual and thereby bind him to its needs

structuralist theories of religion   Lévi-Straussian and other views that interpret ritual, myth, and sacred behavior as manifesting unspoken basic categories and oppositions that underpin cultural and social organization

symbolism   exchange of perceptible things (gestures, emblems, words, etc.) as signs standing for culturally categorized referents, such as ideas, relationships, feelings, or natural domains

tambo (Q II? SQ)   way station

tinka (Q)   libation, act of sacrifice by scattering or pouring out a liquid

tinkunakuy, gananakuy (Q II? HQ)   ritual battle

tinkuy (Q, SQ)   encounter between complementary parts, kinds, or domains

tinya, tinyar (Q, SQ)   ritualized song with single-skin drum

totem   species or object as emblem or essence of a social category, such as a descent group or moiety together with its nonhuman congeners

the **transcendent social**   in Maurice Bloch's analysis, society imagined or felt as an overarching, eternal virtual entity that empowers but also consumes its members

trusku, tawa   respectively the QI and QII terms for the numeral 4

tsaki chakra (Q)   dry field, i.e., unirrigated agricultural plot

tumanku (Q)   colonial-era term for rainbow

unancha, unanchay, unanza, unanzar (Q, SQ)   mark of ownership such as colored tassel, brand, or initials

unir las aguas (S)   to fortify the celestial flow of water in rain by ritually mixing seawater with lake water

ururu (Q)   an edible alga

varayo (HQ, SQ)   balterno

vincha (Q, SQ)   diadem

visitador (S)   judge-inspector

voluntad (HQ, S)   will power and goodwill

wachay (Q)   to give birth

wak'a, huaca (SQ, Q)   in colonial usage, a place or thing manifesting a superhuman being

wayi (Q)   house

winaychaniy (Q)   *comunero* household's share of *reparto* from the communal harvest

wiya (Q)   belly, sack for ritual use

yunka (Q)   mid- or lower-valley warm lands, or population associated with them

INDEX

Notes: Bold numbers refer to Glossary entries. Surnames with *de, la* are alphabetized under main noun.